Clash of Crowns

Clash of Crowns

William the Conqueror,
Richard Lionheart, and Eleanor of Aquitaine
A Story of Bloodshed, Betrayal, and Revenge

Mary McAuliffe

ROWMAN & LITTLEFIELD PUBLISHERS, INC.
Lanham • Boulder • New York • Toronto • Plymouth, UK

Published by Rowman & Littlefield Publishers, Inc.
A wholly owned subsidiary of The Rowman & Littlefield Publishing Group, Inc.
4501 Forbes Boulevard, Suite 200, Lanham, Maryland 20706
www.rowman.com

Estover Road, Plymouth PL6 7PY, United Kingdom

Part pages image: Floral decoration from the portal of the Coronation of the Virgin, the northern portal of the western façade of Notre-Dame de Paris, Paris, France. © J. McAuliffe.

When not otherwise noted, all translations are by the author.

British Library Cataloguing in Publication Information Available

Library of Congress Cataloging-in-Publication Data
McAuliffe, Mary Sperling, 1943–
    Clash of crowns : William the Conqueror, Richard Lionheart, and Eleanor of Aquitaine : a story of bloodshed, betrayal, and revenge / Mary McAuliffe.
        p. cm.
    Includes bibliographical references and index.
    ISBN 978-1-4422-1471-2 (cloth : alk. paper) — ISBN 978-1-4422-1473-6 (electronic)
    1. Richard I, King of England, 1157–1199.   2. Philip II, King of France, 1165–1223.
3. Great Britain—History—Richard I, 1189–1199.   4. France—History—Philip II Augustus, 1180–1223.   5. Plantagenet, House of.   I. Title.
    DA207.M425 2012
    942.03'20922—dc23

                                                                        2011050778

Printed in the United States of America

For Mavyn

Contents

❦

Part Four

Part Five

Illustrations

Part divider pages: Floral detail, from Notre-Dame de Paris

Preface

꧁꧂

$\mathcal{A}$ number of years ago, prompted by our friend Earl Foell, my husband and I first visited Les Andelys and Château-Gaillard. Foell, former editor of *The Christian Science Monitor*, loved nothing better than to explore the byways of France. Following his example, Jack and I took to the back roads, thoroughly enjoying our discoveries along the way. We fell in love with numerous places, but it was Château-Gaillard to which we regularly returned, charting its many years of restoration with innumerable slides, photos, and (more recently) digital pictures, as the scaffolding moved from one part of the vast complex to another.

From Gaillard it was natural to follow in Richard Lionheart's footsteps, whether along his great post-imprisonment dash from Barfleur to the rescue of Verneuil, in Normandy, or the scene of his death at Châlus, in the Limousin. Along the way, we explored castles built by his forebears along the Loire valley, castles over which he held sway in the Dordogne, and his burial place at the Abbey of Fontevraud. We included Eleanor of Aquitaine's Poitiers in our explorations, as well as medieval remnants in and around Rouen, in whose cathedral Rollo the Viking, William Longsword, and Henry the Younger are laid to rest, as well as the great heart of Lionheart himself. It was easy to be enchanted by Henry I's favorite hunting grounds, the still-peaceful Forêt de Lyons. But it was along the river Epte, that bloody dividing line between the Norman and the French Vexin, that we found the most fascinating evidence of the long-term struggle between the French and the English crowns—the struggle that culminated in the great clash at Château-Gaillard. Not surprisingly, sometime along the way all of this began to shape itself into a book.

My subsequent research brought me into contact with several local historians, who generously shared their time and knowledge with me. In Les Andelys, I am especially grateful to historian Yvan Parrault and to Christian Letourneur, then assistant mayor for tourism and culture. In Saint-Clair-sur-Epte, I was fortunate to encounter Françoise Henry, then assistant to the mayor, who unlocked the ancient church of Saint-Clair for us, literally and figuratively. Without her generosity, we would not have seen the church's eleventh-century interior walls or known that the church foundations date from the ninth century—thus were already in existence at the time of Rollo and the 911 treaty.

I love libraries as much as I love the open road, and I am especially grateful to the Library of Congress and to the splendid research facilities of the New York Public Library. In both of these institutions I discovered a surprising wealth of now published manuscripts and chronicles from the period as well as many fine scholarly studies, to which I have given specific acknowledgment in both notes and bibliography.

My deepest thanks to my editor, Susan McEachern, and to my production editor, Jehanne Schweitzer. I am indeed fortunate to have benefited from their endless patience, support, and guidance for this and my previous book, *Dawn of the Belle Epoque*. Many thanks as well to editorial assistant Grace Baumgartner and to my copyeditor, Catherine Bielitz. I am also indebted to Joanne Amparan-Close and to the late Sally Wecksler, who read this manuscript in its early stages and provided important criticism and encouragement.

My husband, Jack McAuliffe, has once again been my partner in what indeed was a team effort. I am deeply grateful for his steadfast enthusiasm and multiple roles in helping to bring this book to fruition. I could not have written it—or visited all those wonderful places in France—without him.

Lastly, a tribute to my daughter, Mavyn McAuliffe Holman, who in between her demanding roles as engineer, wife, and mom somehow manages to read, critique, and offer support for my various endeavors.

Mavyn loves a good story, and so it is especially fitting that I dedicate this book to her.

❧

For further insights into *Clash of Crowns* and Mary McAuliffe's other books, see her Facebook photo blog via www.ClashofCrowns.com.

Overview, Château-Gaillard, Les Andelys, France. © J. McAuliffe

Introduction

❦

*H*igh upon the chalky cliffs of Andely stands the twelfth-century stronghold Château-Gaillard, once the mightiest castle of its time. Now a romantic ruin, it began life as an insolent bully, a bastion of astonishing proportions and capabilities unlike anything Western Europe had ever seen before. Flung up in record time in the face of Richard Lionheart's archrival, Philip of France, it effectively called a halt to French encroachments in Richard's hereditary lands in Normandy. But even more forcefully, it sent a direct signal to Philip that Richard, king of the English and ruler over half of France besides, was Philip's superior in everything that mattered to a medieval monarch.

Not that this was anything new. Ever since William, duke of Normandy, seized the English crown in 1066, English monarchs had run circles around their French counterparts, outshining them in glamour as well as in territorial possessions and sheer power. Significantly, glamour counted—as much in those distant days as in our own. Richard Lionheart was the culmination of more than a century of larger-than-life forebears, from William the Conqueror to the equally legendary Henry II of England and his queen, Eleanor of Aquitaine, who seized the stage of Western Europe and bestrode it like colossi. Beside them, the kings of France appeared pitifully weak and—in some intangible way—less kingly.

Richard, the golden child of Henry II and Eleanor, came to center stage with the confidence of a legend in the making, having extraordinary abilities of his own. The heir of a by-then magnificent empire, he was also an unrivaled warrior and leader of men. By comparison, Philip II of France seemed distinctly lackluster.

And yet Philip, like his forebears, possessed an amazing degree of tenacity. Despite the odds, he refused to give up. In a lesser man, this might have placed him directly on the short road to trouble, but Philip also possessed great abilities of his own, including a talent for administration and a remarkably clever—some would say scheming—mind.

Early on, this intelligent and crafty man set his sights on redressing the long-standing imbalance of power between the two royal houses. Not surprisingly, as he watched Château-Gaillard spring forth upon the Rock of Andely, Philip seethed. "Were its walls of iron, I nonetheless could seize it!" he contemptuously cried.

"Were its walls of butter, I could defend it!" Richard roared back.[1]

Verbal posturing, to be sure, but even more an exercise in raw power, for the medieval castle was both symbol and embodiment of dominance, and the presence of a state-of-the-art bastion like Gaillard on the very boundary of the French royal domain signaled a fundamental challenge to the French monarch. Philip read the challenge rightly and responded in kind.

What follows is a story of a remote time and a deep-rooted conflict, whose unexpected denouement here, on the Rock of Andely, set the stage for epic struggles between the French and the English for centuries to come.

Part One

Merlin's Prophecy

The Eagle of the broken covenant . . .
Shall rejoice in her third nesting.

—Geoffrey of Monmouth, "The Prophecies of Merlin"[1]

*T*hey found the tomb deep in the earth between two stone monuments erected so long before that no one could remember what they signified or what the words inscribed upon them meant. Digging deep, as the king directed, they at last encountered a wooden sarcophagus of great size, which they carefully drew up and opened. There they discovered two sets of bones—the huge ones of a man and, at his feet, the smaller and more delicate bones of a woman. Word spread quickly. The bodies of King Arthur and his queen, Guenevere, had at last been found.

From the outset, accounts of the discovery differed. Neither of the two men who first chronicled the event—Ralph of Coggeshall and Giraldus Cambrensis—was present at the scene, although Giraldus visited soon after. A monk named Adam of Domerham wrote of the exhumation a full century later, but he seems to have drawn upon eyewitness testimony. Adam was a monk of Glastonbury, the abbey in Somerset where King Arthur's body was discovered and where details of the marvelous find must have been told and retold long after. Their very own abbey, the "glassy isle" that in the Saxon tongue had become "Glastingeburi," had turned out to be the legendary isle of Avalon.

Yet according to legend, Arthur—who was a special hero of the Celts—had not died at all and would someday return in messianic fashion to lead his people to victory over all their enemies. Quite probably in response to this legend, as well as to the widespread Celtic unrest that simmered along his kingdom's borders, England's Henry II had set out to find Arthur's remains and settle once and for all any question of the ancient king's return.

The result was the remarkable discovery at Glastonbury. Almost as remarkable was the fact that it was Henry who told the monks where to dig. According to Giraldus Cambrensis, the king "had heard from an ancient Welsh bard, a singer of the past, that they would find the body at least sixteen feet beneath the earth, not in a tomb of stone, but in a hollow oak." Giraldus then goes on to describe the dramatic scene of exhumation. Opening the coffin—wooden, although Giraldus specifically calls it a hollow oak—the monks discovered the bones of a man and a woman, the man's of remarkable size. The woman's hair still glinted gold, but when an overeager monk reached out to touch it, the hair crumbled to dust in his hand.

There could be no doubt about the contents. Above the coffin lay a lead cross bearing the words, "Here lies buried the renowned King Arthur with Guenevere his second wife in the Isle of Avalon."[2] Rejoicing, the abbot and monks of Glastonbury bore the precious bones into their abbey church, where they placed them in a marble tomb before the high altar. There, according to John of Glastonbury's fourteenth-century account, they remained until 1278, when King Edward I and his queen opened the tomb and confirmed its contents with their seals and an accompanying inscription.[3]

It is of course quite possible that the monks of Glastonbury, in response to pressure from the king or simply a desire for renown (and the wealth that a flood of pilgrims would bring), had successfully passed off a couple of old skeletons as Arthur and Guenevere. Even Edward I's seal did no more than certify that the tomb's contents were plausible; the king had no way of knowing for sure.

Bogus or not, the news of the Glastonbury discovery created a sensation. Henry II, however, did not live long enough to be gladdened by the news, for he died in 1189, shortly before King Arthur was found. Many had already taken due note of the relevance of some of Merlin's prophecies to current events.[4] Henry's death brought to pass one of Merlin's most famous prophecies: that the eagle of the broken covenant—which the twelfth century understood to mean Henry's queen, Eleanor—would rejoice in her third son, or nesting. The broken covenant referred to her first marriage, to France's King Louis VII, which ended in divorce. As for rejoicing, she certainly had cause. Upon the death of Henry II, who was her second husband, their third son—Richard Lionheart—became ruler over all the vast Plantagenet realms.[5]

❧

Richard was the apple of his mother's eye. Born in 1157, two years after Prince Henry and a year after the death of three-year-old William, Richard from childhood was singled out as Eleanor's designated heir, the future ruler of Aquitaine and Poitou.

He seems to have been a handsome lad, muscular and deep-chested like his father, but tall and long-limbed, with red-gold hair and a ruddy complexion. Named for his Norman forebears, he embraced his remarkable heritage with enthusiasm, devoting himself with rigor and single-mindedness to the pursuits of war. Without question, Richard loved nothing better than a good fight. By the time he was sixteen, he was a blooded warrior, and while his older brother, Prince Henry, contented himself with tournaments, Richard seems to have been dissatisfied with anything less than the real thing. Fierce and single-minded when focused on warfare (which he generally was), he soon mastered the combatant's skills and moved on to the commander's, absorbing the larger lessons of siegecraft and assault, fortress-building and defense, to such remarkable effect that—as Giraldus was quick to point out—scarcely a castle could hold out against him. The roll call of fortifications that crumbled to Richard, generally in record time, constituted one of the marvels of the age.

Far narrower in his interests than his father, whose talents lay in governance as well as war (and who preferred the former), Richard seems to have been bored by administration and little intrigued by the realm of ideas. Had he been born in the tenth or even the eleventh century, he would have bathed his steps in blood and never bothered to wash for dinner. Instead, under Eleanor's tutelage, he became something far more complex—a very model of chivalry.

Eleanor adored him.

❧

Bernard of Clairvaux had never much liked Eleanor. The saintly monk had never liked Henry, either, but he had a particular aversion to Eleanor and her family, the house of Poitou. Although renowned for his obliviousness to the things of this world, Bernard seems to have had a sharp eye when it suited him. He understood the appeal of Cluniac art and architecture, even as he rejected it, and he just as clearly noticed and understood the appeal of Louis' first queen. Bernard did not necessarily speak for all ecclesiastics, as the Church had never been a seamless whole, whether in the exercise of power or opinions. Even as bishop jostled bishop and Cistercian took on Cluniac, Bernard did not sit well with all higher prelates, including the powerful Abbot Suger, whom Bernard had once scolded for worldliness. Always the politician and statesman, and ever devoted to the house of Capet, Abbot Suger tried to keep Eleanor—and her vast lands—by Louis' side. But Bernard, who had early concluded that Eleanor was a bad seed descended from evil stock, pressed Louis to free himself from her influence. At length—after Suger's death—Louis reluctantly did as Bernard urged.

For once, although for vastly different reasons, Eleanor and Bernard were in agreement. Still, her subsequent marriage to Henry of Anjou must have confirmed whatever evil the saintly monk believed of them both. She and Henry began married life in mutual defiance of Louis, with the bright overtones of sexual as well as political triumph. The thirty-year-old countess pleased her nineteen-year-old husband, and just as important, he pleased *her*. Both were passionate and strong, dangerous as well as attractive to the opposite sex. Henry had the more legalistic mind, while Eleanor was the more romantic—but neither gave place to the other in intelligence or wit.

Eleanor bore this lion of a husband eight children, five during the first six years alone—something of a record given the two children she had managed to conceive during her fifteen years with Louis.[6] Even more remarkably, all but one of this strong brood survived infancy. Between them, she and Henry founded a dynasty.

In December 1166 or early 1167, at the age of forty-five, Eleanor gave birth to her last child, John. Henry had by this time taken firm hold of his empire, consolidating control over England and his extensive Continental domains—stretching from Normandy and Anjou down through Poitou and Aquitaine—as well as extending Plantagenet authority over Brittany. He also managed to put down rebellions in Wales, while preparing to bring Ireland and Scotland into the fold. It was an enormous undertaking, and Henry held his far-flung territories together by sheer tenacity; he was constantly in the saddle as he rode the considerable length of his strung-out domains.

Given Henry's constant wars and travels, he and Eleanor had never seen much of one another—although the time they did spend together appeared to be productive, as Eleanor conceived little Plantagenets with remarkable regularity. Yet by the late 1160s, Eleanor's childbearing years had come to a close. She had lived up to and even exceeded all expectations for a medieval queen, for Henry certainly required no more sons. The larger question, in fact, appeared to be how best to provide for them all.

Henry's solution emerged early in 1169, at Montmirail, where he announced his intention of dividing his realm. His eldest, Prince Henry, who was heir to England, would receive his father's own inheritance. In recognition of this, the young prince now did homage to Louis VII for Normandy and Anjou—his father's lands, but subject to the French crown. Richard, as expected, bent the knee for Eleanor's vast lands in southwestern France, while Geoffrey, the third living son, paid homage to Prince Henry—and through him, to the French king—for the English king's recent conquest, Brittany. These youngsters—aged thirteen, eleven, and ten, respectively—now held the titles to go with their expected inheritances. The following year, Henry even had his eldest son crowned king.[7] This was not an unusual procedure, as the Capetians and others had been doing it for years to secure the succession. The problem lay in the homage that these heirs of Henry II had now paid to Henry's hereditary rival, Louis VII of France.

Exacerbating this potentially explosive situation was the inevitable question of when Henry's sons would receive the lands, revenues, and responsibilities to go with their titles. To Henry, the answer was obvious: upon his own death. Yet in the following years, as the boys grew to manhood, they became restless under the restrictions their father imposed. Even Richard, who as duke and count of his mother's lands had considerably more independence than the rest, was held on a tight leash. But it was Henry's oldest, the duly crowned young king, who chafed the most, for by 1173 he was eighteen years old and a married man. To his mind, his father was treating him like a child.[8]

Henry the Younger (or the Young King), as this young man was known, was the handsomest of all the Plantagenet brood, a striking fellow with an engaging manner and easy ways. A spendthrift and something of a dandy, he was surrounded by friends and hangers-on who urged him to claim what was rightfully his.[9] After all, hadn't his father received Normandy from *his* father, in fact as well as in name, when he was still in his teens? Marriage to Princess Marguerite of France only worsened the situation.

This remarkable union had taken place many years earlier, after Louis VII's second wife most disappointingly gave birth to yet another daughter. Contemplating the English king's growing brood of male children, Louis set pride aside and—looking to the future—proposed a marriage alliance with his erstwhile rival. If a Capetian son did not seem destined to rule over France, then perhaps a grandson could rule over France as well as the vast Plantagenet realms. Sweetening the deal, Louis offered an especially strategic piece of property between French and English crown lands called the Norman Vexin, which he had extracted from the Plantagenets some years before.[10] The outcome was the betrothal of baby Marguerite to three-year-old Prince Henry, with the all-important Norman Vexin as her dowry. Marguerite, aged six months, went to be raised in the court of her future husband, as was the custom, while Louis sat back, prepared to retain control over the entire Vexin until Marguerite and her young prince reached marriageable age.

He failed to appreciate the wiliness of the elder Henry, who quickly outmaneuvered him, marrying off the youngsters—by now two and five years old, respectively—and reeling in the Norman Vexin before Louis could sit up and take notice. It was a brazen move, made possible only because a pope in dire need of Henry's support was willing to overlook the extreme youth of the bride and groom and cast his blessing on the marriage. Louis himself, thoroughly preoccupied in the tumult surrounding the unexpected death of his second wife (while giving birth to yet another girl) and his almost-immediate remarriage to Adele of Champagne, did not catch what Henry was about until it was too late.

King Henry II of England had thus most grievously jeopardized relations with his Continental overlord, the king of France, on the heels of yet other causes for hostility (a tedious list for the reader, but not for the French king). It was hardly surprising that Louis' animosity now grew increasingly open, as his marriage to Adele of Champagne so clearly signaled. Certainly neither Adele nor her brothers—the powerful Theobald of Blois and Henry of Champagne—were friends of the Plantagenets.

More than this, in the year 1165, Adele at long last presented Louis with a son.

❧⚜☙

It was a sweltering August night, and twenty-year-old Giraldus Cambrensis—drawn to Paris like other young students of his time—had retired from the heat to his room in the Cité. A zealous student (by his own account), he had remained up studying until well past midnight. At last, thoroughly exhausted, he collapsed upon his bed. But no sooner had he fallen into slumber than a great commotion of clanging bells awakened him. Fearful that a great fire had broken out, he dived toward his window and leaned out. The city was ablaze with bonfires, and people rushed westward toward the king's palace, lighting the narrow streets with torches as they went.

"What is it?" he cried out as two old crones hastened by.

Recognizing from his accent that he was English, the one called out, "This night a boy is born to us, who by the blessing of God shall assuredly be a hammer to your King!"[11]

At long last, at the age of forty-five, Louis VII had fathered a son. They named him Philip, but they called him Dieudonné (God-given), for God had finally answered their prayers. Bolstered by the event, Louis seems to have developed more sprightliness. He now took it upon himself to stir up flames of rebellion wherever they appeared within his rival's vast empire, whether in Wales or Scotland, Aquitaine or Brittany. Most particularly, he offered asylum to Thomas Becket, archbishop of Canterbury, who had recently evolved from the English king's closest friend into his bitterest enemy. Henry countered by marrying off his eldest daughter, Matilda, to the powerful Henry the Lion, duke of Saxony, and threatened to join with the German emperor in supporting a rival pope. It was at this moment that Louis decided to raid the Norman Vexin. Henry replied with a brilliant sack of Louis' heavily fortified arsenal on the French side of the border, at Chaumont-sur-Epte. Louis in turn sacked the nearby town of Andely.

Thirty years later, Richard Lionheart would choose Andely as the site on which to build his magnificent castle, Château-Gaillard. But for now, Henry and Louis called a truce. This was the occasion that brought Henry and his three eldest sons to Montmirail in early 1169. And this was the place where Henry proposed to divide his realm, while Louis agreed to betroth the youngest of his four daughters, a princess by the name of Alais, to young Richard. Just as her older sister had brought the invaluable Vexin to Henry as her dowry, Alais promised to bring portions of the equally significant borderland of Berry into Henry's hands.[12] Louis, in turn, received homage from Henry and his sons, plus the promise of eventual joint Capetian-Plantagenet rule over the greater part of Henry's realms. Both sides had reason to be pleased.

Yet Louis had reason to be wary as well. Becket, whose case figured large at Montmirail, warned the French king that Henry was not to be trusted, and Henry's subsequent actions only heightened Louis' concerns. Once again, the rivalry between the king of England and the king of France exploded into war, only this time—the year was 1173—there was an astonishing difference.

This time, in an amazing turn of events, Henry's queen, as well as his three oldest sons, allied with Eleanor's former husband, the king of France.

⌘

Sometime during the late 1160s and early 1170s, the dazzle faded and the remarkable marriage between Eleanor of Aquitaine and Henry II took a dismal turn. Eleanor left Henry and established herself at her court of Poitiers. Henry's biographer, W. L. Warren, concludes that Eleanor was aggrieved because her marriage to Henry had brought "neither the power nor the influence she—a duchess in her own right, and a queen before she married Henry—thought to be her due."[13] This possibly accounts for it, for in Poitiers, Eleanor—with her favorite son and heir by her side—proceeded to establish herself in charge of her vast and turbulent lands to a degree quite impossible had she remained with Henry.[14] Still, the acrimony that continued to grow between Eleanor and Henry has encouraged speculation that something more was afoot. Had Eleanor been merely dissatisfied or even aggrieved with her role as Henry's queen, her years at Poitiers, in control of her own lands and court, should have brought her a measure of peace and satisfaction. Instead, Henry now was her mortal enemy, and marriage—all marriage—was a sham. Eleanor—still strong and beautiful, still the recipient of troubadours' sighs—was behaving like a woman scorned.

If Giraldus can be trusted, it was not Henry's infidelity per se that sent Eleanor packing, for over the long years of her marriage, Eleanor must have known what everyone else knew. Fidelity in a husband in those times was unusual—in Louis' case, possibly even boring—and Henry was often far from her side. His many casual liaisons would have been beneath her contempt, and for years she seems to have successfully ignored them. Yet Rosamond Clifford was different.

The shock would not have been that Henry had taken a mistress; what seems to have been unique, and devastating, was how he loved this one, treating her as if she were his queen. In the fair young daughter of Walter de Clifford, the unsophisticated offspring of a simple knight, Eleanor of Aquitaine had most unexpectedly met her match.

The affair was a long one, lasting from around 1166 to Rosamond's death in 1177, but Eleanor probably learned of it in its first bloom, while in England to give birth to John. This would explain, at least in part, the bitterness of the estrangement that arose between her and Henry following John's birth, including Eleanor's subsequent departure for her own court in Poitiers. Under her guidance, Poitiers became the most brilliant court in Western Christendom, as well as a hotbed of intrigue. Here, encouraged by Eleanor, troubadours sang of romantic love, knights learned courtly chivalry, and Eleanor's four surviving sons learned to hate their father.

It was not a difficult task. A crafty and unreadable man of sudden and violent temper, Henry demanded total loyalty and utter dependency. Giraldus says that he was a kind father during his sons' youth and childhood, "but as they advanced in years looked on them with an evil eye, treating them worse than a stepfather." Giraldus, who himself harbored considerable resentment of Henry, having been denied a much-coveted bishopric, nevertheless could be perceptive: "Whether it was that he would not have them prosper too fast," he ruminated, "or whether they were ill-deserving, he could never bear to think of them as his successors."[15]

According to Giraldus's contemporary, Walter Map, Henry acquired this particular trait by training as well as by instinct, for his mother, Matilda, had taught her son to "spin out all the affairs of everyone, hold long in his own hand all posts that fell in," and "keep the aspirants to them hanging on in hope." She supported this Machiavellian observation with the analogy of an unruly hawk: "If meat is often offered to it and then snatched away or hid, [it] becomes keener and more inclinably obedient and attentive."[16] Map thought this teaching offensive, but concluded that it explained Henry's less attractive qualities. Certainly Henry, who was an avid hawker, seems to have readily taken to it, baiting his filial as well as other relationships with hunger, and holding the choicest tidbits just out of reach.

Henry Plantagenet was thus a difficult and even dangerous man. Not surprisingly, his sons showed similar promise, although on a meaner scale. Young Henry, the heir, was handsome and a general favorite but, in the end, weak and pathetic. Geoffrey was a schemer, with a talent for behind-the-throne manipulation. John, the baby, was shamelessly crooked, with neither the talent nor the interest to disguise it. Richard, Eleanor's favorite, was also flawed. Yet of the four sons who survived infancy, Richard showed the greatest promise, and Eleanor showered her affection on him.

It should therefore have come as little surprise when the discontented older sons, aided by their bitter mother and her former husband, Louis of France, led a general uprising against Henry of England. But even before this, Eleanor had carried on her own form of rebellion in Poitiers. There she not only turned Henry's offspring against him, but undertook to turn the scruffy, blood-soaked sons of the nobility into gentle knights in the service of love, beauty, and fair womanhood.

Although historians now question whether Eleanor's famed court of love ever existed, the ideals behind courtly love were unquestionably held in high esteem at the court of Poitiers. Key to the concept was a new role envisioned for women, in which the suitor became his beloved's vassal in love, learning to please her in any way she chose—from nicer table manners and gentler speech to more sophisticated and refined methods of courtship. Rugged young knights, accustomed to rowdy camaraderie and the smell of the stables, could be persuaded to clean up and behave if such sacrifice promised something interesting in return. Under sufficiently enticing circumstances, their more courteous and chivalrous behavior might become long-term or even permanent.

Behind it all lay the assumption—reinforced by the typical marriages of the time—that marriage had little to do with love. Everyone knew that marriages were essentially political or economic mergers, moves on the great chessboard of life. From there, it was but one step to the extreme statement, made by Andreas Capellanus, that love and marriage do not mix. Andreas put these scandalous words into Eleanor's mouth in his treatise on the art of courtly love,[17] and although there is nothing to indicate that she ever spoke them, there also is nothing to indicate that she would have found them repugnant. Indeed, the role of women in courtly love represented but another aspect of Eleanor's striving in the personal and political realm for independence and power.

The fashions of Poitiers spread rapidly throughout the courts of Western Europe. Yet for all of their influence, it is questionable whether they accomplished any substantive change in the relationship between the sexes. Beneath the more colorful and civilized surface they encouraged, attitudes and relationships appear to have remained pretty much the same. The troubadour warrior, Bertran de Born, who had a particular interest in inciting Henry the Younger to war against his father, enthused about the joys of seeing castles besieged and smashed. His poems extolled the sound of trumpets and the flourish of pennants, which for him were rousing reminders that the world was good. Unquestionably, it still was a man's world, and men continued to live for war.

Henry Plantagenet may have thoroughly enjoyed discussions with men of letters, but he could not be troubled with an elaborate code of etiquette or the sophisticated lifestyle it entailed. Furthermore, the barely masked subversiveness of Eleanor's court at Poitiers was accompanied by outright treason. With some difficulty, Henry brought the great rebellion into check, granting surprisingly lenient terms to his sons. But toward Eleanor he was not in the least magnanimous. Swiftly Henry closed down her court at Poitiers and brought the totally unrepentant queen back to England and imprisonment.

There she remained for fifteen years, until Henry's death.

⚜

Following Henry's victory over all his enemies, he sent Richard, now aged seventeen, to subdue the insurgency that still raged throughout Aquitaine. Richard was not yet the warrior his father was, as Henry had made abundantly clear when he roped him in at the rebellion's end. Still, the teenager took on his military duties with enthusiasm, razing castles and cowing his unruly subjects so convincingly that he won a lasting reputation for military prowess and savagery.

Peace now extended throughout Henry's vast realms, giving him the appearance of invincibility. His sons subdued, the French king defeated, and even the German emperor shattered by the Lombards, Henry had no real rivals either at home or abroad. With all his other troubles for the moment resolved, he now took steps to rid himself of his queen.

Henry's grounds for divorce were solid: certainly treason would do, if consanguinity would not. Yet he had no intention of allowing Eleanor to remarry. And so Henry now seems to have sought the pope's help in agreeing to a divorce, followed by the queen's permanent retirement from the world as the Abbess of Fontevraud. Over the years, Fontevraud had become wealthy and fashionable, a most suitable final destination for a former queen. Even more to Henry's purpose, Fontevraud was located on the border between Poitiers and Anjou, near his castle of Chinon. He could readily keep an eye on Eleanor there.

Yet Eleanor was not about to be bundled off to Fontevraud—not even as an alternative to imprisonment. She protested mightily, and her sons promptly took their mother's side. Adding to the furor was the persistent rumor that Henry had plans to remarry, repudiate his ungrateful sons, and father a new and better lot. By 1177, after fair Rosamond's death, rumor even had a name for Henry's new choice as queen: his son Richard's betrothed, the French princess Alais.

Alais and Richard had been betrothed for many years but had not yet wed—a surprising omission, given the bride's rank and the fact that she was now seventeen (almost an old maid by medieval standards). Why, court gossips wanted to know, had Henry put off marrying her to his now twenty-year-old son? Given Richard's inclination to find his way to Paris, in his older brother's footsteps, an obvious answer was that Henry was reluctant to provide yet another tie between his difficult progeny and the French king. But gossips soon had another and far more titillating answer: Henry had decided to wed the young princess himself. Indeed, tongues wagged that Henry, seeking solace for the dead Rosamond, had already made Alais his mistress. It was even said that Alais bore Henry a daughter, who did not survive.[18]

Louis now complained to the pope and demanded that Richard marry Alais, as originally agreed. Henry (whose appeal to Rome for a divorce had come to naught) temporized and finally said the marriage would take place, but only if Louis gave up the city of Bourges as well as the French Vexin (Princess Marguerite's dowry had included only the Norman portion). Louis did not accept—indeed, could hardly be expected to accept—and said nothing further about Alais or her marriage to Richard.

More than this, the Church (which had ordered Henry, under threat of interdict, to wed Alais to Richard or return her to her father) now grew remarkably quiet on the subject. Henry retained custody over Alais, and there was no interdict. Since it could not be expected that the pope would "openly countenance, much less use the authority of the church to enforce, a marriage between a man and his father's concubine,"[19] the Church's sudden silence underscores the distinct possibility that the rumors were true. Certainly, from this point on, the pope's interest in Alais' fate came to an abrupt halt.

⚜

Meanwhile, Philip, heir to the French throne, was growing up. With his knightly training well under way, he could look forward to his kingly consecration, which Louis planned for August 1179. On that date, Louis' dearly beloved son would turn fourteen.

Louis himself was ready to turn over the reins of government to Philip as soon as possible. Almost sixty, he had never possessed Henry Plantagenet's restless energy or strength, and his long battles with the Plantagenets had taken their toll. A gentle man, he now napped frequently and seemed to be slipping toward a more permanent repose. One much-cited scene finds him sleeping virtually unprotected in the palace garden. When discovered, his courtiers admonish that he has placed his life and kingdom in considerable jeopardy. To which Louis mildly replies that he could hardly be in any danger, for he has no enemies.[20]

It was true. Even Eleanor, who despised him, did not hate him, and Henry's wrath seems to have fallen upon his own sons rather than upon the French king. Thus it was that when young Philip became severely ill just prior to his coronation, Louis did not hesitate on his course. In a dream, he beheld a vision of the martyred St. Thomas Becket beckoning him to pray for Philip's recovery at Canterbury. Despite dire warnings from his barons, Louis donned a pilgrim's habit and departed immediately for England. Steeling himself for the Channel crossing, he landed safely at Dover just as the king of England hove into sight, having ridden all night to meet him.

There never was a question of Louis' safety on this his only visit to England. Henry accompanied him to Canterbury, where Louis gave copious gifts and prayed. Then, still in Henry's company, Louis returned to Dover, where he once again set sail for France. There, to his infinite relief and joy, he learned that his only son had recovered.[21]

Louis himself could not attend the coronation for which he had risked his life. En route home he became severely ill and spent his remaining months as an invalid. In September of the following year, he died, garbed in the modest robe of a monk.

He left a fifteen-year-old to rule as king.

⚜

It is possible that had Henry II been born eight centuries later, he would have made just as memorable a leader of a modern government as he did of his medieval realms. Personally unostentatious, with a talent for administration and an energy so boundless that he virtually wore out everyone around him, he was a creative ruler, a man of thought and action, a charismatic leader who—according to Giraldus, a longtime member of his household—never forgot a face.[22]

Left to his own devices, this dynamo might have spent the 1180s in subduing, binding together, and providing the building blocks of government for his vast empire. But Henry had enemies, made over a lifetime of molding others to his will, and so he spent much of the last years of his life at war—with his barons, with his sons, and with the king of France.

Unlike Louis VII, who had begun his reign under the auspicious circumstances of civil war in England and a German empire in disarray, young Philip found himself pitted against the wiliest and most powerful ruler of his time. Heavily outmatched, he bided his time, poking a little here and a little there until at last he found the agent for his devices— Henry the Younger, the dissatisfied heir to the English throne.

Bored and aggrieved, young Henry took no interest in the government of those realms he would someday inherit and instead looked with envious eyes at his brothers, especially Richard, who had a realm of his own and warfare to occupy him. Young Henry, feeling sadly out of pocket and misused, drifted southward from a glittering but evanescent season of tournaments and soon found men eager to claim his leadership on behalf of their own causes. Brother soon fought brother, with Geoffrey taking the elder brother's side against Richard, count of Poitou. Philip, watching closely, sent his own mercenaries to keep the pot boiling.

At length, fearing that his sons would tear each other as well as the Plantagenet empire apart, the elder Henry entered the fray on the side of the beleaguered Richard. Young Henry wiggled and squirmed, desolating the land and its religious sanctuaries as he tried to keep to the field and desperately sought to avoid defeat.

The end came suddenly, in the small town of Martel. There, young Henry fell into a fever and died. He was twenty-eight years old.

Suddenly Richard, Eleanor's favorite, stood to inherit a crown. His father, looking for a way to provide for John as well as to contain Richard—who was far more of a threat than young Henry had ever been—now seems to have carved up his realm according to a different plan. Richard would inherit England and Normandy as well as Maine and Anjou, but John would receive Poitou and Aquitaine. At this, Richard—who had made Poitou and Aquitaine his business for years—became incensed. He had no intention of losing one iota of what he thought due him, nor had he any intention of assuming his dead brother's empty titles and thankless role.

Philip of France was most interested by what he heard. Yet it was not Richard but Geoffrey who first bolted for Paris. Geoffrey still retained the promise of Brittany, but he had been denied additional territory and was bitter about it. Geoffrey, who was perhaps the brightest of the family, was also the most devious. He had, Giraldus commented, "more aloes than honey in him," while his tongue was "smoother than oil." Geoffrey was above all a master at persuasion, with a "sweet and persuasive eloquence" and an extraordinary talent for dissimulation.[23] It was Geoffrey whom Giraldus suspected of being the mainspring behind young Henry's revolt, and it was Geoffrey who now repaired to Paris, where Philip received him like a brother, carefully nurturing his grievances.

Still, despite his calculation, Philip could not foresee all events. In the summer of 1186, Geoffrey's sojourn in Paris abruptly ended with his death—probably from wounds received in a tournament.[24] Soon it would be Richard's turn to visit Paris and seek Philip's friendship. In the meantime, Philip demanded the return of the Norman Vexin (his widowed sister Marguerite's dowry) as well as the marriage of Alais to Richard.

It was a reasonable demand. Marguerite's husband, young Henry, was dead, and Alais had been betrothed to Richard for more years than anyone cared to remember. Yet Henry Plantagenet resisted, on the grounds that the French monarchy had lost any right to the Norman Vexin when Marguerite and Henry the Younger originally wed. At length, with Marguerite on the verge of marrying a second time (to King Béla III of Hungary), Philip agreed to leave the Norman Vexin with the king of England in return for a hefty yearly monetary payment to Marguerite[25] as well as Henry's solemn oath that Alais and Richard would soon wed.

It is unclear whether or not the Norman Vexin now became Alais' dowry.[26] But from this point on, her fate and that of the Vexin would be intertwined.

⚜

With Geoffrey's death, Henry was left with two sons, the elder of whom he did not trust. Richard, Eleanor's pet, was a formidable warrior, but John—still in his teens—had yet to impress anyone on any grounds whatever. Rude, prone to vice, "more given to pleasures than to arms, to dalliance than to endurance,"[27] he was the least as well as the last of all Henry Plantagenet's sons. Henry—believing that he would outgrow these traits—now pinned all his hopes on him. Although John had proven a disaster in Ireland, where Henry originally planned to set him up as king, Henry now intended to use this unpromising lad to keep Richard in line.

By this time, Philip had reached his early twenties and was showing a thought-provoking willingness to assert the prerogatives of the French crown. Demonstrating that he understood the importance of protecting and enhancing his growing capital city, he went to the considerable expense of paving the streets of Paris as well as constructing a wall around the city's new outskirts.[28] And then, bolstered by the birth of a son and heir,[29] he once again confronted the English king.

Alais and the Norman Vexin remained the outstanding issues. Alais still was not married to anyone, and Philip, tired of Henry's evasions, wanted both the princess and the property back. Henry, despite a demonstrated willingness to pay homage to his French overlord for his French territories, had little inclination to let this young whippersnapper tell him what to do. The Norman Vexin was his, by God, and he was going to hold on to it. Philip thought about this briefly and then presented his answer to this powerful yet disobedient vassal: he invaded that other source of contention between the two kings, the disputed territory of Berry.

Henry responded, as was his wont, with massive force, but Philip did not back down as Louis would have. Perhaps judging his young rival in a new light, Henry now agreed to a truce. What he did not anticipate was this determined and calculating young king's next step. Coolly assuming the initiative, Philip now undertook to turn Richard against his father.

Richard soon found his way to Paris, where Philip treated him as a brother—or, as some have recently contended, as a lover.[30] They ate from the same dish—a common-enough indication of friendship, for trenchers generally were shared—and slept together in the same bed.[31] Again, such accommodations may simply have amounted to a sign of close friendship, without necessarily implying sexual overtones, for beds were scarce and frequently joint-tenanted. Still, there would have been beds aplenty for the king and his royal guest, should they have chosen to sleep separately, and in light of Richard's subsequent behavior, it seems possible that Philip calculatedly accommodated him.

It is possible that Philip previously had a similar relationship with Geoffrey as well, for their friendship appears to have been unusually intense, even for the emotion-laden twelfth century—where men readily cried, and a gift for tears was a valued asset. Philip seems to have been so overcome with grief at Geoffrey's death that he could scarcely be restrained from hurling himself into his friend's grave. In any case, whether or not fraught with sexual overtones, Philip and Richard's relationship seems to have been a close one, and Richard left the court of the French king persuaded that his father was on the verge of disinheriting him in favor of John. Philip even hinted that Henry planned to marry John to the much-abused Alais.

Upon Henry's urgent appeals, Richard at length returned. But young Lionheart fretted that his father remained decidedly mum about the succession. News from the Holy Land added urgency to Richard's concerns, for he had recently taken the Cross and longed to be off on crusade. Yet he was understandably reluctant to leave while John stood ready and waiting to step into his place.

For a time, Richard's attention was taken in fighting off rebellion in Aquitaine (which Henry may have instigated to keep his son diverted), while Philip continued to prowl and prod along the most vulnerable of Henry's borders. Henry, feeling up to whatever Philip was inclined to dish out, was in a feisty mood when the two once again met in the summer of 1188 along the banks of the Epte, near Gisors.

In the shade of a giant elm, under which the dukes of Normandy and kings of France had traditionally conducted business, Philip returned to the question of Alais' marriage and the Norman Vexin. Henry, however, refused to discuss anything but Philip's most recent incursions into what he considered Plantagenet property. At loggerheads in the sweltering heat, the two sides almost came to blows. At last, driven beyond endurance, the French fell in a fury upon the giant elm under which they had parleyed, hacking it to pieces. As a symbol of where relations stood between the two houses, this sudden act of violence could hardly have been more pointed.

Henry now renounced his vassal's allegiance to the king of France and went to war. The conflict promised to be drawn out and expensive, leading the two kings once again to meet. With considerable concern, Henry heard Philip offer to withdraw from Berry and allow Richard to retain disputed lands in Toulouse if Henry would only marry Richard to Alais and have his barons swear fealty to Richard as his heir. Furious, Henry flatly refused.[32]

And now Richard suddenly stood forth. As Henry and his lords watched, thunderstruck, young Lionheart removed his sword and knelt before Philip, openly doing homage to the French king for all the Continental domains he claimed by inheritance, and swearing fealty to him "against all men."[33]

At last it had come to this.

❦

Little happened for a time, as frantic intermediaries unsuccessfully sought to avert the inevitable. But at length, with the end of Lent, the open season for war arrived.

Repeated efforts to avert the upcoming tragedy met with repeated failures, while the last attempt—at La Ferté-Bernard, just over the border into Henry's territory of Maine—gave clear evidence of just how hopeless the breach had become. Philip demanded that Alais marry Richard and that Richard's inheritance be acknowledged. Richard added that, for his own security, he would not go on crusade unless John went with him. Henry flatly refused and, according to Roger of Howden, introduced the highly delicate subject of marrying Alais to John.[34]

Ever since, people have wondered exactly what game Henry was playing. Had he indeed decided to disinherit Richard for John, as Richard now so plainly believed? Or was he merely "trying to discipline Richard by keeping him in uncertainty," and then was caught in the coils of his own deviousness?[35] Henry never could forget his eldest son's rebellion after being crowned successor. But neither could Richard forget the abrupt way his father had removed Aquitaine and Poitou from his inheritance and given it to John.

The tragedy now proceeded to its grueling conclusion. Philip and Richard fell upon Le Mans, where Henry had taken refuge, and soon flames enveloped the entire town. Henry managed to escape, but Richard pursued him. Only the timely intervention of William Marshal, one of Henry's most renowned warriors, saved the king from capture—or worse.[36]

Instead of fighting his way back to Normandy, where he could mount an army or set sail for England, Henry fled to his great Angevin fortress of Chinon, high above the river Vienne. The old lion was defeated and he knew it. His body, which he had relentlessly pushed for years, no longer could be willed into action. Deathly ill, he awaited his end in the summer heat.

Castles and towns now promptly fell to Philip and Richard, suggesting that their inhabitants sensed which direction the wind was blowing. Even the city of Tours fell into Philip and Richard's hands. At that body blow, Henry agreed to come to terms.

Henry consented but was so ill he could scarcely ride. Even Philip was moved to pity when he saw him. But Henry would have none of it, refusing the seat that Philip offered and remaining bolt upright in his saddle—supported by attendants—as he listened to the victors' terms. These were rugged. He was to renew his homage to the king of France and pay a heavy indemnity for Philip's trouble. He was to acknowledge Richard as his heir, and call upon his barons to swear homage to his eldest remaining son. Alais was to be turned over to a guardian of Richard's choosing, who would keep her in safety until Richard wed her, upon his return from crusade.

As Henry listened, a roll of thunder broke forth. He nodded his assent, and yet another roll of thunder burst from the heavy summer sky. But perhaps the worst blow was yet to come. For when he sent for the list of names of those who had gone over to Richard, the first name on the list was that of his youngest son, John.

Château de Chinon, overlooking the river Vienne, Chinon, France. A Plantagenet strong-hold and a primary residence of Henry II, who died here and was buried in the nearby Abbey of Fontevraud. © J. McAuliffe

After that, death came quickly. In anguish, Henry "cursed the day on which he was born, and pronounced upon his sons the curse of God and of himself." And then, knowing that he was sick unto death, he ordered that he be carried into the chapel, where he received communion and absolution before wearily drawing his last breath.[37]

While Roger of Wendover reported a sedate funeral, with Henry lying in state in appropriately royal splendor, William Marshal (who was present) described a far more humiliating scene. According to the Marshal, Henry's attendants stole his belongings, leaving the body naked until someone took pity and covered it with a cloak. With panicked courtiers tending to their own welfare, it was difficult to find anyone to enshroud the body or prepare it for funeral and burial. According to Giraldus, no one could even find an appropriate ring for the dead king's finger, let alone a scepter or a crown.[38]

Giraldus, keen to report the fall of the great, may have embroidered or exaggerated, but his dramatic account of Richard's last encounter with his father is corroborated by both Roger of Wendover and Roger of Howden. When Richard, who had pursued Henry to the end, approached the body, all present were stunned to see blood suddenly burst from the dead king's nostrils.[39] *An omen of the first order!* they whispered among themselves. A curse on the living from the dead!

Yet Richard, a Plantagenet through and through, remained unshaken. He now was undisputed lord of England, as well as the vast Plantagenet holdings in France, and the future was his.

Merlin's prophecy had indeed come to pass.

✸ 2 ✸

Turning Point

$\mathcal{Q}$uite understandably, Richard Lionheart may not have been giving much thought to German affairs as he buried his father and seized the English crown. But even as Richard took ship for London and coronation, a German duke with a vendetta was making waves that would soon reach England's shores. Indeed, Duke Henry the Lion was in particularly fine form that autumn of 1189. Returning to his lands in Saxony, he swept all before him with truly magnificent fury, reigniting his rivalry with the German emperor and reclaiming all that had once been his.

Once lord of sixty-seven castles and forty towns, not to mention all of Saxony and Bavaria, Henry had married royally—Henry II and Eleanor's eldest daughter, Matilda Plantagenet. This reinforced his status as one of the wealthiest and most powerful rulers in Western Christendom, a rival to the German emperor as well as a worthy match for the daughter of a king.[1] But being duke of Saxony and Bavaria was not a peacetime occupation. The Lion was a warrior, with enemies in high places. And his most exalted enemy was the emperor himself.

The red-bearded emperor, Frederick Barbarossa, was of the ambitious house of Hohenstaufen, while the Lion was of the equally proud and ambitious house of Welf. By the time of Duke Henry's return to Germany, the families had been battling each other for decades—the chief object of their dispute being the imperial crown.

Earlier in his reign, Barbarossa had maintained an uneasy peace with his great rival. But as the Saxon Lion grew increasingly powerful and his alliances ever more threatening, the arrangement slowly unraveled. In particular, the Lion's marriage to the daughter of mighty Henry Plantagenet clearly signaled his growing independence of the emperor and an interest in a broader scope for his talents than the Welf family lands.

Barbarossa pondered this situation carefully, for it placed him in grave difficulties. His own lands, stretching from Swabia down into Lombardy, centered in what today is southern Germany. The Lion, occupying a clean sweep through Saxony and Bavaria, was far better positioned within Germany itself. Yet in terms of the empire as a whole, which extended clear down to the Papal States, Barbarossa held an advantage, which he exploited from the outset—or would have, had the city-states of Lombardy (in today's northern Italy) not put up such a fierce resistance to his imperial rule. Year after year, Barbarossa sent armies southward across the Alps to subdue the Lombards. Year after year, he met with fleeting victories and more notable defeats. At last, weary of the struggle and anticipating the Lion's desertion to the enemy, Frederick suddenly and decisively changed his course. In 1177, after yet another defeat at the hands of the fractious Lombard cities, he unexpectedly made his peace with their powerful ally, the Church.

This event was all the more remarkable given the long history of bitter political antagonism between Church and empire. The Church had for years fortified its claims to supremacy by reminding one and all that a pope had crowned Charlemagne as well as subsequent German emperors. (Centuries later, remembering the controversy, Napoleon took no chances and snatched the imperial crown from the pope's hands, crowning himself.) Frederick had taken a direct and highly unorthodox response to the problem, even supporting a series of anti-popes of his choosing rather than acknowledge the hostile popes in Rome. It was Barbarossa, after all, who first termed the empire over which he ruled "Holy." And it was Barbarossa who, in unsubtle reinforcement of the point, had his anti-pope promote Charlemagne to sainthood. Recognizing the exact nature of the emperor's threat, the Church dived swiftly and effectively into the political fray, cultivating alliances with the German nobility and following a variety of courses to undercut the imperial dream.

So it was an event of the greatest magnitude when, in 1177, Emperor Frederick Barbarossa unexpectedly made peace with this longtime antagonist. Political realities alone governed his decision. The Church was allied with the Lombard cities, which had just handed Frederick another decisive defeat. Even more important, the Church was a natural ally of Duke Henry the Lion.

Henry the Lion's fate now unfolded with brisk and ruthless precision. He had seized Church lands in Saxony and appointed his own candidates to important ecclesiastical sees, neither of which he cared to undo. This served Frederick with the pretext he needed. Moving decisively, Frederick abruptly outlawed Henry and relieved him of all his lands—reassigning these to other presumably more grateful recipients, and swinging important members of the contentious German nobility to the emperor's side. Even a duke as powerful as Henry could not survive such totally unfavorable circumstances.

It was a splendid checkmate. Duke Henry had no choice but to pack up and leave Germany, bringing his family and sizable retinue to the court of his father-in-law, Henry II of England. There the Saxon Lion passed several years during the 1180s, awaiting the precise moment for revenge.

It came in 1189. At Easter, the aging Barbarossa—in his fourth decade of rule—departed on crusade for Jerusalem, leaving his son and heir, Henry Hohenstaufen, in his place. Young Hohenstaufen, already designated as his father's successor and co-regent, was clever but inexperienced. The Lion, with his accumulated experience of more than sixty years, sensed the situation's possibilities and determined to strike.

In the autumn of 1189, Henry the Lion returned in vengeance to Saxony, routing his enemies and reclaiming the lands he called his own. Victory followed victory, and none of his opponents—even young Henry Hohenstaufen himself—could stop him. The Saxon Lion was in magnificent form indeed.

It must have been galling for young Hohenstaufen, especially as childless King William of Sicily had departed this world shortly after the Lion's return. Barbarossa's son and heir had eagerly anticipated William's death in order to pounce on the enticing kingdom of Sicily. But now, occupied by the Lion's maddening forays into Saxony, his hands were completely tied.

Turning points come infrequently in history, but it soon became clear that the year 1189 marked a fundamental change for the leading actors on Europe's stage. Henry Plantagenet died ignominiously that summer, allowing Eleanor to emerge triumphantly from prison and see her dearest son, Richard, don scepter and crown. Henry the Lion swept back into Saxony that autumn, righting old wrongs and setting Barbarossa's son and heir on his ear. Victory must have seemed even sweeter when, not many months after, word arrived that Barbarossa himself had departed this world, drowned en route to the Holy Land.

Quite suddenly, Europe stood at a crossroads—two of its most important leaders abruptly removed from the scene and the power relationships they dictated gone topsy-turvy. Richard Lionheart and Philip of

France were comrades and allies in war, not bitter rivals, while Richard was related by marriage to both Henry the Lion and the royal house of Sicily. Frederick Barbarossa, clearly seeing his own options, had allied his empire with Philip and France, but now what? Henry Hohenstaufen, about to emerge as Emperor Henry VI, saw trouble on all sides. He could ill afford the luxury of heading off on crusade, as had his father. The crusader's laurels would have to go, as always, to the golden Plantagenet, Richard Lionheart.

Yet the old rivalries and antagonisms did not in fact disappear as easily as the leaders who had caused them. And although Richard did not yet know it, trouble lay directly ahead.

Part Two

Rollo the Viking

*R*ichard had of course inherited a long tradition of rivalry and conflict between the French and English crowns, one that dated from his great-great-grandfather, William the Conqueror. But the incendiary juxtaposition of English and French royal lands along the Norman border, which regularly fueled these clashes, had its origins back further still—with Richard's distant ancestors, the Vikings.

In that sense, it all began with Rollo—Rollo the Walker, as he was known, for he was a tall man, too long-legged for any horse to carry. A legend in his time, this imposing Viking had already distinguished himself with a long career of rapine and plunder before unexpectedly encountering defeat in pitched battle outside the walls of Chartres in A.D. 911.

This surprising news seems to have prompted Charles the Simple, the beleaguered king of the Franks, to think more constructively on how best to deal with Rollo and his plundering hordes. Charles's predecessors had tried to end the Viking devastation by buying off the marauders, only to discover that bribery merely whetted their appetites. Instead, Charles decided to offer these barbarians a stake in what they were decimating—lands in the valley of the lower Seine, in return for peace and their conversion to Christianity.

According to the much-disputed eleventh-century testimony of Dudo of Saint-Quentin,[1] this agreement took place in autumn of the year 911, in the little village of Saint-Clair-sur-Epte—possibly in the ancient church of Saint-Clair, whose ninth-century foundations still remain. Whether this arrangement warranted the formal term of "treaty," and whether the talks between warring parties even took place in Saint-Clair-sur-Epte, has been lost to history. Rollo may even have already hacked his way to control over the lands to which Charles now solemnly gave him legal authority.

But what does emerge from the mists of time is that territory in the area of the lower Seine was indeed ceded to Rollo the Walker at about this date and that, soon after, he and many of his followers received baptism from the archbishop of Rouen—a simple sequence of events that bound Rollo and his heirs to this chunk of territory and began their absorption into the Frankish population, thereby changing the course of history.

The land that Rollo received consisted of a strategic wedge between Paris and the sea, including Rouen and several of its dependent districts. Pushing outward from this base, he and his family rapidly subjugated lands as far east as the river Bresle and as far west as the rivers Orne and Vire. Soon after Rollo's death, his son, William Longsword, swept all the way to the Atlantic, hammering together the territory that would soon become known as Normandy—the land of the Normans, or Northmen.[2]

This land over which Rollo's descendants ruled was—and remains—beautiful and astonishingly varied, from the lush and pastoral landscapes of its interior to the wind-blasted heights of its western coasts. There are not one but many Normandies, and even the geological strata on which the region rests divide between the limestone country through which the Seine flows and the granite country to the west.

Such diversity promises interest to the traveler but headaches to the administrator and defender—especially if, as in Normandy's case, the region has no obvious natural borders on its landward side. Apart from the waters of the Atlantic and the Channel, the rulers of Normandy—down to Richard Lionheart himself—had to content themselves with merely a series of small streams to mark their duchy's southern and eastern extremities. Such flimsy boundaries quite naturally invited armed disputes, and in the years to come, Norman dukes would constantly be at war along their borders, whether with the counts of Flanders to the east or the rising house of Anjou to the south.

Yet of all Normandy's contentious borderlands, none would prove more dangerous than the portion of Charles the Simple's first territorial cession stretching between the Seine and two of its tributary rivers, the Andelle and the Epte. This vital piece of property bordered what would in time become known as the Île-de-France—those lands surrounding Paris that served as the heart of the French royal domain. Exercising due caution, Charles retained the territory extending below the river Epte to the river Oise, which became known as the French Vexin. Rollo's share, the Norman Vexin, looped southeasterly along the Seine from the river Andelle to Vernon, at the Epte's mouth, and extended eastward to Gisors. The Rock of Andely went to Rollo.

The agreement of Saint-Clair-sur-Epte thus made these Viking warriors and the Frankish king near neighbors. This created a potentially uncomfortable situation for both parties—although, given the king's weakness, a discomfort that promised to weigh more heavily on him. Yet the pitiful proportions to which Frankish kingship had shrunk by no means signaled a power vacuum on Rollo's frontiers. There were other powerful lords in the neighborhood who, like Rollo, had seized upon a welter of opportunities to become more powerful still.

Prominent among these was Hugh the Great, who bore the titles of count of Paris, marquis of the lands between the Seine and the Loire, and duke of the Franks. Rollo's heirs must have found it of considerable interest when, in the year 987, Hugh's son, Hugh Capet, became king of France.[3]

ের

The exact relationship between Normandy's tenth-century rulers and their overlords remains murky—as it may well have been at the time. While Charles seems to have believed that the lands he gave Rollo rendered the Viking chieftain his vassal, with the specific feudal obligations this entailed, Rollo seemed to think otherwise. Behaving as if the lands were a gift outright and the oath he had taken at Saint-Clair-sur-Epte called for little more than ceremonial homage, Rollo proceeded to do as he pleased—much as he probably had throughout the course of his long and bloody career. His successor, William Longsword, may not have seen the relationship substantially differently.[4]

It would hardly be surprising if these Vikings—for they unquestionably still were Vikings—had not fully understood the political arrangements of the land they were more accustomed to looting than cohabiting. Nor for the moment did there seem any good reason to learn. In the freebooting atmosphere of tenth-century France, there remained little but the exercise of raw power to persuade Rollo and his successors to rein in their ambitions and independence. Noble lords bashed their fellow lords with abandon, picking up the pieces and accumulating lands and authority as they went, while the sad remnant of Charlemagne's empire crumpled.

Hugh the Great was one of those who had consolidated his family's power at the expense of the monarch. He also played power politics with the Normans—a practice that his son, the future king, energetically followed. Hugh Capet even married off his sister to Rollo's grandson, Duke Richard I.

Whatever the relationship's exact legal implications, the willingness of Norman dukes and Capetian kings to help each other in distress proved essential during these early years. Hugh Capet's grandson received aid from Duke Robert of Normandy while battling a younger brother for the throne. Once king, he in turn recognized Robert's bastard son, William, as heir to Normandy, intervening decisively on William's behalf at the pivotal battle of Val-ès-Dunes.

It was only after this battle, which trounced an army of Norman rebels and securely established William as duke of Normandy, that the trouble between Norman dukes and French kings began.

❧❦❧

Several miles west of Andely, in a pretty ravine at the foot of Falaise's ducal castle, seventeen-year-old Robert of Normandy first encountered the local tanner's daughter, washing clothes. Her name was Arlette, and she was beautiful. Robert could judge this clearly, for she was knee-deep in the natural spring that welled up here, her skirts hiked high. Given her station, Arlette was not fit to wed the son of a duke, but there were other alternatives. And so the smitten young man lifted the unreluctant beauty upon his horse and brought her back to the castle—proudly, at her insistence, by the front door.

Or so goes local legend. Historians reject the flourishes but retain the essence.[5] What remains undisputed is that there in Falaise, in the year 1027 or 1028, Arlette bore Robert a son—William the Bastard, as he was most commonly known, until he seized events and became not only duke of Normandy but king of England.

William's father, Robert, became duke when his older brother sickened and died, suspiciously soon after inheriting the title. Whispers of "poison" began to circulate, and the duchy plunged into warfare. After quashing the immediate peril, Robert unexpectedly decided to leave on pilgrimage for Jerusalem—in penance, many knowingly suggested, for his brother's death. First persuading the king and the Norman nobility to recognize William as his heir, Robert set forth. He never returned, leaving an illegitimate seven-year-old to claim the title.

William's chances for survival, let alone recognition as duke of Normandy, were slight, and for several harrowing years he barely escaped with his life. Fortunately for him, the French king still vividly remembered the aid he had received from William's father and came to the lad's rescue.

Statue of William the Conqueror in his birthplace, Falaise, France.
© J. McAuliffe

This made all the difference; William now took effective rule over Normandy and never looked back.

He proceeded to marry magnificently, wedding Matilda, a daughter of the mighty house of Flanders. He successfully challenged the count of Anjou at several strategic points along their mutual frontier. Even more arrestingly, he now claimed that his cousin, Edward the Confessor, king of England, had named him as his successor. By itself, this development would have sufficiently alarmed the French king, but in company with these other triumphs, the news was chilling.

William now conquered the contested territory of Maine, attacked Brittany, and kept one eye on affairs in England. The tanner's grandson was about to become a king.[6]

✦

Judging from the vivid details of the Bayeux Tapestry, the transport vessels that bore William and his warriors across the Channel in 1066 looked much like the warships that had carried Rollo and his men up the Seine a century and a half before. Although William's own ship, the *Mora*, bore the figure of a golden boy blowing a horn pointed toward England, the tapestry shows that some among his fleet still used the fierce dragon figurehead to strike terror as they came.[7]

Yet the Normans who scanned the Channel's horizon little resembled the Viking warriors who had once sacked, then settled, Norman shores. Their Viking ancestors had lived among and married native Franks for five generations, obscuring Scandinavian bloodlines and absorbing Frankish manners, laws, and customs, until their descendants had become—and, even more importantly, thought of themselves as—Franks, or French.[8] The language they now spoke was the language of northern France.[9] Moreover, if any among this lot knew how to write (their intrepid leader was not among them), the language in which they took quill to parchment was Latin.

"Here the English and the Franks [*Angli et Franci*] have fallen in battle," the Bayeux Tapestry reads, in words embroidered across one of the scenes depicting the Battle of Hastings. Again, words above another scene helpfully explain, "*Hic Franci Pugnant*"—or, "Here the Franks are fighting."[10] Bishop Odo of Bayeux, William's half-brother and probably the impetus behind this remarkably vivid and intentionally persuasive length of stitchery, had no doubts about who it was that conquered the

English in 1066. It was the Franks. Not the heirs of the Vikings, nor even the Normans, but the Franks.

Not that everyone agreed. In particular, the twelfth-century monk and historian, Orderic Vitalis, thought otherwise. Chalking up the impressive list of conquests by Normandy's sons, he soon found an explanation for their successes in the very ancestry that they were so quick to disavow. Orderic (whose father was Norman but whose mother was English) asserted that the Normans' unique roots had in fact driven and defined them as a people, endowing them with both the ability and the drive to conquer. He wrote:

> The Normans are an untamed race, and unless they are held in check by a firm ruler they are all too ready to do wrong. In all communities, wherever they may be, they strive to rule and often become enemies to truth and loyalty through the ardour of their ambition. This the French and Bretons and Flemings and their other neighbours have frequently experienced; this the Italians and Lombards and Anglo-Saxons have suffered to the point of destruction.[11]

Other contemporary chroniclers were quick to concur,[12] even though by the time that Orderic wrote, the Normans' genetic as well as cultural absorption into the Frankish population was almost complete. And yet Orderic's vivid history so persuasively accounted for the sudden burst of Norman conquest, from the Mediterranean to the English Channel, that until recently this view has prevailed.[13]

Myths of ethnic or racial superiority die hard. When clothed in high romance, their death comes harder still. But to attribute the source of the Conqueror's overwhelming energy, drive, and ruthlessness to a genetic mix that had diluted the Viking bloodline on his father's side and may not have existed on his mother's side at all presses credibility. Scandinavian blood, in Haskins's words, may have been "numerically small in proportion to the mass," but the likelihood that (as Haskins concluded) it "leaven[ed] the whole" seems remote.[14]

More than nine centuries after the Battle of Hastings, it is time to recognize that, using new methods of warfare—mounted knights and the cavalry attack—William the Conqueror brought a thoroughly Frankish form of combat to England's shores.

Philip was an unusual name for a future king of France. Charles (with its obvious linkage to Charlemagne) and Louis (derived from Clovis) had been the more traditional choices of Charlemagne's French heirs, and the Capetian line abounded with Roberts and Hughs. But Anna of Kiev, Philip I's mother, brought the name westward from her birthplace, and in 1052, Henri of France bestowed it on his newborn son. Eight years later, Henri died, leaving a young boy who would have one of the longest reigns in French history (1060–1108).

Philip survived the six years of his minority without notable incident, but the French monarchy continued its meltdown, even as the power and exploits of the French nobility reached legendary proportions. To the south, Raymond of Toulouse swashbuckled his way to glory in the First Crusade, while William the Great of Aquitaine behaved in all respects like a king. In the north, Brittany remained virtually autonomous, while the count of Flanders ruled uncontested over his strategically important lands. Even Burgundy, although adjacent to Capetian holdings and closely connected to the royal family, retained its independence, while upstarts such as the counts of Anjou and Blois set themselves up in the fashion of the older and greater lordly houses, disdaining subservience and helping themselves to lands well within the Capetian territorial base.

And then there was Normandy. Even before acquiring a crown of his own, William had been little inclined to do homage to the king of the French. Now, following his conquest of England, he was even less interested in so doing.

From William's point of view, no one needed to worry about this state of affairs but Philip I, the young and inexperienced French king. After all, despite his legendary girth, Philip was the metaphorical ninety-pound weakling of the French political scene. But during the years while William was far away from Normandy, establishing and rounding out his royal conquest, the balance of power in northern France began to shift in significant and troubling ways. The house of Anjou revived, unleashing conflict along Normandy's southern borders. Rebels threatened from the west, digging in along the Breton frontier. And just when William least expected it, crisis erupted in the French Vexin, leaving the territory up for grabs. Philip exercised his kingly prerogatives and grabbed first, immediately occupying the Vexin right up to the Epte, along the Norman frontier.[15]

Absorbed in subduing England and in serious family quarrels, William did not confront Philip in the Vexin for a full decade. Then, in the summer of 1087, the French insolently threw down the gauntlet, sending raiding parties from the garrison of Mantes into the Norman Vexin, where they ravaged lands and took prisoners. "This," says the Norman chronicler Orderic Vitalis, "provoked the warlike King William to anger, and he laid claim to the whole Vexin."[16] Cloaking his action in somewhat dubious legal claims,[17] William now decided to put an end to the French threat along his frontier.

Armed to the teeth, the grizzled old warrior led his troops to the fortified town of Mantes, devastating the countryside as he went. Although he had put on considerable weight, William still was a commanding figure—at five feet ten inches, a towering one for his times. Not long after, a monk of Caen wrote that King William was "great in body and strong, tall in stature but not ungainly," adding that "if his voice was harsh, what he said was always suited to the occasion."[18] One wonders what orders this violent man bellowed as he urged his followers onward in the sack of Mantes, one of the most brutal of his career.[19] According to Orderic, the king's troops raged out of control, torching Mantes' churches and houses as well as its castle.[20] Many townspeople died in the terrible conflagration, which left Mantes desolate.

Yet Mantes had its revenge. For as William rode through its burning streets, his horse stumbled, throwing the portly monarch against the high pommel of his saddle and causing internal injuries. Some accounts merely say that he fell ill from the stench and heat, but whatever the cause, the king painfully made his way to Rouen, where he took to his bed. Soon it became obvious that he was dying.[21]

As his strength ebbed, the king made his confession and received absolution. He then distributed his kingdom and treasures among his sons, the churches, and the poor. In penance, he sent a large donation to the clergy of Mantes, to pay for the churches he had burned there. And then, after receiving Holy Communion from the archbishop of Rouen, William "departed this life, and, as we believe, went happily to his rest."[22]

The good monk of Caen who told this tale either did not know or did not care to report the Conqueror's truly sordid end, the worst of which occurred when his portly body proved too large for its waiting tomb. Harried attendants, forcing the corpse into its unyielding resting place, caused the decaying body to burst. Such a terrible smell spread throughout the church that everyone—including the priests—quickly fled.

Orderic, who tells this story, found ample material here for comment on the transiency of human glory.[23] Had he lived to see the rest of his century, he might well have expanded his thesis to include the fate of the star-studded dynasty that William founded.

❧ 4 ❧

Fathers and Sons

$\mathscr{B}$y the time of his death, William the Bastard had claimed his father's duchy and conquered a kingdom. He had subdued with the sword and ruled with an iron hand. He had also fathered four sons.

Three of these—Robert (known as Robert Curthose), William (known as William Rufus), and Henry— survived to adulthood. Having thus produced an heir and two spares, William could reasonably expect his line to continue. What he seems not to have expected was the rebellion of Robert, his eldest son. Although William had placed Normandy under Robert's care while busy subduing England, he was quick to remove his adult son's authority and independence once the Conquest was completed. Angered by this, Robert argued violently with his father, who was infuriated by such insubordination and, in any event, unwilling to lose control over Normandy. Showing Robert the door, William banished him from his lands. Not surprisingly, Robert now found his way to Paris and to the more welcoming court of the French king.

Philip I, who was no fool, received the young man warmly and proceeded to install him in the muscular castle of Gerberoy, along the simmering Vexin frontier. Reacting with typical bluntness, William fortified his neighboring Norman castles and besieged Gerberoy, with Robert in it. But Robert refused to back down, sallying forth with his own men to engage the besiegers in battle.

William was still a formidable fighter, but Robert was far younger and—as his father may not have recognized—an outstanding warrior in his own right. Engaging his father at sword point, Robert managed to unhorse and wound him, forcing proud William to withdraw to Rouen—a defeat of the most humiliating kind.

Frantic efforts by Robert's mother at last brought reconciliation. But after her death, trouble between the two broke out again. Despite William's reluctant recognition of Robert as his heir in Normandy, Robert still had no real authority there—nor was it William's intention to give him any. Exacerbating the situation, William regularly insulted Robert in public. Even Robert's nickname (Curthose, or "Short Boots," a joking reference to his height) became a verbal brickbat from the far taller father.

At length, William once again sent the discontented young man into exile, where he still was knocking about upon the Conqueror's death. It may well have been Robert, in fact, who fomented that surge of trouble between Philip and William in the Vexin that led to the Conqueror's demise.[1]

Persuaded on his deathbed to do right by Robert, William gave him Normandy, as promised. But he refrained from giving him anything else: England went to the second son, William Rufus, who had played his cards right, while the youngest, Henry, received a large sum of money. In time, as in the fairy tales, the youngest would end up with the entire kingdom. But in the meantime, strife broke out between the two older brothers,

Ruins of Château-sur-Epte, overlooking the river Epte. Constructed in the late eleventh century by William Rufus to guard this portion of the all-important boundary between the Norman and the French Vexin. Henry II subsequently added to its fortifications. © J. McAuliffe

with William Rufus supporting Robert's rebellious barons, and Robert in turn receiving aid from the French king.

In gratitude, Robert gave Philip the eastern anchor of the Norman Vexin, at Gisors—in effect handing over Normandy's eastern gateway to the king of France. William Rufus took quite a different approach to the matter. Several years later, when Robert gave Normandy to his brother as security for a loan to take him on crusade, William Rufus immediately fortified his Vexin borders with a vengeance—most notably at Gisors, where he piled up a steep artificial hill with a large tower on top (see illustration in chapter 10). He carried out the same plan at other locations along the Epte, including Château-sur-Epte. Unlike his brother, William Rufus was taking no chances with the French king.

⚜

Philip I was leery of William Rufus as well, for it was no secret that this boldly acquisitive English monarch (crowned as William II) wanted the French Vexin, and even entertained dreams of the French crown—a "detestable ambition," as Abbot Suger caustically put it.[2] Paris, which straddles the Seine upriver from Normandy, lay little more than forty miles from Norman frontiers, and at one point in his Vexin wars, William Rufus advanced as far as Pontoise—virtually at Paris's door.

But William Rufus's opportunities stemmed from more than geographic proximity. As he well knew, Philip I had only one son and heir. The chance that this heir—young Louis—would survive to adulthood was in those uncertain times far from likely. The Capetian monarchy was in fact a breath away from extinction, and William Rufus (who was related to the French royal family through his mother) sat ready and waiting to administer last rites.

Philip, in the meanwhile, nurtured and prepared this single heir. Under his watchful eye, young Louis grew into a capable warrior, well able to deal with the various baronial insurgencies that repeatedly cropped up throughout Capetian lands. In addition, Philip formally associated his son with him on the throne.[3]

Philip's detractors have suggested that the old king merely passed along to his offspring what he had come to be too lazy to do for himself,[4] and it is possible that his motives may have been mixed. Still, Philip's willingness to allow his son and heir an active role in the royal government went a long way to ensure that the monarch who would someday take his place would be an effective one. Indeed, Louis turned out to be a good and successful ruler, credited by historians with consolidating lands and power in a meaningful fashion and starting the Capetian monarchy on its spectacular rise.[5]

Of course, no one knew that things would work out that way. William Rufus was betting that Louis would not live long enough to receive the royal crown, and Philip, too, worried about this. Indeed, it probably was this concern that prompted Philip to remarry, putting aside his first wife, who had proven incapable of bearing him further heirs. But instead of securing the succession, the children from this second union created a new threat to Philip's legitimate heir. Indeed, Philip's death in 1108 precipitated a crisis in which a "conspiracy of wicked and evil men" tried to crown Louis' young half-brother in his place.[6] Louis (Louis VI) received his crown on the run, in Orléans—the first time that a Capetian monarch had not been anointed and crowned at Reims.

As if these perils were not enough, Louis' most dangerous foreign enemy, the king of England, soon appeared on Normandy's shores. But the king Louis now faced was not William Rufus, who had been shot by a longbow while hunting in the New Forest.[7] Instead, it was the Conqueror's youngest son, Henry, who had seized the crown.

Unlike his father and his brothers, Henry did not thrill to personal combat. A balding man of average height, with fleshy body and brawny chest, he was fond of saying, "My mother bore me [to be] a commander, not a soldier."[8] Beauclerk, he was later called, in tribute to his reputation for learnedness.[9] Still, he was as ruthless and aggressive in his own way as either his father or next-older brother, and he was perfectly capable of mounting a successful campaign, even as he was quite capable of winning what he wanted through means other than war. Within six years after William Rufus's death and Henry's assumption of the crown, Robert Curthose was Henry's prisoner for life.[10] Robert never was Henry's match.

Thus it was that as young Louis VI of France fought to save his crown, the Norman duke he faced was neither William Rufus nor Robert Curthose, but the far more dangerous Henry I of England. Refusing to pay homage for Normandy to the new king, Henry now arrived on Norman shores.

꧁꧂

As a military objective, Paris at the opening of the twelfth century lacked distinction. Half a millennium before, Clovis had made it his capital, and his successors favored it as well. But the last of Charlemagne's

heirs had preferred Laon, and for most of the eleventh century the Capetian monarchs resided in Orléans. Paris in the eleventh century was in fact
one of the smaller towns in Capetian domains. Yet by the century's close,
Philip I was spending an increasing amount of time there, and eventually
his son, Louis VI, established Paris as his capital.

The site—a hill-ringed basin lying at the Seine's confluence with the
Oise and the Marne—certainly was propitious. Centuries before, the Romans had taken due notice, driving out the Parisii Celts and establishing
what they called Lutetia at this junction of a major overland route between
southern France and the North Sea. Erecting a temple and administra-
tive buildings on the largest of Lutetia's islands (now the Île de la Cité)
and settling to the south on the hill later named for Paris's patron saint,
Geneviève, they created a small metropolis—with a forum near what now
are the Luxembourg Gardens, extensive baths abutting the present-day
Musée du Moyen Age, and an arena alongside the present Rue Monge.
They also built an aqueduct leading in from the south.

Lutetia's role as a strategic crossroads grew, with bridges (now the
Petit-Pont and Pont Notre-Dame) linking what now is Rue Saint-Martin
on the Right Bank with Rue Saint-Jacques on the Left. By the second
century A.D., this metropolis contained a population of more than ten
thousand—considerably less than the eighty thousand of Lyons or the one
million of Rome itself, but still of respectable size.

With Rome's decay and the onslaught of Germanic invaders, Lutetia's role as a Roman outpost withered. Yet the town (by now called Paris,
after its first inhabitants) continued to function as a trading center, even
while the third-century arrival of Denis, the first bishop of Paris, added
a new element to the mix. Although St. Denis' mission ended in martyr-
dom, he succeeded in creating a foothold for Christianity. When Clovis,
first king of the Franks, converted to Christianity in the early years of the
sixth century, he established his capital here.

By this time, a cathedral dedicated to St. Étienne dominated the
eastern end of the Île de la Cité. Clovis made a significant addition to
this ecclesiastical presence by building the church on the Left Bank later
known as Sainte-Geneviève.[11] Not many years later, Clovis' son, Childebert, founded the monastery that became known (after St. Germain,
bishop of Paris) as Saint-Germain-des-Prés. Members of the royal family had their final resting place here from Childebert on, until Dagobert
changed the royal burial site to the Abbey of Saint-Denis.

During the years immediately following Clovis, Paris managed in a
modest way to prosper. But after the Viking onslaught and the collapse of

Charlemagne's empire, little survived. Shrunken to scarcely more than the walled Cité, the town became a tangle of marsh and weeds.

Still, several of the great churches and their huddles of dependent villages remained. Recovery began during the eleventh century, and in the following years the city gradually grew to encompass these ecclesiastical bastions, slowly spreading to the marshy *marais* of the Right Bank as well as to the Left Bank of the Seine.

By this time the great fairs of nearby Champagne had begun to draw merchants from as far as Italy, spawning new traffic on roads and rivers leading everywhere. Wool from England and cloth from Flanders exchanged hands for spices, silks, and precious ornaments wrought of gold. These goods then made their slow return along the dusty Gallo-Roman roads, bringing quickened activity and prosperity as they came. Although Reims benefited most from the increasingly lucrative Champagne fairs, Paris, too, profited from its superb situation on the Seine. Port facilities had already sprung up along the river's northern and wider arm by the time Louis VI transferred the markets to the Right Bank from the increasingly crowded Île de la Cité. Later in the century, Philip II would build covered warehouses on the site, soon to become known as Les Halles. He also expelled the Jews from the Cité; they eventually reestablished themselves on the Right Bank, which was becoming the commercial heart of town.

But in Louis VI's day, most Parisians still lived on the Seine's largest island, the Île de la Cité. Here at the western end lived the king, in a small palace that the second Capetian monarch, Robert the Pious, had erected on the site of an ancient Roman citadel. To the east, near the cathedral, resided the bishop of Paris and a growing throng of students, who flocked from great distances to listen to and debate with the likes of William of Champeaux and, the star of them all, Peter Abelard. In between these secular and ecclesiastical domains, perhaps three thousand craftsmen and tradespeople lived cheek by jowl, jostling each other along the cramped and muddy lanes as they cried their wares and scurried from place to place.

Here, amid the cacophony, mud, and stench, Louis began to fortify his palace, strengthening it not only against possible Norman attack, but also—and more imminently—against the welter of powerful lords that surrounded him.[12] With this in mind, Louis linked the Cité to the growing port along the Seine's right bank via a great stone bridge directly connecting the island with what now is Rue Saint-Denis, securing access with a stout fortification, the Châtelet.

Rue Saint-Denis, one of two major routes leading northward, led directly to the royal Abbey of Saint-Denis, founded centuries before at the burial site of the martyred saint.[13] Here, even as Louis VI was building Paris into the seat of a reviving Capetian monarchy, Abbot Suger was planning a new abbey church that would reach to the very heavens. His church, with its arched and pointed vaults and astonishing deep-blue windows (of such brilliance that many believed the glassmaker had infused his molten glass with sapphires), led the twelfth century into those soaring Gothic realms where Chartres, Notre-Dame de Paris, and countless others would soon follow. But more than this, Suger created in Saint-Denis a fitting tribute to the saint who by this time was evolving into a political as well as a spiritual powerhouse.

Centuries of close ties between the Abbey of Saint-Denis and the royal crown had quite naturally lent a certain aura to the martyred saint's reputation. Since the late sixth century, members of the royal family had been buried there, and from about the same time the court had deposited copies of royal documents there for safekeeping. The royal regalia used at coronations came to be kept at Saint-Denis as well, although the coronation itself continued to take place at Reims, the site of Clovis' conversion and coronation. Dagobert's recognition of St. Denis as royal patron further enhanced the abbey's reputation as the royal abbey, as did royalty's extension of numerous special privileges, which freed the monks from the usual fees and obligations.

Yet these were evidences of royal favor, with power residing in the benefactor. Indeed, for more than a century, when the monarchy sank to its nadir, the abbey stood in danger of losing its independence to the real source of local power, the counts of Paris.

Still, as Abbot Suger was quick to recognize, the king held the French Vexin as a fief from the Abbey of Saint-Denis—in theory, from the saint himself, although in practice from the abbey and its abbot (who during Louis VI's reign was, of course, Suger). A minister to the king during the reigns of both Louis VI and Louis VII, and regent during Louis VII's long absence on crusade, Suger held a formidable position in the Capetian court. Clearly the fortunes of the Capetians and those of Suger were intertwined, for while this energetic abbot sent the arches of his abbey cathedral soaring toward the heavens, he was also hard at work erecting a political construct that would set the Capetian king at the pinnacle of feudal power—worldly power for, as Suger argued, the monarch was in turn vassal to the long-dead St. Denis. That the Abbot of Saint-Denis was the martyred saint's agent here on earth did not at all intimidate Suger, who did not shy away from the obvious conclusion.

Suger's political construct was at heart a simple one, positing a neat and tidy theory of landholding. According to Suger, the French territorial princes held their lands in fiefdom to the Capetian monarch in much the same way that lesser lords had traditionally held their lands within the hereditary Capetian realms. In Suger's view, the count of Auvergne held his lands from the duke of Aquitaine, who in turn held his vast realms from the king of France. To Suger, Normandy and Aquitaine and all the rest were simply part and parcel of the kingdom of France—a neat and tidy theory, filled with possibilities for the Capetian monarchs. The only problem was that the territorial princes did not view things that way. As far as they were concerned, the king of the French could do what he liked in his own hereditary lands, but he had no business whatsoever in theirs.

Suger's political construct thus did not yet represent reality, for feudalism, with its fundamental elements of loyalty and protection, landholding, and military service, was still evolving out of the disorder that had accompanied the widespread collapse of central authority in the ninth and tenth centuries. Certain of its elements had ancient roots, but tradition faltered in the face of raw aggression. Local conditions varied enormously, and men of power—whether great or small—simply demanded and took what the traffic would bear.

By Suger's day, many of these arrangements had acquired a certain stability and even sophistication. But the messy and overlapping structure of French political society in the early twelfth century did not even remotely resemble a pyramid, and certainly not one with the king at its apex. Feudal relationships still were widely diffused, focusing on dukes and counts and even local lords rather than the monarch. Although Suger's theory presented a kind of blueprint for power, the Capetian monarchs could not expect power to come their way by some sort of divine right but would have to impose it upon their recalcitrant subjects.

St. Denis pointed the way. With Suger's encouragement, the king acknowledged that St. Denis was not only his spiritual patron but his feudal overlord as well. Facing invasion from the German emperor, Louis VI hastened to the Abbey of Saint-Denis. There he begged the martyred saint to defend his kingdom. Then he took from the altar the military standard of the Vexin—a forked scarlet banner embroidered with golden flames that legend ascribed to Charlemagne.[14]

In all humility, Louis received this silken banner in a manner that acknowledged his vassalage to his saintly overlord, St. Denis.[15] He then called for all of France to rally around him against the common foe. The response was impressive, with many of France's most powerful barons flocking to his side. Reconsidering, the emperor decided to head for other parts (German historians insist that he had more pressing business elsewhere). Rejoicing in this turn of events, Louis returned the banner to the abbey in triumph.

"It is neither right nor natural that the French be subject to the English, but rather the English to the French," Suger gloated, anticipating days of glory that still lay well ahead.[16] But for the first time a king of France had caught a whiff of the possibilities. For nearly three centuries thereafter, the French would go into battle bellowing their famous war cry, "Monjoie Saint-Denis!" and carrying before them the flame-colored silken banner of Saint-Denis known as the Oriflamme.

Already, this banner was emerging as the royal standard of France.

⚜

"Louis, king of the French," wrote Suger, "conducted himself toward Henry, king of the English and duke of the Normans, as toward a vassal, for he always kept in mind the lofty rank by which he towered over him."[17] As duke of Normandy, in other words, England's Henry I was Louis VI's feudal dependent, no matter what other titles he bore. For years, Henry resisted this logic, and this recalcitrance lay at the heart of Henry's struggles with the French king.

Louis in turn countered by rallying to the cause of the imprisoned brother, proclaiming Robert Curthose's son—an attractive young man by the name of William Clito—as the rightful Norman duke and English king. Until his untimely death, Clito served as a rallying point for all of Henry's enemies, which was exactly what Louis had in mind.

William Clito was not the only son upon the political chessboard, for Louis and Henry each had sons. In a reversal of previous generations, Henry had but one legitimate son, while Louis was blessed with eight.[18] In much the same spirit as his father, Louis designated the eldest of these as his successor and associate in the crown, while the next in line, a mild lad by the name of Louis, departed for a monastic career.

Henry I's son, known as William Aetheling, was but seventeen years old when Louis VI appealed the cause of William Clito to the pope, with such success that Henry had to scamper to protect both his duchy and his crown. To ensure his son's succession in Normandy against William Clito's claims, Henry now agreed that young Aetheling would do homage to Louis for Normandy—a significant concession, although not quite the same as the king himself bending the knee. William Aetheling did as he was directed and then prepared to return to England on the White Ship, the newest and finest vessel in his father's fleet. It was a lovely evening in late November, and he and his young friends were prepared to party all the way.

The king set sail first in a light breeze, just before twilight. Delayed by their festivities, young Aetheling and his friends did not push off until well after dark, with a crew that by this time was almost as drunk as the passengers. Catching sight of the king's ship well ahead, the passengers called out that "those who were now ahead must soon be left astern." The ship fairly flew, "swifter than the winged arrow."[19]

Too late, the crew saw the rock that rose above the waves. As the boat impacted with a grinding crash, the young nobles cried out in alarm, suddenly realizing their peril. Out came the oars and boat hooks, as the crew tried in vain to force the vessel off. But the rock had split the prow, and water now came pouring in.

Amid the terror, as frantic bodies fought the sea, someone thought to launch the single skiff and push the prince inside. Well on his way toward shore and safety, he heard one voice above the others—his illegitimate half-sister, the young countess of Perche, who shrieked out for him not to abandon her. Overcome with pity, William Aetheling ordered the little boat to return, thus sealing his fate: "for the skiff, overcharged by the multitudes who leaped into her, sank, and buried all indiscriminately in the deep."[20]

There was but one survivor, a butcher who managed to seize the mast and keep afloat until morning. He alone remained to tell the terrible tale. Lost were countless sons and daughters, the cream of England and Normandy's young aristocracy. Scarcely a noble family went untouched.

Worst of all was the king's loss. For now Henry, duke of Normandy and king of England, had no legitimate son and heir.

The White Ship had changed history.

❋ 5 ❋

The Virgin and the Queen

𝒥t was summer in the year 1137, and Louis VI lay dying. Nearly sixty years of age, he had by this time grown so huge that he was called "the Fat"—a sobriquet not even bestowed on his obese father. Yet despite the terrible heat and his debilitating illness, he seemed at peace. His people loved him, and his domains—although still small—were well ruled and secure.

His great opponent, Henry I of England, had died two years earlier, leaving his own broad realms without a male heir. Remarrying soon after William Aetheling's tragic death, Henry—who had fathered countless illegitimate children—fathered no offspring by his second queen. But he had a daughter, Matilda, who at a tender age had married the now dead German emperor. With no prospect of legitimate male heirs, Henry now induced his barons to recognize Matilda as his successor. And then he married off the protesting twenty-five-year-old widow to fourteen-year-old Geoffrey of Anjou.[1]

It was an interesting move. Since the time of Fulk the Black in the tenth century, the house of Anjou had constituted a major threat to Normandy's southern frontiers. During the intervening years, the Angevins and the kings of France had predictably found much in common. It was this particular alliance between French king and Angevin count that Henry of England now sought to break up.

Matilda, who keenly resented her demotion from empress to countess, treated her teenaged husband with contempt, which he fully reciprocated. It was a miserable marriage. Yet after some rocky early years, it accomplished what Henry had hoped: it permanently broke up the

Angevin-Capetian alliance and promised to absorb Anjou's territories into the empire the Norman Conqueror had created. For although Matilda and her young husband had little love for one another, they eventually did their duty and managed to produce three sons.

Of course, from the Angevin perspective it would be an Angevin count who would someday acquire Normandy and the English crown. But Henry chose not to see it that way. And he lived to see the birth of his first grandson, a little namesake who would in time become England's Henry II.[2] Not only had Henry I of England provided for an heir, but he had also created a major territorial alignment that threatened to overshadow the slow but steady territorial gains of the house of Capet.

Louis VI, looking out from his sickbed, could see the full implications of this threat, but he could see as well the uncertainty of all human plans. For immediately following Henry's death, Stephen of Blois (Henry's nephew) had seized the English crown, plunging England into almost two decades of dynastic warfare.

Louis had suffered his own reverses as well. His heir, young Philip, met an untimely death while riding the dank streets of Paris—victim of a snoozing sow who toppled both horse and prince into the muck. Most fortunately, Louis had other sons. But the next in line, another Louis, was only eleven years old and of far milder disposition than seemed altogether appropriate in a king.[3]

Unlike his father or older brother, young Louis was not a warrior born. Indeed, he seemed quite suited for the archbishop's role originally envisioned for him. But now, with no other choice, the old king hauled this youngster out of the monastery and began his knightly training. Indeed, upon Suger's recommendation, Louis VI soon had his adolescent son anointed and crowned.[4] Then, in the summer of 1137, as the old king lay dying, he sent his young successor southward, toward a political coup of the most magnificent proportions.

For news had reached Louis concerning Guillaume, count of Poitou and duke of Aquitaine. Guillaume, who had not shrunk from life's banquet, had died en route to the shrine of St. James of Compostela, where he presumably thought to find forgiveness for his many and varied sins. He left as his heirs two orphaned girls, the oldest of whom—Eleanor—was only fifteen. This event quite properly riveted King Louis' attention, for the young heiress's domains would make a truly noble addition to the still-small territory controlled by the kings of France. Better yet, the placement of these lands would squeeze Normandy and Anjou between the Île-de-France and Poitou.

At last, Louis had a response to Henry I's move in Anjou. Acting swiftly, the French king launched his by-now seventeen-year-old heir and namesake on a mission to southwest France to claim the heiress as his bride.

Young Louis marched off in the blistering heat with a retinue sufficiently fierce and splendid to strike terror and admiration into the hearts of any possible competitors. Within a month he had arrived at the ducal city of Bordeaux and, on a wilting Sunday in midsummer, married the beautiful and sophisticated young duchess. It was as the newlyweds returned to Paris that word arrived of Louis VI's death. His son now was king, and Eleanor of Aquitaine had most suddenly vaulted from duchess to queen.

What Eleanor thought of this unexpected turn of events, we do not know. For all his lack of polish, Louis seems to have been a reasonably attractive young man, tall and slim with shoulder-length blond hair. More to the point, he now was king of France. While his royal domains lacked heft, a royal crown was not to be sneezed at—especially as Eleanor's own lands would go a long way toward correcting any of her husband's territorial deficiencies.

And so the royal bride set off in a splash of silken banners with her young husband, who from all indications was completely besotted with her. Quite properly so, for Eleanor was no ordinary fifteen-year-old, even as her inheritance comprised no ordinary aggregation of lands. In size alone her territories boggled the imagination, stretching from the Loire to the Pyrenees, and from the shores of the Atlantic to the heights of the Massif Central. Moreover, Eleanor's lands were as beautiful and open to pleasure as the duchess herself—and, from all accounts, just as independent.

Independence seemed to come with the territory, for the dukes of Aquitaine had never enjoyed the same authority over their lands as had the dukes of Normandy. Although Norman barons were inclined to rebel whenever opportunity arose, their most recent rulers had given them as little opportunity as possible. By contrast, Aquitaine's history redounded with rebellion, and the names of Lusignan, Limoges, and Angoulême instantly summoned up images of trouble. Retreating to their cliff-top castles, high above rivers that sheared their way through limestone to the sea, these lords of the South enjoyed the bounty of their petty tyrannies and stoutly resisted all ducal efforts to rein them in.

The dukes of Aquitaine did not appreciate such thoroughgoing insubordination, but in turn managed to behave in much the same way toward their own sovereign overlords, the Capetian kings. Not only powerful, the dukes of Aquitaine were a particularly lusty and unrepentant tribe. Disinclined to follow anyone's rules but their own, they took on their neighbors and the clergy with equal enthusiasm. They had no regrets. Eleanor's freewheeling grandfather, Guillaume the Troubadour, had led scores of men to their doom in the Holy Land, only to desert his wife and abscond with another married lady upon his return. He never had any difficulty in justifying his behavior.

Nor would his granddaughter, who in time would prompt certain members of the clergy to recall her family ties to a woman most appropriately named Dangereuse.

⚜

Once upon a time, so goes the story, there was no true love. And then, from a breath of air and two pairs of lips, the troubadours invented the kiss, and true love began.

It's a nice story, which of course is not true. Except that, as with most legends, it hints at a reality. For sometime toward the end of the eleventh century, the influences of nearby Moorish Spain filtered through the Pyrenees and, mixed with the particular light and warmth of southern France, created a new and softer ethos, one hospitable to love. Under the leadership of Eleanor's grandfather, the legendary Guillaume the Troubadour—a poet in his own right, and a patron of the first magnitude—the troubadours of southern France brought together the subtle sensuousness of Moorish traditions with the open pleasures of Provence to create a new and highly original secular poetry of love.

At first unique to southern France, the earliest troubadours were wanderers with a talent for song and an acquaintance with courtly ways. Unlike the minstrels who traveled from court to court throughout the later Middle Ages, these early troubadours claimed ties with noble households, whether as offspring of the serving staff or as scions of lesser lords—younger sons of younger sons. Whatever their origins, most had little in the way of prospects and were dependent upon their patrons. In some instances this meant the lord of the castle, but more frequently their patron was the castle's lady.

These troubadours entertained their patrons with songs of love, creating a new ideal—a feminine ideal of romance and love—even as the earlier *chansons de geste* had ennobled the thoroughly masculine preoccupation with war. It was necessary. Life, especially for the aristocratic woman, was invariably dull and often brutal. Married off at an early age to a husband she could not love, the typical lady of the castle spent the remainder of her days confined within the castle walls. She was perfectly capable of defending those walls during her husband's absences, which were frequent. Yet this sort of excitement could not have given much pleasure, except in contrast to the usual routine. Otherwise, apart from her primary function of giving birth to healthy heirs, much of her days would have passed in devotional duties or in stitching.

As an alternative to rapine, bloodshed, and destruction, this cloistered existence had its advantages. Certainly the peasant wife would not have hesitated to exchange her hard lot for the safer boredom of the lady of the castle. Nor would the lady willingly have exchanged places with her social equal from an earlier and more primitive period. Still, dissatisfaction hung like a pall. "I have lived here in this castle like an anchoress in a cell," the dying Duchess of Brunswick told her confessor. "What delights or pleasure have I enjoyed here, save that I have made shift to show a happy face to my servants and gentlewomen? I have a hard husband (as you know) who has scarce any care or inclination toward women."[5]

Louis VII was not a hard husband, but his marriage to Eleanor proved a similarly dismal arrangement. Monkish by inclination and training, his habits and preferences set the tone for the entire French court. During the fifteen years she endured as his wife, Eleanor put up with a gray and somber existence, enlivened only by occasional scholastic disputes in a Paris littered with disputing scholars. Eventually this marital mismatch was blessed by the birth of two children. Yet since both of the children were female, Louis' well-wishers began casting about for the cause of their godly king's bad luck. Eleanor, whose contempt for her husband as a marriage partner was notorious, had long since concluded that they did not have far to look. But Louis' supporters chose to put a different slant on matters, blaming Eleanor for Louis' undeserved punishment.

After all, wasn't this the woman who had ridden to the Second Crusade dressed as an Amazon? Wasn't this the woman whose scandalous behavior with her uncle, Raymond of Antioch, shocked Louis' court, reminding one and all of her infamous ancestry? What Eleanor actually had done or not done seems to have been lost in shadows, but the rumormongers had a field day. With the queen's reputation in tatters, the saintly Bernard of Clairvaux now proceeded to make matters perfectly clear. Put off this woman, he warned Louis—put her off before she brings ruin to the entire house of Capet.

Louis resisted. Astonishingly enough, in an age where love and marriage had but passing acquaintance, this mild-mannered king loved his beautiful and spirited wife. She dazzled him. She was everything he wasn't, and despite all arguments to the contrary, he longed to forgive and keep her.

To Eleanor's evident relief, he failed. The grounds for divorce were the usual ones—consanguinity, or too close a blood relationship between the parties. Louis' and Eleanor's distant family ties had not bothered anyone, pope included, at the time of their marriage, and over the years the pope himself had even offered his exalted services as a marriage counselor—but to no avail. Everyone well understood that consanguinity existed for the purpose of putting asunder for reason of state what reason of state alone had joined, and in Louis' case the dynastic justification for divorce was overwhelming: Eleanor had been Louis' wife for fifteen years and had yet to produce a male heir.

Given these clear dynastic requirements, the still-young king and his consort at last separated, Louis freeing his beloved to return to the sun-washed land of her birth. Immediately withdrawing to his retreat of a castle in Paris, he failed to give adequate attention to the powder keg he left behind. Although by now thirty years old, Eleanor still was beautiful and, most important, still was duchess of Aquitaine and countess of Poitou. She would unquestionably marry again.

❧

Just as unquestionably, Eleanor's world remained a man's world. The former queen undoubtedly was captivating, but neither she nor any mortal woman commanded center stage. A softer and more feminine ethos may have begun to permeate the south of France, but men everywhere still gloried in the epic song of Roland, the tragic hero of Roncevalles. Roland's great death scene, which countless fighting members of the nobility seem to have committed to memory, reveals a curious oversight—a hero so preoccupied with the glories of war that it never occurs to him to think of his betrothed, the beautiful Alda.

Alda did not interest the men who hung on every word of this great *chanson de geste*, while Roland's sword, horse, and best friend, Oliver, did. Chivalry was still completely masculine in orientation, just as the *Chanson de Roland* was a totally masculine tale.[6]

One woman alone during these years commanded unhesitating loyalty and devotion, and this was Mary, the Blessed Virgin herself. As early

Virgo, the virgin or maiden. Relief from the portal of the Coronation of the Virgin, the northern portal of the western façade of Notre-Dame de Paris, Paris, France. © J. McAuliffe

as the ninth century, the Western Church had begun to venerate her. But it was the twelfth and thirteenth centuries that turned to her in special appeal, as a maternal intercessor with enough love, pity, and power to combat the rigors of a still-brutal world.

She arrived from the East, where she had always been held in special reverence, to shed her light and love in Western Christendom. The Church of Rome still was a Church militant, with a fighting clergy and a sternly watchful and wrathful God. Yet it was the warriors themselves who discovered and brought her home with them, an unexpected prize of the First Crusade and the Norman conquests of Byzantine Sicily and southern Italy.

Western Europe, and especially France, took to her with relief and joy. She was the Mother of God. She understood. Noble houses and whole towns hastened to declare themselves her subjects, expressing their humble and devoted vassalage by flinging up glorious and light-filled cathedrals dedicated to Notre Dame. They loved and revered her, and she rewarded them in turn, flouting conventions and overturning judgments. Unlike her Son, the Blessed Virgin was neither monarch nor lawgiver nor judge. She was a mother and, so long as they remained in her service, she rewarded the endeavors of all her children, saints and sinners alike.

On her feast day of the Annunciation, they blessed the seed for the coming year's crops. On her feast day of the Assumption, they blessed the fruits of the harvest, the orchards and meadows, the fields and farms, oceans and boats—all the places where her devoted followers worked and cultivated their daily bread. Her blessing rained down showers from heaven, and the sun shone with a special radiance from her love.

Who would not willingly serve such a gentle and all-forgiving, yet powerful queen?

⚜

It was spring, and Empress Matilda, countess of Anjou, lay dying. All had rejoiced at the birth of her second son, but joy soon made way for sorrow as her condition became clear. Surrounded by hovering attendants, Matilda weakly supervised the distribution of her goods, and then asked to be buried at her beloved Abbey of Bec-Hellouin, across the river from her deathbed in Rouen. No, her father insisted, that would not do; she would be buried at Rouen's cathedral church like a proper daughter of a Norman duke, alongside Rollo the Viking and William Longsword.

With steely determination, the dying Matilda persevered. She would be buried, she argued, at the Abbey of Bec. And then, with steelier determination yet, she mooted the entire argument by recovering.[7]

In a man, this kind of resolve and indomitability would have won praise, but in a woman it aroused wholesale anger and derision—especially as Matilda's temper seems to have been none too sweet, and stories of her arrogance circulated widely among her foes. She was, one of her contemporaries remarked, "of the stock of tyrants."[8] All these traits had to one degree or another characterized the first three Norman kings of England, and they would prove no strangers to her son as well. Yet in a woman, something more in the way of modesty and gentleness was expected. As Matilda was to find, it was difficult enough for a strong and forthright woman to live up to the twelfth century's standards of fair womanhood: this woman was expected to do so while seizing a crown.

Matilda's rights as heiress were murky, but not out of the question. The twelfth century expected its monarchs to be warriors. Yet her father had, after all, extracted his barons' allegiance to her. Rapid action on her part, such as William Rufus had taken upon the death of the Conqueror, or Henry upon William Rufus's own demise, would have assured her a coronation, if not an untroubled reign. As it was, her cousin Stephen got to Winchester first, and with such dazzling speed that Matilda was left to play catch-up for the better part of twenty years. Throughout these years, the fact that the rival claimant to the crown was a woman did not in the least help Matilda's cause.

Two months pregnant with her third son, Matilda responded to the news of her father's death and Stephen's coronation by racing to secure the Norman border castles—an effort that would not have been necessary had her father (unprepared, in Orderic's words, to "set anyone above himself as long as he lived, or even to suffer any equal in his house or in his kingdom")[9] given over these very castles to Geoffrey as he had originally promised. This unfortunate grasping quality, which had also distinguished the Conqueror, may have meant the difference between success and failure for Henry I's daughter, who—with her husband—now had to establish her Norman foothold before crossing the Channel to England.

There, no mass uprising greeted her arrival. Yet enough supporters turned out that Stephen, despite his vastly greater resources, was unable to crush the threat she offered, which remained a real one throughout the entire course of his unsettled reign. While her husband remained to fight in Normandy, Matilda and her illegitimate half-brother Robert, earl of Gloucester, pressed on toward London. There she came within a breath of attaining her goal, until she so alienated the Londoners with the magnitude of her financial demands that they chased her out of the city, forcing her to retreat to Oxford.

Despite Stephen's subsequent capture (followed by an exchange for the indispensable Robert of Gloucester, who had also fallen into enemy hands), it at length became clear that Matilda never would win the crown. By the same token, a sufficient number of English lords possessed Norman properties that they looked with considerable interest at the progress her husband Geoffrey was making in Normandy. At last, urged by Robert of Gloucester and others, Matilda came to realize that her best hope lay in her firstborn, Henry, whose claims to the throne were rapidly gaining ground with every year.

Earl Robert first brought young Henry back with him from Normandy when the lad was only nine, and for the next two years the youngster remained in England, training for knighthood and kingship. By this time, with the exhaustion of Stephen's royal treasury, the two sides had come to be more evenly matched. Matilda kept up her resistance, even as Geoffrey continued his successful battling in Normandy and young Henry grew closer to assuming his mother's cause in his own name. Under these conditions of almost constant warfare, the boy very quickly became the man, absorbing lessons in administration and government along with his study of letters (on which his father insisted) and the indispensable lessons in war.

Henry seems to have first entered the fray on his own behalf at the age of fourteen. With a teenager's hotheadedness, he raised a small force of knights and crossed the Channel from Normandy, intent on doing whatever damage he could to Stephen's cause. Although at first creating something of a sensation, he quickly learned that his band of warriors was too small to do much damage. In want of loot or any other sort of reward, he had to apply somewhat sheepishly to his mother for money to pay his men.[10]

Stephen also had a son, named Eustace, of about the same age as young Henry. Eustace represented the same threat to Matilda's cause that young Henry did to Stephen's, and so it was quite natural for Stephen to press to have Eustace immediately crowned as his successor. He also was perfectly willing for Eustace to do homage to the king of France for Normandy, to ensure his smooth succession in that land. But Geoffrey of Anjou continued to pursue his Norman claims, at length capturing Rouen and claiming the ducal title, for which he did homage to Louis VII. He may even have given up Gisors in the Vexin, in return for the French king's reluctant recognition.[11]

In due course both Eustace and young Henry were knighted (Henry by his great-uncle, the king of Scotland), and each of these sixteen-year-olds was now prepared to rule the contested lands of England and Normandy. Although Stephen still kept to the field, Henry assumed his mother's cause in his own name, while Matilda retired to Rouen. England's crown still lay beyond Henry's reach, but thanks to Geoffrey, the duchy of Normandy was his.

At length, the French king agreed to meet with the Angevins. Thus it was that in August 1151, Geoffrey of Anjou and young Henry arrived at the royal court to make their peace with the king and claim the duchy on Henry's behalf.

They must have created quite a stir. Geoffrey (known as Geoffrey the Fair or Geoffrey Plantagenet, after the golden wildflower that so dashingly floated from his helmet) was devastatingly handsome, while his by-now eighteen-year-old son was a natural leader of men, bred for kingship and already a warrior of considerable renown. Henry's prospects, although still far from certain, surrounded him with a certain aura. Eleanor, Louis' unhappy queen, could not but have noticed.

The price Henry paid for Louis' recognition as duke of Normandy was a large one. Louis was not inclined toward recognition, and he required a significant prize: the rest of the Norman Vexin, which Henry now turned over to the king.[12] But as Henry perhaps already suspected, the price that Louis was about to pay for this encounter would, in the long run, prove infinitely greater.

❧❧❧

From the devil they came, to the devil they will go.
—attributed to St. Bernard of Clairvaux[13]

On his mother's side, Henry Plantagenet was impeccably descended from William the Conqueror and greatness. But on the paternal side, rumor had it that he was descended from the powers of darkness—from Fulk the Black and an unknown dervish, who gave birth to Fulk's children and then reportedly escaped Holy Communion by wafting out an open church window in the form of a witch. It gave much cause for comment, especially when Fulk's descendant and Henry's father, Geoffrey of Anjou, unexpectedly took ill and died after uttering an astonishing blasphemy within hearing of the entire French court.

The gossip was delicious. Yet for all that, Geoffrey does not seem to have departed this life in a fit of anger. His blasphemy—quite in character with his hair-trigger temper—had exploded on the heels of quite another controversy and was a passing matter. Instead there is strong evidence that Geoffrey of Anjou had good reason to be pleased with himself and the prospects for his son and heir. In fact, few later doubted that during his sojourn at the French court, Geoffrey held certain conversations with Eleanor, queen of the French. It was upon his return to Anjou, anticipating events to come, that he most unexpectedly took ill and died.

Henry Plantagenet, the successor of Fulk the Black as well as William the Conqueror, now became duke of Normandy and count of Anjou.

It was six months later, in March 1152, that Louis VII and his queen divorced. Immediately following the lofty synod of ecclesiastics that sanctioned this momentous event, Eleanor speedily departed for her own lands—minus her two daughters, who were awarded to their father. Haste was necessary, for she had metamorphosed from married queen into the richest marriage prize in the realm, and in fact had two narrow escapes from marriage en route from the divorce proceedings (both claimants, including Henry's little brother, being enterprising younger sons, whose idea of courtship was to seize the lady). Eleanor was wily enough to evade both attempts. She could do better than younger sons and was about to prove it. Scarcely two months later, she married Henry, duke of Normandy and count of Anjou.

Louis had not expected that. Nor for that matter had anyone else. Eleanor was notoriously independent, but as duchess of Aquitaine she was Louis' vassal. Louis had been fool enough to believe that she would seek his permission to remarry. In fact she did no such thing and, to make matters even more humiliating for her first husband, chose for her second husband the French king's most powerful political and military rival. Eleanor, who already was countess and duchess over all of southwest France, had proceeded to marry the count and duke of virtually all of northwest France, who was claimant for England to boot.[14]

Her audacity appeared unbounded, and it was only barely outdistanced by that of her young second husband, Henry Plantagenet of Anjou. Not surprisingly, the rumor soon circulated that the late lamented Geoffrey had bedded the French queen before secretly making arrangements to wed her to his son.[15]

A rotten business, to be sure. But what any man might have given to bed Eleanor, queen of the French!

Henry certainly seemed to enjoy his wife's bed—at least, during the early years of their marriage. To his exultation and Louis' despair, Eleanor promptly presented Henry with a male heir, soon followed by four more sons and three daughters—a dynastic bonanza for the young Plantagenet. In the meantime, Henry grasped and seized the crown of England and, with his firebrand of a wife, forged the Plantagenet realm into one that completely eclipsed that of the Capetians—rivaling the legends of Charlemagne and King Arthur himself.

For the second time in her career, Eleanor had become a queen.

⁂

By this time, the Vizir, or Wise Man, in the game of chess had also become a Queen—a transformation that has baffled subsequent centuries. The game itself arrived from the East by the early eleventh century, and the Vizir—known in Arabic as the Firz, or Firzan—came with it. Sometime after his arrival, he changed both name and sex, giving rise to some interesting speculation.

Typically, the French had the most engaging solution. According to a paper presented to the French Academy in 1719, the earliest French chess players had merely confused the words "fierge" (derived from "fers" and the Arabic "firz") with "vierge." "Vierge," of course, means "virgin," and the French, according to this account, quite naturally made the associational leap to the Queen of Heaven. The Vizir became the Virgin and then the Queen.

The less fanciful twentieth century concluded that renaming the figure "Queen" provided a kind of logical symmetry to the already-existing figure of King. As a symbol, the chess Queen also showed a certain transition in the game's focus, from the warlike imagery of the eleventh century to the imagery of the state, in which a queen had a role to play.

Yet the Queen in twelfth-century chess, although presumably grateful for the opportunity to make her presence known, was not a strong figure—weaker, certainly, than the Knight or Rook, and weaker than the King. Despite the twelfth century's escalating attention to women and all things feminine, this attention had not been translated into power—as the Empress Matilda painfully came to realize, and as Eleanor was about to learn.

Women remained of value chiefly as heiresses or as links to powerful families, and in this sense still amounted to little more than pawns upon the great chessboard of Europe. Not until the close of the fifteenth century would the chess Queen acquire astonishing new powers—powers that totally changed the game. There is no medieval precedent for the Queen moves that suddenly emerged. The Queen now became the most powerful figure on the board, and her moves, along with similarly extended moves granted the Bishop, propelled the game into speeds and levels of sophistication the Middle Ages never dreamed of.

But the Middle Ages never dreamed of real-life queens with power, either. Not until the sixteenth century, when monarchies no longer depended to such a degree upon the fighting facility of warrior kings, did Elizabeth I prove that a woman could rule England in her own right.

Empress Matilda, whose toughness under fire was legendary, and who proved entirely capable of ruling in Normandy as vice-regent for her son, had perhaps been born four centuries too early. Empress to her emperor husband and mother of a king, she received as consolation prize the title "Lady of the English," but never England's crown.[16]

Eleanor, too, although by now a queen twice over, would soon discover the limits of power placed on any twelfth-century woman—whether she was duchess of Aquitaine and countess of Poitou in her own right, or consort to England's increasingly powerful and indomitable young king.

Part Three

✹ 6 ✹

The Golden Table of Sicily

$\mathscr{A}$ golden table twelve feet long and eighteen inches wide now enters the story. This, along with twenty-four golden plates and cups, sixty thousand loads of grain and wine, one hundred galleys equipped for two years, and a silken tent large enough to seat two hundred knights, was the rich legacy bequeathed by his royal highness King William II of Sicily to his father-in-law and intended fellow crusader, Henry Plantagenet of England.

All of Eleanor's daughters—two by Louis of France and three by Henry of England—had made splendid matches. Marie and Alix, daughters of Louis, went respectively to the powerful houses of Champagne and Blois, while Matilda Plantagenet went to Henry the Lion, and young Eleanor Plantagenet to Alphonse, king of Castile. But it was the youngest Plantagenet daughter, Joanna, who at the tender age of eleven stepped with particular élan onto the chessboard of European dynastic politics by wedding William of Sicily, the most opulent monarch in the West.

Small Joanna linked Sicily and the Plantagenet empire by marriage. Yet these powerful houses already shared common roots, dating back to those great Norman warriors who sailed for the Mediterranean at about the same time that William the Bastard set his sights on the English crown. Normans were everywhere in eleventh-century Europe—the Battle of Hastings was scarcely the only Norman conquest. These Normans, with names like Rainulf and Drogo, were by all accounts feared brigands and cutthroats. More important, they were empire-builders, the stuff of which mighty dynasties are made. William the Bastard became William the Conqueror, but those who chose sunnier shores than England on which to warm their ambitions did no less well, swarming into southern

Italy and wresting it from the Byzantines and a welter of local potentates. They then crossed the straits of Messina, seizing Sicily from its feuding Muslim lords.

The second generation of Mediterranean Normans was as bloodthirsty and successful as the first. Roger the Great of Sicily forged himself a mainland and island kingdom, the legendary Kingdom of the Two Sicilies. Green and fertile, with magnificent harbors and perfect sea position, Sicily in the hands of an ambitious warrior such as Roger threatened the empires of both East and West, as well as the sea republics of Genoa and Pisa and the papacy itself. Roger's enemies were numerous and impressive, but Roger was not easily impressed. He aimed at dominance in the Mediterranean, and in this spirit unhesitatingly annexed a large portion of the North African coast, raided the Byzantine Empire, and captured a pope.

Roger's son, William the Bad, continued to deal severely with his house's enemies, but with a significant and ominous decrease in energy. Already the luxury and oriental splendor of the Sicilian court had begun to take its toll. William preferred the harem to the battlefield, and his son, William II, or William the Good, was similarly inclined. Not that the royal house's ambitions had in any way declined—this king of Sicily, too, dreamed of Mediterranean dominance and Byzantine conquest, and ended his life aspiring to lead the Third Crusade. Yet although William II managed to keep unprecedented internal peace in Sicily and established a valuable alliance with the papacy (which feared Emperor Barbarossa more than the Normans to the south), he preferred to remain in silken seclusion in his palace and leave the work of government and conquest to someone else. It was a far cry from the relentless energy of Henry Plantagenet, the persistence of Philip Augustus, or the unflagging leadership of Frederick Barbarossa, who in his seventieth year did not hesitate to set off at the head of his troops on the long, grueling overland journey to the Holy Land. Despite William's evident interest in the crusade, no one really expected him to put in a personal appearance.

Roger the Great had thus carved out a kingdom of consequence, but he did not succeed in founding a sufficiently steely dynasty to maintain it. All of Roger's legitimate sons died young, and his grandson could not produce an heir. It was of little surprise to anyone when, in the autumn of 1189, the last of this brief line died childless, leaving the Normans' hard-won kingdom up for grabs.

Barbarossa, who dreamed his own dreams of securing Italy for his empire, had already shrewdly married his son and heir, Henry Hohenstaufen, to Constance of Sicily—who, as William the Good's aunt, stood next in line to the throne. William, embattled with the Byzantines and focusing eastward, must not have fully appreciated the danger. Although Barbarossa was newly at peace with the Church and with the Church's Sicilian ally, he was no friend. Nor was his son—who, as it soon would become clear, had ambitious and daring imperial plans of his own. With Sicily in his pocket, Henry Hohenstaufen could bend the surrounded papacy to his will and even dominate the Mediterranean. If William's death had not caught him at just the unfortunate moment when he was staving off Henry the Lion in Germany, young Hohenstaufen would have immediately rushed southward to secure his wife's claim. But German affairs demanded his reluctant attention, leaving Sicily for the moment free from imperial designs. From Hohenstaufen's view, the Lion's timing could hardly have been worse.

Given this momentary lapse in external danger, the Sicilians took the opportunity to quarrel among themselves. They were quite good at it, and soon the entire kingdom was up in arms, torn between rival Norman claimants to the throne. The winner was Tancred, count of Lecce, a bastard descendant of Roger the Great himself. Tancred lacked the royal look—he was small and ugly—but carried himself with assurance, effectively battling his way to the crown. But scarcely on the throne, he found himself facing yet another challenging situation—two major monarchs who had dropped anchor at his door.

Crisis was at hand in the Christian kingdom of Jerusalem, and Philip of France and the newly crowned Richard Lionheart were bound for the Holy Land.

❧

As all of Western Europe was only too well aware, both city and kingdom of Jerusalem had recently fallen to the great Muslim warrior Saladin, following his crushing victory at Hattin. Even the Holy Cross now lay in infidel hands. The news from the Holy Land had not been good for years, but now it was disastrous. In response, the quarreling monarchs of the West momentarily stepped back from their brawling and prepared to help.

Even the notoriously disinterested Henry Plantagenet had been ready to provide aid, but just as promptly became embroiled in warfare with Philip of France and his own son. After Henry's death in the summer of 1189 and Richard's coronation the following September, Richard and

Philip agreed to set off on crusade together from Vézelay, in Burgundy. A date was set, then broken and set again when Philip's young wife, Isabelle of Hainaut, unexpectedly died. But the need for a crusade remained compelling, and the two monarchs consequently spent the winter months raising funds and arranging for the safety of their kingdoms until their return.

They also kept a wary eye on one another. Although once bedfellows and trencher-mates, that was light-years before, when Richard was his father's worst enemy and the French king's most loyal vassal and dearest friend. Now Richard had inherited his father's enemies as well as his father's scepter and found, to his surprise, that the world had a different look from beneath the Plantagenet crown.[1]

Thus when Philip and Richard finally met with their respective armies in Vézelay in the summer of 1190, a marked tension had sprung up between them. Richard had mustered his troops and received his pilgrim's scrip and staff at Tours,[2] while Philip—who brought with him the Oriflamme, the great standard of Saint-Denis—had received his pilgrim's insignia at Reims.[3] Both joined, with their armies, at the shrine of Vézelay in early July. The French wore crosses of red and the English wore white, while the Flemings proudly wore crosses of green.[4]

Here, some forty years before, St. Bernard had preached the Second Crusade to avid throngs spilled out upon the hillside to hear his impassioned words. Here both Louis and Eleanor had taken the cross and, caught up in the fervor, prepared to follow God's will eastward. Now once again men crowded the steep and narrow street that led to the vast Cluniac church, shrine of the sacred relics of Ste.-Marie-Madeleine and one of the major points of departure for pilgrimages to St. James of Compostela.

Here above the rolling hills of Burgundy the armies for Christ assembled, the fortunate few sheltered in the great shadowy church narthex beneath the moving depiction of Christ with arms outstretched. Then, to strains of a crusading hymn, this mighty throng at last began to march, faces firmly set toward Jerusalem.

The Third Crusade had begun.

❧

Richard himself had no inclination to look back, even though he might well have done so. Eleanor was most capable of defending his interests at home, but he had left her with a difficult set of interests to defend. At the age of thirty-two, this new monarch had yet to do his duty of

Western façade of the Abbey Church (now Basilica) of Sainte-Marie-Madeleine de Véze-lay, in Burgundy. This Romanesque masterpiece was the site where St. Bernard preached the Second Crusade and where Richard Lionheart and Philip II of France met with their respective armies before departing on the Third Crusade. © J. McAuliffe

marrying a suitable princess and providing his vast and unwieldy kingdom with a son. Richard's sole surviving brother, John, had already indicated that he would be more than happy to serve as heir, but there were few, especially Eleanor, who relished this prospect. Yet there were also few who expected John to sit quietly by and let the kingship slip from his fingers. Richard had indeed left behind an extremely volatile situation. Despite the loyalty and devotion of his troops and the obvious color and leadership he provided, many wondered at the sense of adventure that drew him so long and far from the shores where he more properly belonged.

Philip, on the other hand, made no attempt to disguise his disinterest. He did not really care to go to Jerusalem in the first place and, once there, desperately wanted to come home. He had left behind an infant son and kingdom in his mother's care, and although his situation was not as precarious as Richard's—there was no French equivalent of John Plantagenet to stir up trouble—still Philip clearly was uncomfortable. This crusade offered little to attract him, and he felt that he was missing out on great opportunities at home.

Indeed, Philip was not an adventurer but a ruler, with a fine-tuned sense of manipulation and intrigue. Eleanor was shrewd enough to grasp this point, but Richard—caught up in the excitement of the moment and a preoccupation with his own splendor—seems not to have noticed. Unlike Philip, Richard was a warrior king, and a grand one. With his daring and dash, as well as his tremendous wealth and genuine relish for war, he cut an extraordinary figure—a commanding presence, the unrivaled leader of the Third Crusade. Philip, as fellow monarch and Richard's sovereign in the Plantagenets' vast lands in France, was technically the crusade's co-leader. Yet in all measures that mattered most to warriors—power, wealth, color, and charisma—Richard clearly outclassed him. Philip never stood a chance of holding his own.

Not that it should have mattered. Philip, eight years younger than Richard, had never striven for the same laurels. And yet Richard's preeminence rankled deeply. From Vézelay onward, Philip's coolness toward Richard grew, fed by Richard's easy dominance and popularity, Richard's bounty and commanding grace. The knights all loved Lionheart—even the French, who turned naturally to him for the counsel and advice that Philip felt more properly came from both together or from him alone.

At Lyons they parted company—probably much to Philip's relief. The French king headed for Nice and Genoa, where he put up for a while to recover from a bout of sickness before sailing on to Sicily. Richard marched for Marseilles and a rendezvous with his fleet, which was late, having been diverted into raiding Lisbon instead. Impatient to be on, he hired other ships and sailed leisurely down the coast of Italy, at last sailing grandly into the harbor of Messina, where Philip had arrived—much more quietly—the week before.

There, Richard was prepared for the most regal of welcomes. After all, his sister, the beautiful and well-beloved Joanna, had been queen of this land for fifteen years. Instead, much to his indignation, he found himself relegated to camping outside the city walls. Philip had already established himself in Tancred's good graces as well as his palace, leaving Richard little room in either. Worse yet, Joanna had not fared well in the new regime; she was being held, virtually a prisoner, in her own palace at Palermo.

Given the imperial threat from the north as well as the Plantagenet alliance with the Sicilian throne, Tancred might have been expected to welcome a Plantagenet with open arms. But there was a fortune at stake. William had endowed Joanna with vast revenues, which Tancred was most reluctant to relinquish. Nor was he any more eager to hand over William's rich legacy—including the fabled golden table—to Henry Plantagenet's heir. Philip noted this and quietly indicated sufficient sympathy and assurance that Tancred immediately opted for the Capetian, moving him into his own palace and leaving Richard to cool his heels outside the city walls.

It was a dangerous decision, for Richard was not in a conciliatory mood. Bluntly, he demanded Joanna's immediate release, along with her revenues. He also demanded the golden table, silken tent, and the invaluable supplies bequeathed to Henry, which Richard now claimed for his own. After all, was he not his father's heir, and was not this rich legacy intended to further the success of the crusade?

Tancred glanced thoughtfully in the direction of Richard's army, camped at his door. At last he allowed that perhaps the king of England was right. Accordingly, he released Joanna, along with her furniture and a million *terrini* for her expenses.[5]

This was not stingy, but it did not come close to the revenues with which Joanna had been endowed nor the legacy that Richard viewed as his. Tancred would have to do better, and Richard was not in a patient mood.

While Tancred reconsidered, Richard reinforced his point by seizing the city of Messina and sacking it. Agreement between the two monarchs quickly followed. In lieu of Joanna's dower, twenty thousand ounces of gold quickly came Richard's way. Warming to the arrangement, Richard agreed to recognize Tancred's claim to Sicily. He further firmed the alliance by betrothing Tancred's infant daughter to Arthur of Brittany, Richard's nephew, whom Richard now acknowledged as his heir if he failed to produce any of his own. An additional twenty thousand ounces of gold now exchanged hands, to be settled upon Tancred's daughter when the marriage took place. Given the fact that such a marriage was unlikely to occur—the prospective bridegroom was only three years old—twenty thousand additional ounces of gold was a windfall for Richard, who in turn renounced his uncertain claims to William II's legacy on the spot.[6]

Still, the galleys and grain of William's legacy were one thing, but the golden table was quite another, and Richard may not have given that up so easily. He had a keen eye and a cultivated appetite for sumptuousness, and when Joanna's furniture eventually arrived, a striking gilded table along with twenty-four golden cups seems to have found its way among the lot.

It was like Richard to be careful in this regard of his sister's interests, and it would have struck no one as odd if these by chance served to enhance his own magnificence. Roger the Great, the first Norman conqueror of Sicily, had been notoriously acquisitive, and Richard obviously shared some of this same blood.

⚜

Richard, like his father and brothers, could be a most determined man. Yet his determination was but a small thing when compared with that of Eleanor, his mother. Bequeath the Plantagenet kingdom to Arthur of Brittany and the infant daughter of Tancred of Sicily, indeed! Richard must wed and provide a proper heir, and the lucky queen-to-be must not under any circumstances be Philip of France's unfortunate sister, Alais.

Thus began Eleanor's remarkable midwinter journey southward across the Alps, to deliver a suitable bride to her son before he could depart Messina on crusade. During the course of her long and eventful career, Eleanor had traveled extensively throughout her own and her second husband's vast domains. She had also, quite notoriously, accompanied her first husband on the gut-wrenching overland journey through the Balkans and desolate mountain wilds of Turkey into Palestine on the Second Crusade. She was no stranger to hardship and had made innumerable Channel crossings, some in the teeth of raging gales. Yet a midwinter Alpine crossing for a woman of almost seventy was a remarkable feat.

Eleanor approached it with complete aplomb, disdaining a litter or any other cushioned contrivance. Accompanied by the customary retinue of attendants, guards, pack animals, and wagons, she departed from Bordeaux in early December of 1190. Traveling up the Garonne River past Toulouse, she then followed the river valley past Carcassonne toward the Mediterranean. There, she progressed from Montpellier to Avignon, where the road headed into Alpine regions. As the track grew ever steeper, her party braved midwinter cold and snow, transferring to mules to make the actual crossing at the Mont Genèvre pass, to the south of the more frequented pass at Mont Cenis. It was at Mont Cenis, a century before, that Emperor Henry IV had made a January crossing in his desperate flight southward to mend fences with an irate pope—a crossing that proved so icy that he could neither ride nor walk the descent, but had to crawl down on all fours. The ladies of his court, including the venerable empress, could not manage even this indignity and had to slide down in ox skins.

Eleanor's crossing through this ice-bound wilderness seems to have gone without incident, and she arrived early in 1191 on the plains of Lombardy in the company of Berengaria, princess of the small kingdom of Navarre. This elegant but plain young woman, whom Eleanor had so carefully escorted across the wintry mountain passes, was not the usual prospect for a king of England. But, then again, there had been special urgency to find a bride of sufficient rank and distance from the Plantagenet family tree who was willing to undergo grave discomfort and danger to marry this particular king. Richard, newly in possession of the English throne, was now encamped in Sicily, preparing to depart for the Holy Land and war. From every standpoint, it was essential that he not leave on such a dangerous mission without a wife and heir.

Whether or not Richard played any part in the selection process is unknown. Some see his hand in the matter, especially in the southward tilt to policy that such an alliance promised, for Richard was a man of Poitou and Aquitaine. Some, especially from generations past, have sought to find a thread of romance in the story. Richard, according to the chronicler Ambrose, had fallen in love with Berengaria several years earlier, when he took part in a tournament in Pamplona. Whether or not Richard's heart was involved, he seems to have treated the princess most courteously on that occasion, saying all the right things about her wit and beauty. Berengaria, whose brother jousted with Lionheart in the lists, seems to have been graciously attentive to these compliments. Eleanor, if not Richard, took ample notice, and in due course Berengaria found herself wending her way southward to her destiny.

It is interesting how little we know about the appearance and distinguishing characteristics of Berengaria or any other woman of this period.

Of the men, especially men of mark, we are blessed with many details, some of them intimate. Who would have guessed, for example, that Henry I of England snored?[7] We know that both William the Conqueror and Henry I had receding hairlines, and that William Rufus and Henry II had florid complexions. We know that Henry II's neck jutted forward and that he was freckled. We know that Richard was taller than average and was a powerhouse, built along the same broad-chested lines as his father and great-grandfather. We also know that Richard's younger brothers, Geoffrey and John, were small and dark.[8] Yet we have not the slightest idea of what the women in their lives looked like, and we are similarly left guessing about these women's personalities.

We know, simply from the way she behaved, that Eleanor was independent, sophisticated, and strong, and we would like to think that she was beautiful. After all, when troubadours sang that they would gladly yield the whole world, from the sea to the Rhine, if only the queen of England lay in their arms, they must have had Eleanor in mind. Such a woman clearly was considered well worth the exchange. But was she light or dark, tall or short, and did her eyes sparkle? Although Richard of Devizes tells us that she was "beautiful yet virtuous, powerful yet gentle, humble yet keen-witted, qualities which are most rarely found in a woman," this is of little help, even if one looks past the expected flattery and focuses where Richard evidently wishes us to, on Eleanor's intelligence and strength.[9]

Similarly, all we are told of Eleanor's future daughter-in-law, the shadowy Berengaria, is that she was a "prudent maid, a gentle lady, virtuous and fair, neither false nor double-tongued."[10] In contemporary jargon, such faint praise would convey its own double message, and indeed, there is some indication that Berengaria was far more prudent than pretty.[11] Still, prudence and virtue were qualities held in great esteem, and whatever medieval males actually thought of those females thus blessed, the women themselves had earned the right to praise. Eleanor—who, despite Richard of Devizes's flattery, had never been saddled with a reputation for either gentleness or virtue—had found Richard a wife in whom he could take pride, a princess of appropriate rank and becoming manner. As for Richard's own feelings on the subject, they hardly mattered. What was wanted was an heir.

It was a most delicate and dangerous mission. Henry Hohenstaufen himself could have no direct objection. Yet Philip of France, Henry Hohenstaufen's ally, would have every objection in the world, for there remained the unfortunate matter of the even more unfortunate Alais. Following Henry Plantagenet's defeat and death, Philip had promptly attended to family honor and his half-sister's fate, insisting that Richard marry Alais immediately. Allowing that perhaps something had been lacking in Plantagenet manners toward their royal guest, Richard had at last agreed to wed the princess after he returned from crusade.

But Eleanor clearly had other ideas. Promptly obtaining her own freedom following Henry's death, she just as promptly locked up the French princess and went shopping for another bride. Richard needed a wife and queen, and it was plain that the unhappy Alais, now Eleanor's own prisoner in the tower of Rouen, would not do. After all, could the queen of England be expected to bestow her husband's paramour in holy matrimony upon her most beloved son?

Richard's part in the selection process is unknown, but in any case, one royal bride would serve the purpose as well as any other. Eleanor agreed only in part, carefully sifting the candidates. Settling at last upon Berengaria, the inoffensive daughter of the king of Navarre, the aging yet still dynamic queen collected the girl and brought her across the Alps into Sicily, where Richard was wintering.

It was en route, in northern Italy, that by extraordinary coincidence she encountered Frederick Barbarossa's heir, young Henry Hohenstaufen, who was on his way to Rome with imperial coronation and a Sicilian campaign on his mind. Whatever they said to one another, it must have been an uncomfortable meeting, given Richard's presence in Sicily and his recent recognition of Tancred, Henry Hohenstaufen's rival for the Sicilian throne.

Richard, of course, felt a legitimate interest in Sicily—at least, to the extent of placing it in Norman rather than German hands. Henry Hohenstaufen's wife may have been heir to the Sicilian throne, but Richard's sister, Joanna, had been William of Sicily's queen. It should have surprised no one, least of all Henry Hohenstaufen, that Richard favored Tancred. Yet it nevertheless could not have made for pleasant dinner conversation between the queen of England and the emperor-elect.

Whatever excuses Eleanor must have made, she certainly did not linger in Henry Hohenstaufen's company, for she had a princess to deliver. But despite all haste, she did not succeed in conveying Berengaria to Sicily before Lent. Arriving in Naples about Ash Wednesday, she and Berengaria were met by ships that Richard had dispatched to bring them to Messina. Philip of Flanders, who had accompanied Eleanor thus far, took advantage of the offer and arrived in Sicily shortly thereafter, but Tancred's men—reflecting yet another bout of political tensions in Sicily—refused Eleanor and Berengaria leave to join him, supposedly because of the numerous attendants who accompanied them. Messina was already full to overflowing, they were told, and they would have to wait.

Eleanor was not accustomed to such treatment, but no matter how quickly Berengaria now arrived in Sicily, a marriage would be impossible before Easter. And so queen and princess, along with the rest of their cavalcade, struck out by land for Brindisi, a journey that took them the better part of a month.

In the meantime, the count of Flanders found a confused state of affairs awaiting him in Messina. Closely connected to both the French and English royal houses, he seems on this occasion to have represented Eleanor in the very sensitive matter of Richard's marriage—a topic which, as it happened, had emerged with considerable fireworks only shortly before he arrived. Philip of France was livid over Tancred's alliance with Richard, especially since Richard had promised away the Plantagenet kingdom without so much as mentioning his impending marriage to the French princess, Alais.[12]

The French king had brooded about this throughout the long winter months in Messina, when wintry gales on the Mediterranean prevented the crusaders from traveling further eastward. At last, upon the pretext of warning Tancred that Richard would break his pledge, the young French monarch promised that if the Sicilian king would attack Richard, Philip would join in. Discovered, Philip accused Richard of inventing the whole story as an excuse for casting off Alais. Richard replied in kind, taking the occasion to declare in public the unpleasantness that everyone had long suspected. The Princess Alais, Richard announced, had indeed been Henry Plantagenet's mistress and had borne him a child. Taking an aggrieved posture, the pure and noble Lionheart demanded to know how he could be expected to marry such a besmirched woman. Agreeing with him, the assembled bishops and barons were in the process of freeing Richard from the indignity of this marriage compact just as Philip of Flanders walked in the door.

Richard seems to have received the news of another bride with suitable equanimity—indeed, he may well have been delaying his departure from Messina until Berengaria's arrival—but the young French king seethed with anger. Even his well-remarked admiration for the beautiful and recently widowed Joanna was not enough to surmount his hostility to Lionheart, who in any case quickly squelched any marital ambitions that Philip may have entertained in the Plantagenet direction by removing Joanna to safety across the straits. Philip of Flanders hastily mediated between the feuding monarchs, and the outcome was a treaty by which

Philip agreed to absolve Richard from his oath to marry Alais, in return for ten thousand marks of silver—a considerable sum.[13]

According to a thirteenth-century English document purporting to be a copy of the original March 1191 treaty, Philip (in consideration of that hefty pile of silver) also agreed to surrender all claims to the Norman Vexin and Gisors—which for decades had been regarded as the dowry, first of Princess Marguerite, then of Princess Alais. Only if Richard were to die without male heirs would this vital border country revert to the French monarchy.[14]

We do not know whether or not this document was authentic. But we do know that the chroniclers are divided in their accounts of what actually transpired in Messina, as well as its import.[15] Some say that this agreement settled all outstanding differences between the two kings, who from this point on became friends. Yet these accounts were all from the English side of the fence, and it seems possible that the English chroniclers were reflecting Richard's view of the matter. Richard dealt openly with problems, and if to all appearances a difference was settled, then it was settled. Philip, however, was far more difficult and complicated, and it may well be significant that the chronicler who gives a totally different assessment of Messina's outcome was French. Indeed, according to Rigord, from this point on the two kings became irreconcilable enemies.[16]

Philip, in any case, seems to have been thinking a great deal about his sister and the Norman Vexin while he was on crusade, for immediately upon returning home in early 1192—well before Richard—he ordered the Normans to turn over Alais and the key fortress of Gisors. As the great seal authenticating Philip's copy of the treaty had in the meantime been lost in shipwreck, the document he presented in substantiation of his claims may well have been a forgery. In any case, the seneschal for Gisors seemed to think so and refused to turn over the fortress upon only Philip's say-so.

For the moment, Gisors—and Normandy—thus remained safely in Plantagenet hands. In any case, as Eleanor and Berengaria wearily reached Brindisi in late March 1191 and took ship for Reggio, where Richard was waiting for them, the fate of Normandy was far from any of their minds. Philip of France was not among the welcoming party, having sailed for the Holy Land that very day. An obvious slight, but one that did not weigh heavily, for the French king's absence removed a certain chill from the proceedings, allowing Richard's staunch troops to provide an unencumbered welcome.

It was a small moment, but a pivotal one. Despite the English chroniclers' assessment of what actually happened in Messina in March 1191, it seems clear that from this point on, the king of England and the king of France were on a collision course.

❈ 7 ❈

To Jerusalem!

$\mathcal{F}$ollowing a suitable celebration, Queen Eleanor prepared for her departure. Continued turmoil in the Holy Land demanded Richard's earliest possible attention, even as unsettling events in Plantagenet lands—as well as Pope Clement's sudden death—demanded her immediate journey home. Someone, after all, had to put in a weighty word in Rome for Plantagenet interests.[1]

She did not even wait for the wedding, for Richard had decided to put it off until he and Berengaria arrived in the Holy Land. This crusade—with unhappy memories of the one that went before—had specifically banned women from accompanying the troops. But Richard, arguing that pressing circumstances made it impossible for him to linger any longer in Sicily, soon received special dispensation to bring his betrothed with him. He and Berengaria would celebrate their post-Lenten wedding ceremony in the Holy Land.

Given these arrangements, Eleanor prepared to depart after only four days on Sicily's shores. It could not have been a joyous leave-taking. Eleanor, who was approaching her eighth decade, had little expectation that she would ever see her dearest son again. Richard, her treasure and her delight, was about to fulfill her hopes and become a married man. Beyond that, no one knew what lay ahead.

Scarcely a week later, Richard and his crusader army set sail for the Holy Land. As with everything this dashing Plantagenet did, his departure from Messina was truly breathtaking. He had found a large ship, or dromond, for Berengaria and Joanna (who as a widow was deemed a suitable companion for the young princess).[2] Such a boat would not have

been particularly speedy but was stoutly built and well able to accommodate the ladies' considerable retinue and baggage. Accompanied by two
escort ships laden with treasure, the royal ladies left Messina in advance
of Richard's fleet.

Behind them, in line after line, came more of these transport vessels,
each holding forty knights and horses, forty foot-soldiers, sufficient sailors
to man sails and oars, plus food to feed the whole lot for a year. Thirteen
of these cumbersome vessels swept after the royal ladies in a line, while
fourteen more followed, their ranks separated by no more distance than the
sound of a trumpet. Within each rank, the ships were sufficiently close that
their crews could call out to one another. Twenty smaller transports took
their places after that, followed by a line of thirty, then one of forty. The
next line, of sixty transports, stretched almost as far as the eye could see.

After that came the warships—long and slender, like Viking ships
of yore—each propelled by two tiers of oarsmen and fully armed for war.
Thirty-nine of these galleys brought up the last line, in the foremost of
which stood Richard himself, rallying his men and thoroughly enjoying
the scene. When all of these ships had passed through the straits into
open sea, the galleys at last shot forward beyond the bobbing crowd of
dromonds and transports to take their place as the advance guard for the
entire fleet.[3]

For two days this armada encountered little wind, leaving the smaller
transports—entirely dependent on sail power—virtually becalmed. And
then on Good Friday a mammoth storm hit, shattering ships and sending
them scuttling across the sea. When the winds at last receded, Richard
counted his fleet; twenty-five ships were missing, including the three
dromonds carrying Berengaria and her escort.

As it happened, Berengaria had survived the storm but now was encountering new dangers. Her ship had washed up on the shores of Cyprus,
while her two escort ships had dashed upon the rocks, where the Cypriots
took the survivors prisoner. Isaac Comnenus, a cousin of the Byzantine
emperor and himself emperor of Cyprus, soon learned the identity of
his beleaguered guests and pressed Berengaria and Joanna to land. Relations between the Byzantine emperors and the crusaders had long been
strained, but Isaac, having made an enemy of Constantinople as well, had
taken matters further yet by linking up with Saladin. Giving due consideration to the politics of the place as well as the fate of their companions,
Berengaria and Joanna understandably hesitated. By the time Richard
finally arrived on the scene, Isaac's troops had assembled on shore with
the evident intention of carrying out their emperor's invitation by force.

Richard was furious. The Cypriot emperor would pay for this! And pay he did, for Lionheart proceeded to lead his warriors for Christ onto Cyprus's thoroughly Christian shores. Emperor Isaac held vast personal treasures, and the island of Cyprus itself was a virtual breadbasket. With any luck at all, Richard would be able to draw upon its largess for months.

Isaac managed to escape, but the victory was Richard's. After this brief and successful diversion, Lionheart decided to celebrate the God-given victory with his wedding. Now that Lent was safely over, a wedding celebration seemed an appropriate way to cap his triumph. Selecting the city of Limassol for the site, he approved plans for a royal wedding and Berengaria's coronation, with an all-out three-day festival to follow.

No one seems to recall what the bride wore for the event, but Richard dressed most memorably for his wedding day. Wearing a dazzling crimson outfit adorned with silver bangles, and sporting a scarlet bonnet drenched in gold, he enhanced this remarkable effect with golden sword and spurs. Topping it off, he pranced to the ceremony astride a spangled Spanish stallion.

The crowds loved it. One only hopes that Berengaria was properly appreciative.

❧

Whether Richard was properly appreciative of Berengaria was of course the larger question, for from this moment, he was rarely by her side. Soon after the wedding, he was at war again, off pursuing the elusive Isaac. After several days of this, he became ill and took time out in Nicosia, at some distance from Limassol. Then he set off once more after the emperor, who at last surrendered. By this time Richard was feeling more chipper, but unfortunately Berengaria was nowhere around, for Lionheart had sent her ahead to the Holy Land. Although the newlyweds may have made good use of their brief moments together, it must have been a strange honeymoon.

In the meantime, Guy of Lusignan had shown up in Cyprus to bid for Richard's support for Jerusalem's throne. Guy, a hot-tempered opportunist who had once attempted to ambush Eleanor, had disappeared from France only to reappear in the East as husband of Sibylle, sister of Jerusalem's sickly king. Following this king's death and the death of the child king who followed, Guy—as Sibylle's husband—assumed the crown. Living by the sword, he boldly took on the Saracens. Yet the infidel's many successes, along with Sibylle's death, left him with significantly dwindling support. The succession now passed to Sibylle's younger sister, Isabelle, and to Isabelle's husband, Humphrey of Toron.

Humphrey, however, seemed reluctant to accept the honor. Unwilling to put up with Guy any longer, and concluding that Humphrey would therefore have to go, the barons arranged for Isabelle's divorce and remarriage to yet another dashing cavalier—Conrad, marquis of Montferrat. Conrad, who now had the heiress, next tried to assume the crown. Much to his indignation, Guy refused to give it up.

As it happened, Guy hailed from Plantagenet soil, while Conrad claimed ties to the Capetians. Not surprisingly, the French and the imperial Hohenstaufen threw their support to Conrad, while Richard—despite that unfortunate episode with Eleanor—found Guy's claims far more persuasive. Philip of France having already made his decision, Richard now made his. At the very moment that the crusading host was en route to rescue the Holy Land from the infidel, local politics were dividing the armies of the Cross in twain.

Still, Richard's arrival in the Holy Land, at the port city of Acre (now Akko), was a triumph. The weary Christian warriors who for two years had been trying to rout the infidel looked up one June evening from their filthy trenches and saw sails on the horizon—painted sails, like the Viking ships of yore. All sent up a terrific cheer. Then, of one accord, those who were strong enough to stand gathered to watch the amazing sight.

Despite shipwreck and storm damage during his passage from Messina, Richard had managed to launch more than 160 vessels from Cyprus. As the combat-worn besiegers of Acre watched and waited, the sea foamed with the churning of a thousand oars, while sails multiplied across the horizon. The sound of distant trumpets skimmed the waves, while a rainbow of banners floated on the breeze. Surely there had never been such a sight!

The royal ladies, whom Richard had carefully sent ahead—possibly with an eye to preventing distractions from this carefully staged event—had arrived a full week earlier and must have watched the landing with almost as much anticipation as the desperate warriors on the shore. Richard was bringing relief—not only men, but food and horses and the assurance of long-awaited victory. Those grizzled and exhausted warriors who awaited him had held on under terrific adversity, battling disease and hunger as well as the enemy, and now they were about to reap their reward. Richard was coming, Richard was coming. And what a show!

As the growing throng upon the shore cheered wildly, somewhere in the distance drums began to beat and horns to blow. Processions of revelers wound their way toward the landing stage, where they amassed in ever-larger numbers. Someone had managed to get hold of skins of wine, which passed from hand to hand among the exuberant crowd, while in the twilight torches and tapers began to glow. "Great was the joyance," Ambrose tells us, describing the scene, for "all the people with one accord rejoiced at his coming."[4]

As the setting sun blazed off the warriors' shields, hung along each oncoming bow, the waves gently washed the first ship on toward shore. A tremor shot through the crowd. It was Richard! Richard Coeur de Lion! The glorious warrior of whom they all had heard but few had ever seen. Yells and huzzahs broke forth as he appeared, standing magnificently on the highest prow, his ruddy hair and beard glinting golden in the red-rimmed twilight.

One can imagine Philip's sardonic evaluation of his rival's magnificent entrance, but Philip was in no position to criticize openly, for he desperately needed Richard's aid. After almost two months in the Holy Land, Philip had failed to make significant headway against the Saracens or provide sufficient supplies and reinforcements for the warriors entrenched outside Acre's walls. Whatever Philip's thoughts, Ambrose tells us that the French king met Richard cordially and accompanied him from the landing stage, keeping ever by his side.[5]

Richard's arrival specifically brought the promise of victory over this critical port city, which the crusaders had been unsuccessfully besieging for almost two years. The siege itself had begun in haphazard fashion when Guy of Lusignan, in the sort of harebrained enterprise for which he was famous, had marched his ragtag army up to Acre's walls. In one respect, Guy had the right idea, for Acre was a key target, having been the major port and western point of entry for the entire kingdom of Jerusalem before falling into Saladin's hands. When Saladin conquered the Holy City, virtually all the crusader kingdom fell with it, except for the northern port of Tyre. Tyre served as a beachhead, and the Christians were grateful for it, but Acre's size and more centralized location made it essential to Jerusalem's reconquest.

The problem was that Acre was a fortress of awe-inspiring proportions, built by the French and currently manned by some of Saladin's finest warriors. Worse yet, Saladin soon encircled Guy's paltry forces with a large army of his own. By this time, Saladin had emerged from years of infighting to become sultan of Egypt and ruler of Damascus, a formidable military leader with the resources of Aleppo, Damascus, Baghdad, and Cairo at his command. All that was necessary to give him a clean sweep of the Middle East was the rest of Syria and Palestine, occupied by crusader states since the First Crusade a century before. Setting to work on the problem in 1187, Saladin swallowed almost the entire Christian kingdom of Jerusalem in one gulp, leaving only Tyre. And then Guy audaciously, unwisely and—in the end—magnificently marched his small army to a hill just outside Acre's walls and set up camp.

At first the effort seemed suicidal. Even with the arrival of more European crusaders, the effort appeared hopeless. The northerners who arrived first—Danes, Frisians, Saxons, and Thuringians, as well as Flemings and French—greatly expanded Guy's besieging army, but not enough to extend it clear around the city on the landward side. The great Sicilian fleet that had saved Tyre, Tripoli, and Antioch the summer before did not return after William the Good's death, but the city-states of Genoa, Pisa, and Venice sent fleets bearing fighters, as well as much-needed supplies.

Still more crusaders poured in—enough to survive the terrible winters, when the Italian fleets could not navigate the Mediterranean, and the Egyptian navy reasserted its command over Acre's sea approaches. Starvation and disease almost wiped out the little band of crusaders during those two winters, when men were reduced to killing their horses and eating grass. Yet somehow the remnant managed to hang on.

The city itself occupied a small peninsula and spilled out onto the mainland, where it was protected on the north and east by thick walls and massive towers, beyond which lay a deep ditch. The crusaders spread themselves along this fortification, grouped together under their own banners.[6]

In July 1190, Henry of Champagne (Queen Eleanor's grandson) arrived, leading an important contingent of French and Burgundian crusaders and bringing Philip's siege engines with him. Henry provided not only significant relief, but also much-needed leadership during those long months when Philip and Richard lingered in Sicily and Frederick Barbarossa abruptly disappeared from the scene.

Barbarossa's death and the subsequent dispersal of his army was in fact a disaster of the greatest magnitude as far as Acre's besiegers were concerned. Relatively few of the Germans who left Regensburg in the spring of 1189 actually completed their journey, and those who made it did not straggle in until autumn of the following year. In the meantime, the Christian army had grown sufficiently large that it now completely surrounded the city on the landward side. Although the Christians had so far failed to take the Saracen-held citadel, Saladin's forces in the hills beyond had failed to shake the besiegers' tenacious hold.

Now Richard's arrival gave the crusaders command of Acre's sea approaches, as well as fresh men and supplies for a renewed attack by land. It was only a matter of time until this fortress, doorway to Jerusalem, fell into the crusaders' hands.

❦

A trumpet by day and a lantern by night had kept Richard's fleet together on its journey, and trumpets and lanterns now played their role in the siege encampment as well, for Richard was a warrior born. There was nothing he loved so much as fighting, unless it was planning for a fight—whether designing his fortresses or selecting the stones for his huge battering catapults. In all things pertaining to war, he was in his element, and his men loved him for it.

Nowhere could there be found a lord or king who attended to the details like Richard. He walked the area beneath Acre's citadel, examining the likeliest way to breach this rocklike fortress. He talked with his sappers and listened to his engineers. He bantered with his foot soldiers. He listened, he learned, he evaluated, and he charmed—for this, too, was part of the role he had assumed as leader of this throng. Even more, he revived spirits, whether through man-to-man camaraderie or through less personal but still stirring reminders of the grandeur and glory for which each had been called.

Not only were these weary warriors buoyed by the invaluable appearance of replacements and supplies, but their spirits seem to have been lifted by the display of banners, the blare of trumpets, and the blaze of torches that now engulfed the camp. Philip of France might scoff at Richard's devotion to show, but there were occasions when such display found its mark, encouraging the weary and dispiriting the foe.

Richard immediately set to work to relieve the disease-ridden and hard-pressed besiegers. Setting up his siege engines—long-range catapults and huge slings with sneering names like "Evil Neighbor"—he beefed up and coordinated the crusaders' battering activities. Simultaneously, Philip's sappers dug beneath the wall, propping up the masonry with timbers until they were ready to set the torch to them, which left the undermined wall sections nowhere to go but down. Although the entire stretch of wall offered numerous targets, one particular tower—at the corner where the wall made a right-angle turn—drew the crusaders' particular attention. Called the "Accursed Tower," it constituted the fortification's chief defense.

Throughout the month following Richard's arrival, siege engines pounded night and day as warriors struggled through the heat, stench, and smoke to get the job at long last done. The sources of the heat and stench were obvious, but the smoke was something Richard's reinforcements had not before encountered. The stuff was called Greek fire, which the Saracens hurled in pots. On impact the pots shattered, and the mixture within—an ancestor of napalm—immediately burst into flames, incinerating anything and anyone it touched. Since water had no effect on this strange and deadly substance, the crusaders quickly learned to cover all wooden objects with hides soaked in urine (the most convenient liquid that repelled it). Adding to the ambience, the whole area was infested with mosquitoes. In no way could this strange war in which the two young monarchs now found themselves be considered glamorous.

Indeed, Richard had scarcely arrived when he took severely ill. This was nothing new, for despite his legendary strength and endurance, Richard seems to have had a fragile side.[7] By the time he reached the Holy Land, he had suffered for many years from some malady that regularly beset him, and his frequent recourse to his sick bed has led some of his unkindest detractors to suggest that he was a hypochondriac. But no one was suggesting this now. Many in fact feared for his life.

Yet Richard was loath to miss out on the action. Mindful of the stirring impact his presence had upon the troops, he insisted on having himself borne about in a litter from post to post, directing operations and encouraging his men. They loved him all the more for it. What could they not accomplish if Richard, on his deathbed, could behave with such a disregard for hardship, even death itself?

Philip of France must have been inundated with this kind of talk, which would have worn a trifle thin—especially as he had also heard of English negotiations with Saladin over chickens for the royal invalid, not to mention Saracen gifts of fruit and snow.[8] He had even heard that Richard sought a personal interview with the Muslim leader.[9] What was Lionheart up to?

Adding to the growing rivalry and mistrust between the two kings, Richard quickly established his leadership over the whole enterprise. As Richard of Devizes graphically put it, "When Richard came [to Acre] the king of the French was extinguished and made nameless, even as the moon loses its light at sunrise."[10] In part, this was the unavoidable result of Lionheart's tremendous charisma and natural leadership abilities, but it was also the outcome of his vastly superior wealth. The king of England had contributed far more than the king of France to the crusading effort, and everyone knew it. Moreover, when Philip announced that he would pay three gold pieces a month to any knight who would fight for him, Richard immediately offered to pay four. Not surprisingly, the combination of Richard's legendary reputation plus his unquestionable largess brought men flocking to his service. Yet it could not have done much for relations between the two kings.

In an effort to hold his own, Philip took advantage of Richard's illness to launch a general assault, despite Richard's strong opposition. It proved an utter failure, and now Philip became gravely ill. Affairs took a nasty turn when the French camp spread the rumor that Richard, on the mend, had maliciously undercut Philip's recovery by telling him that his infant son had died. It seems that young Louis Capet indeed fell seriously ill at this time, although in fact he made a full recovery, living to succeed his father on the throne. Still, this kind of rumor boded ill, especially as Philip (whose hair and fingernails had fallen out) claimed he had been poisoned, and that traitors were responsible. Richard, of course, was the chief suspect.

Richard, who seems not to have engaged in this sort of psychological warfare—possibly because it never occurred to him, but more likely because he did not have to—continued about his business with renewed energy, setting up a kind of protective shed beneath the Accursed Tower itself. From this minimally protected shelter, he personally directed the action, even on occasion arising from his convalescent's cushions to let fly a few well-placed crossbow bolts himself.

The citadel and surrounding camp had by this time become an inferno of smoke and fire, where day and night were barely distinguishable. The Christians manning the siege engines worked like dervishes, even as their companion miners feverishly continued to undermine Acre's walls. At last, one of the turrets fell, followed by yet another, and soon the besiegers had cracked open a huge breach in the outer wall.

Countless crusaders had died to take this city, but Acre's fate at last was sealed. On July 12, 1191, the white flag finally rose. At long last, the crusading host stormed inside.

❧

Yet Richard's troubles had just begun. Having managed to take Acre, the crusaders now fell to fighting among themselves. Despite the two kings' care to divide the city between them, there were other contenders—less powerful, yet in their own eyes just as worthy of reward. Since there was no room in Richard and Philip's scheme for other plunderers, this contributed to considerable bitterness among those left out. Even as Richard's standard went up over the royal palace, Leopold of Austria daringly ran up his own standard beside the king's, in a bid for a share of the spoil. In the ensuing melee, Leopold's standard was torn down and cast in the dust.

Richard probably thought little of it, but the Germans marked that particular insult well. Significantly, the French—despite their privileged status—joined in the murmurings directed Richard's way, and it was not long before Richard's many rivals and enemies found endless opportunity to decry his arrogance and hint at future retribution. Let Richard Lionheart think the victory belonged to him and him alone! They knew better, and speculation quickly spread in certain quarters on the inevitable consequences of overweening pride.

Philip himself seems to have been chief among the malcontents, for he had already demanded half of the Cyprus bounty, on the grounds that he and Richard had previously agreed to split the crusade's booty. Richard flatly refused, arguing that this agreement applied to the Holy Land alone. Philip—still ill and unquestionably sick of the Holy Land— waited only until Acre was taken before announcing that he was going home.

In true twelfth-century fashion, his bombshell was accompanied by ready tears, although everyone knew the French king could hardly wait to be on his way. He shied from personal combat and had never enjoyed the warrior's life. Now, having given due consideration to the impossible hardships of Acre and the difficulties ahead, not to mention Richard's insistence on hogging the glory as well as the Cyprus plunder, he decided to throw in the towel.

Yet Philip being Philip, he was also interested in getting his hands on certain lands of the count of Flanders, who had recently died beneath Acre's walls.[11] Undoubtedly, he was giving considerable attention to Plantagenet lands as well. Richard certainly thought so, for he took care to obtain Philip's most solemn oath upon holy relics that he would leave Richard's lands well alone.

Philip sailed from Acre in late July, leaving his army under the leadership of the duke of Burgundy, who immediately turned to Richard for a considerable loan to tide him over. Philip, never magnanimous at best, had chosen to rely upon his share of the ransom money from Saladin's garrison (about 2,600 men) to pay for the French troops' upkeep. Unfortunately for this plan, Saladin—who had not been directly involved in the final truce negotiations—had no intention of paying, and possibly could not pay the huge sum the Christian kings demanded.

Days and weeks passed, and the final day came for Saladin to restore the Holy Cross into Richard's hands and pay two hundred thousand gold pieces for the hostages' safe return.[12] By this time Richard had become most thoroughly angered by Saladin's long delay, and as midday came and went without a word from the defeated foe, the English king now led his army to the middle of the plain and sent for the hostages, who were dragged into the army's midst. There, Richard ordered each and every one of the 2,600 massacred.[13]

This ghastly bloodbath may have sent a message that Richard meant business about holding to agreements, but it certainly did little to improve relations with the Saracens. Nor did it solve the problem of paying the French, who in any case had become a dubious asset, having grown resentful of the English king and reluctant to aid his quest for glory.

While Richard thus proceeded with an iron fist, the French king was proceeding with a velvet glove, subtly conveying the wrongs done him to attentive ears along his homeward route. Richard, he confided, was a dissembler and a thief, not to mention a would-be murderer. Lionheart, he concluded, deserved nothing less than to have certain French properties wrested from him at the earliest possible date. Encountering Henry Hohenstaufen north of Rome, Philip did not hesitate to relate all the indignities done to Leopold of Austria and Isaac of Cyprus, who were Henry's relations. Philip seems to have waxed especially eloquent on the captivity of Isaac's small daughter (given into Berengaria's hands), as well as the destruction of Leopold's banner following Acre's fall. Both monarchs agreed that Richard deserved to be severely punished. And both were eager to do the job.[14]

❧

Almost immediately after butchering the Saracen hostages, Richard prepared to march southward along the coast to Ascalon (now Ashquelon). Each member of his army carried provision of biscuit, bacon, and wine sufficient for ten days, while the ships that followed carried more provision still.[15]

He was headed, of course, for Jerusalem, but like those before him rejected a direct (and diagonal) overland route for one that began with a coastal march. This allowed him to keep his supply line as short and secure as possible once he turned eastward from the shore.

He had divided his infantry in two, setting identical lines to march in parallel—one inland and one along the sea. With Saracen attacks expected upon the inland-marching troops, Richard was prepared to alternate his two identical armies of foot soldiers when those bearing the burden of the fight grew fatigued. It was a clever plan, especially since it provided protection for the irreplaceable cavalry, which was to remain between the infantry at all times.[16]

Not surprisingly, Richard gave special attention to this part of his army, letting his foot soldiers—who fought with spear and crossbow or simple bow and arrow—take the brunt of the punishment. This was the course of things in an age when human lives, especially non-noble lives, meant little, but it was especially noticeable in times of war. Not only were the invaluable knights protected by infantry, but they were also clad in chain mail. Indeed, by the latter part of the twelfth century, knights headed for battle had added chain mail gloves and leggings to their long coats and hoods of interlocking iron rings. In addition, they sported hefty helmets—some still of the conical variety, although the flat-topped canister (completely enclosing the head) was coming into fashion.[17]

By contrast, the foot soldier had to make do with a jerkin made of leather or heavy quilting. While this could be sufficient to stop Saracen arrows (foot soldiers were reported to continue fighting after taking so many arrows they looked like hedgehogs), it nevertheless afforded nowhere near the protection of chain mail. Richard would lose a good many infantrymen on his march south.

Undoubtedly his troops knew this, and as Lionheart prepared to march, barely half of his army responded to his call. Some of these no-shows were the usual stragglers, but most had purposely lagged behind, reluctant to leave the many brothels and taverns that had sprung up after Acre's fall. Months and years of hardship outside Acre's walls had instilled a certain attachment to the creature comforts the liberated town now so fulsomely offered.[18]

Still, as the hour for departure neared, the scene was sufficiently grand to stir the most hardened warrior's blood. Pennants and banners of every description waved above this gallant throng, whose helmets and lances gleamed boldly in the sunshine. Everywhere, surcoated knights directed men and baggage.[19] In the harbor, the fleet prepared for launching, loaded with provision and supplies. And in the midst of this furor, foot soldiers with no carts or packhorses staggered under the weight of food and gear. It would be a slow and anguished march for these Jerusalem-bound warriors, even without the fighting that was sure to lie ahead.

Suddenly a trumpet pierced the clear blue sky. Slowly the crusading host began to move, the great Standard in its midst. Mounted on wheels, this iron-covered pole bearing the royal banner soared above the entire army, serving as both its inspiration and its guide.[20] Surrounded by Normans, who had the special honor and responsibility for its protection, the Standard provided a rallying point for the cavalry in battle as well as a sign for the entire host.

With their faces set toward Jerusalem, these Christian warriors now were following their glorious leader into an expected, God-given, victory.

⚜

According to Ambrose, the army that departed Vézelay under Richard and Philip was a hundred thousand strong, but this clearly was an exaggeration. This was an era when contemporaries regularly overestimated the size of armies by wild amounts. Much like the biblical "forty," any reference to "thousands" in medieval chronicles seems to have meant, quite simply, "a lot." Richard and Philip may have brought with them somewhere between three thousand and six thousand men,[21] and Richard's army as he marched southward certainly was of this scale rather than the hundred thousand that Ambrose so breathlessly reported.[22] Such a mythical army and its baggage wagons would have stretched for miles.

As it was, Richard had a sufficiently difficult task in keeping his line together, especially under the constant harassment of mounted Saracen archers. It was a grueling march along a road that—once a Roman thoroughfare—now was little more than a trail through burning sands. Despite the presence of the renowned Knights of the Temple in the vanguard and the equally experienced Knights of the Hospital in the rear, the Saracens seized every opportunity to harass the line, shadowing it from behind the sand hills to the west and darting out to kill men and horses or, when possible, make off with supplies.

The key role played by both the Templars and the Hospitalers in holding the line was hardly surprising, considering the pivotal role that these military orders had come to play in the politics and warfare of the Holy Land. Although founded to provide aid and protection to pilgrims traveling to and from Jerusalem, both the Templars and the Hospitalers, whose knights took religious vows and fought for Christ, had evolved into powerful and wealthy organizations, boasting fighters of renown. In particular, the Templars—distinguished by a red cross on a white ground— had been fighters from the outset, and their order had steadily attracted some of the toughest warriors of the land.[23]

Richard's immediate goal was to seize the great fortress of Ascalon, which commanded Saladin's sea and land communications with Egypt, the main source of his manpower and supplies. United, Damascus and Egypt represented an impossible obstacle to retaking and keeping Jerusalem, but separated by a strong Christian presence at Ascalon, each of these powers could be contained. Richard had also concluded that by taking the entire seaboard, from Acre to Ascalon, he would secure his own supply base far more dependably than if he simply struck out directly inland for the Holy City itself.

Surviving the heat, the sandy wastes, and the marshes, the crusaders at length approached a wilder country, so choked with undergrowth that the cavalry and heavy baggage carts could not make their way. Richard now decided to cut up the left bank of the Dead River to an inland road. Here progress was physically easier but more dangerous, for the Saracens swarmed like flies. Even the king was wounded—a light javelin graze on his side. Still, despite the constant harassment, the Christian warriors doggedly continued their advance, holding tightly to their formation and only breaking rank to allow the cavalry to pass through for an occasional charge.

That evening they camped near the Salt River, where they killed and ate the wounded horses. And then, after a brief respite, Richard marched his men into the Forest of Arsuf, where it was said that Saladin—who had been marching on a parallel course—awaited them with three hundred thousand men. Holding tightly to their formation, the crusaders proceeded warily but steadily forward, ready for trouble but finding surprisingly little to hinder them.

Only when they emerged into open country did they see the entire Saracen army massed before them upon the plain.

⋇

The subsequent battle of Arsuf, one of the most famous of Richard's career, has traditionally been portrayed as a pitched battle[24]—something of a rarity in European warfare at the time. Warring lords generally avoided it, for within a few hours the careful creation of years could go up in smoke. Richard was not unfamiliar with pitched battle, but he was by far more experienced in siege warfare and the ravaging and skirmishing that accompanied it. Despite the presence of an entire field army at his back, Acre had been a confrontation to his taste; he knew exactly how to deal with it. What he now was approaching has been depicted as something entirely different.

Yet a close examination of contemporary sources indicates that what Richard did at Arsuf was perhaps not all that different from what he had been doing ever since leaving Acre—that is, fighting on the march. To make Arsuf into a classic pitched battle scenario, historians have pictured Richard's men as spread out in battle array against the enemy, with Lionheart in the center, his vanguard on the right flank, and his rearguard on the left.[25] But Ambrose—who admittedly is confusing, yet got his material firsthand—never talks in terms of left and right flanks. Instead, he makes it clear that the Templars were in the vanguard and the Knights of the Hospital in the rear, with Bretons, Angevins, Poitevins, Normans, English, and all the rest disposed in tight and orderly fashion between.[26]

There were no vulnerable baggage wagons or pack animals in this marching column, for Richard had sent these to relative safety along the seashore. Henry of Champagne took charge of protecting the column's landward side, while foot soldiers guarded from behind, who "closed the line of their march."[27] In other words, Richard's men were marching— slowly and leisurely, to be sure, for this was a confident and swaggering lot—but marching, nonetheless. The major difference between this incendiary occasion and all that had gone before was that now, for the first time, these crusaders—some of the finest warriors in Christendom—were advancing directly into a major clash with Saladin's entire army.

Unquestionably, they were looking forward to it. This was an assembly of stars: Robert of Dreux, cousin to the French king; Philip, the fighting bishop of Beauvais; James of Avesnes, the grizzled leader of Acre's siege, and Robert, the new earl of Leicester. Robert the elder had died en route to the Holy Land, and Lionheart himself had girt the youngster with the father's great sword. Now Robert, small and untested, was taking his father's place, and his look clearly told the waiting warriors that he "would not in any wise have been elsewhere."[28]

The clash began an hour before Terce[29]—still early in the day. Riding furiously to the accompaniment of blaring trumpets and pounding drums, the Saracen horsemen bore down hard upon the Christian host, shooting walls of arrows as they came. The crusaders kept their tight formation and soon were completely surrounded by a sea of howling enemy. Fighting and hacking on all sides, the Christian warriors could scarcely hear their own voices over the piercing trumpets and wildly pounding drums. Amid the chaos, riderless horses galloped panic-stricken, while knights whose horses had gone down beneath them continued the fight on foot.

The day was growing horribly hot, and the air had become clogged with a black and choking dust. Saracens were throwing themselves with particular violence upon the rearguard, and as this assault intensified, the Hospitalers pressed Richard to allow them to charge. Yet Richard refused. Exact timing was critical to a charge's success, and he was waiting for that precise moment when the foe was exhausted and Saladin had committed all his reserves to battle. Unleash his knights too soon, and Richard would endanger his men and throw away the chance to annihilate Saladin's army. No, he told them. Hold fast and withstand the assault.

For a time the Hospitalers held up under this near-impossible demand. But at length—infuriated by the Saracens and unable to restrain themselves any longer—they broke ranks and charged, drawing countless others after them.

A Frank on horseback, according to one awed observer, "is irresistible; he would bore his way through the walls of Babylon,"[30] and this particular lot fell on their assailants like thunderbolts. Yet an uncoordinated charge—especially a mistimed one such as this—invited disaster. Small groups of warriors, however heroic, could be surrounded and overcome. Worse yet, it was virtually impossible to call these warriors back to mount another charge. Judging the danger, Richard immediately acted to save the situation by signaling the trumpets to sound the general charge.

Richard's quick action turned a possible disaster into a triumph, for the crusaders now sent the Saracens flying. Many a reputation was made that day, including that of young Robert of Leicester, who acquitted himself heroically.

Yet despite the legends that have grown up around the Battle of Arsuf, the Christian warriors did not crush their foe. The crusaders failed to do the job. Indeed, although Saladin suffered heavy losses, the Muslim leader still had an army in the field. And as Richard's warriors were about to discover, that army remained a formidable barrier between them and Jerusalem.

The Lion at Bay

That evening, exhausted crusaders combed the field of battle and returned to camp laden with loot. They also carried back the body of James of Avesnes, whose face was hacked almost beyond recognition.

They laid James to rest the next day, on the feast of the Nativity of the Blessed Virgin. And then Lionheart and his men continued their march southward toward Joppa (now Jaffa), where the weary warriors rested and recuperated outside the city's battered walls.

A century before, Joppa had been the seaside staging area for the First Crusade, and many among Richard's barons—primarily the French—now pressed him to build up Joppa's port and use it, instead of Ascalon, as his base from which to march on Jerusalem. While they argued, Saladin raced to destroy Ascalon, effectively preventing it from falling into crusader hands. Richard was appalled, but now there was no choice. He would have to advance on Holy Jerusalem from Joppa.

He would also have to advance with a rapidly dwindling army, for deserters were piling onto the returning supply ships. Worse yet, word had it that Conrad of Montferrat, Philip of France's unsuccessful candidate for Jerusalem's crown, was angling for an alliance with Saladin—one that would exclude Richard. Alarmed, Richard hastened back to Acre to strong-arm the deserters as well as put a stop to Conrad. Working quickly, he returned within a fortnight, bringing large numbers of deserters with him. He also brought Joanna and Berengaria.[1]

While the Crusaders rebuilt Joppa's walls, Richard spent much of his time hawking and reconnoitering with his men. He also spent many hours negotiating with Saphadin, Saladin's brother. Anxious that Saladin not ally with Conrad of Montferrat, Richard may also have been entertaining serious second thoughts about the entire crusade. While stating that he hoped to take Jerusalem by January,[2] he confided to others that he was rapidly exhausting his health and strength, not to mention his money.[3] Although this may have amounted to little more than a plea for men and financial aid, it could in fact have been an indication that the great Lionheart was beginning to wonder whether he could accomplish all he had set out to do. Jerusalem, as he was learning from those who knew the land well, would be difficult to take—especially with a Muslim army in the field, led by a formidable foe.

Evidently delighting in the game he was playing, Saladin (and Saphadin) listened attentively to the English king's proposals. These included the astonishing idea that Joanna, the widowed queen of Sicily, wed Saphadin, and that the two rule Jerusalem together. According to this plan—which Richard seems to have proposed with some enthusiasm—the Christians would recover their sacred relics as well as access to their holy places, and all of Palestine would be Joanna's dower.

It was a long shot, but one of several proposals that both Saphadin and Saladin seemed willing to consider in the attempt to encourage these blond barbarians to go home. Saphadin even went so far as to allow Richard to dub him a knight.

But whatever the proposal's merits, it quite certainly did not take Joanna's feelings into consideration. Normally, these would have made little difference, but as a widow and former queen, Joanna occupied the one position in twelfth-century life where a woman had some leverage. To Richard's evident dismay, she was furious. Marry a pagan, indeed! She would call upon all the clergy to witness her most just defiance!

Richard put up a last-ditch protest, reminding her that her great-grandfather, Fulk of Anjou, had sat upon that very throne. But Joanna was adamant. Quickly reevaluating the situation, Richard called a retreat.

His little sister could be formidable.

Not long after, Richard moved his forces closer to Jerusalem, while Saladin withdrew into winter quarters within Jerusalem itself.

Winter soon set in, leaving the crusading host mercilessly exposed. Armor rusted and clothing molded. Salted meat rotted and biscuit became so soaked it putrefied. Rain and hail beat down upon the tents and ripped them, while floods turned the encampment into a river of mud. In this hostile environment, both man and beast sickened and died, and still the rains poured on.

Richard celebrated Christmas at the nearby castle of Latrûn, with the two queens and Guy of Lusignan. After Christmas we hear no more of the two queens, and Richard moved still closer to Jerusalem, headquartering his army in the Judean hills at Beit Nûba. Here the rains and misery continued. At last, deciding that any attempt to besiege Jerusalem in winter was utter folly, Richard decided to pack up and retreat to the coast. They would move to Ascalon, he told his disheartened warriors—as he had intended from the outset.

Men whose sole reason for persevering had been the expectation of taking Jerusalem now made their bitter way back to the coast, through mud and mire and driving sleet. When at last they reached Ascalon, they found it completely desolate. The place was such a shambles of rubble and ruins that they could not even find a way inside.

At length, after slipping and sliding up and over the wet rocks that had once formed this city's proud fortifications, the remnants of Lionheart's fighting force cobbled together a pitiful sort of shelter inside, among the ruins. There they eked out a bare existence. The seas were too rough to allow supply ships to land, and most of the food they had brought with them had either rotted or been lost in the journey.

Not surprisingly, the steady stream of deserters turned into a flood.

⚜

In the days and weeks that followed, word filtered back to Acre that Richard's sally on Jerusalem had failed. Having pressed within twelve miles of the Holy City, Lionheart had retreated. Yet from the outset, he had considered Ascalon the key to taking Jerusalem, and as the sun once again began to shine, Richard rallied his men to clear the ruins and rebuild Ascalon's walls.

Richard's ability to encourage his troops under the most difficult circumstances was extraordinary, and soon a surprising number heeded his call. But even as the walls of Ascalon were starting to rise, ominous messages began to arrive from England, where John was setting himself up as ruler of the realm.[4]

As if this were not enough, Conrad of Montferrat was again angling for Jerusalem's crown. The remaining French among Richard's troops now deserted for Tyre and Acre, where they trumpeted Conrad's cause.

Torn between reconquering Jerusalem for Christendom and returning to England to save his throne, Richard now acted to put a stop to the infighting over Jerusalem's crown. Realizing that Guy of Lusignan's star was almost extinguished, he agreed to recognize Conrad.[5]

It was a realistic political decision, aimed at encouraging the crusaders to stop their squabbling and refocus on their ultimate goal. No one, though, had reckoned on the terrorists.

⚜

For almost a century—ever since the crusades began—true Christian warriors had fought and betrayed their brethren in the Holy Land. The Hospitalers and the Templars, those two great Christian military orders, had become powers in their own right, subject to no king, while the crusader states themselves—Edessa, Antioch, Tripoli, and Jerusalem—had for years been hotbeds of strife and sedition.

Within Muslim ranks there was similar disunity and disarray, heightened by conflict between Shiite and Sunni—a conflict that by the time of the First Crusade had led to the formation of a revolutionary Shiite brotherhood of Assassins, sworn to secrecy and to the destruction of their far more numerous Sunni foes. Headquartered in the remote reaches of Syria, the Assassins carried out a systematic—and very public—elimination of their enemies. Sometimes they did the deed by poison, but more often by dagger. Since each member of the brotherhood fully expected to die a martyr's death (and reap a martyr's reward), the Assassins rarely failed to carry out their missions.

By the time Lionheart reached the Holy Land, the order's head was a remote being mentioned only in whispers as "the Old Man of the Mountain." Although he and his organization had come to look upon the Christians as sometimes useful allies, the fanatical Assassins—who had accumulated a powerful roster of enemies, including the mighty Templars[6]—added an unpredictable and highly explosive element to the Holy Land's already-combustible mix. As Christians and Muslims battled one another for the Holy Land, the Old Man of the Mountain persisted in sending out his secret orders of death and destruction from the unreachable Alamut, or "Eagle's Nest." Armed Assassins—disguised as beggars, merchants, or even Christian household servants—continued their reign of terror throughout the Land beyond the Sea.

This terror now struck with devastating swiftness. Soon after being chosen king of Jerusalem, Conrad was attacked one night on his way home from dinner. One assailant drew his attention, while the other thrust a dagger in his back. His murder, so totally unexpected, rocked the

Christian community. The murderer was caught and (under torture) confessed; he was one of the dread Assassins. Yet many doubted whether the Old Man of the Mountain was to blame. Some thought that Saladin was the real culprit, but Richard's enemies pointed at Richard himself. Richard immediately protested and referred his critics to a long-simmering feud between the Old Man and the dead man, who had refused to make proper reparations after murdering and robbing one of the Old Man's followers of a considerable sum of money.[7]

Politics in the Holy Land being what they were, Conrad's widow, Isabelle, was given little time to grieve. Having already given up two husbands for Holy Jerusalem's sake, she now was called upon to marry yet a third time for the same cause. All the factions at last agreed upon Henry, count of Champagne, who as grandson of Eleanor and Louis was nephew to both the current French and English kings. Having fortunately been well removed from the murder site when the deed was done, and therefore absolved of any part in the bloodshed, Henry soon wed the beautiful Isabelle.

The awkward matter of Conrad's death thus smoothed over, a rare spirit of unity at last emerged among the Christians in the Holy Land. Still, insofar as Richard's enemies were concerned, the subject of Conrad's murder was far from settled, and they added it to their growing list of black marks against this golden monarch of the West.

❧

Well aware that he had to make up for lost time, Richard now was in a hurry. Sending his engines of war by ship, he set off for Darum with a small band of trustworthy warriors from his own domains.

Darum was an important fortification that—since Ascalon's fall—had served as a major base for Saladin's troops and supplies coming out of Egypt. Accompanied by Robert of Leicester and other faithful followers, Richard galloped southward out of Ascalon, pounding along the sandy byways and sending up great clouds of dust as he came. By late afternoon he and his men reached Darum, where they pitched their tents before its seventeen strong towers. Being too few to encircle the place, they camped together along one side while they awaited their battering devices.

The Saracens who looked down on them from Darum's walls found them laughable. But by morning, Richard's ships with the battering engines had arrived. Since Darum was a solid fortification, built against the rock, the best offense was to pound the lot to pieces. Richard's stonehurlers promptly went to work, launching their missiles in a round-the-clock assault that stunned the Saracens. Richard himself took the largest siege engine under his command, aiming it directly at the huge keep. Men from Poitou manned a second hurling device, while a group of Normans pounded away with a third.

While the siege engines flung their missiles at Darum's walls, Richard's sappers worked to undermine them. Within record time they reached the fortress's foundations and began to tunnel under, ready to burn the wooden props behind as they left. Above them, Richard's bowmen let their arrows fly whenever they saw one of the enemy so much as move from his protected perch.

Thus pinned in place, the garrison watched helplessly as the siege engines shattered the castle gate, which the crusaders set on fire. After only four days of siege, the disheartened Saracens offered to surrender in return for their lives—an offer that Richard characteristically refused. Soon one of the towers fell with a terrible crash. His warriors immediately rushed in through the breach, raising their banners above the walls and killing or capturing the entire garrison.

Lionheart's conquest of the entire seaboard, from Acre to Darum, was now complete, and he could direct all his considerable energies into taking Jerusalem.

⁕

But Jerusalem was not Darum, and despite the recent accord reached among the crusaders, Lionheart's chances for taking Jerusalem had significantly dwindled. In numbers, names, and quality, the crusading host of June 1192 was not at all the one that had marched south with Richard to Arsuf the previous September. Indeed, hardship and disease had sided with the Saracens, reducing Richard's army to a shadow of its former strength.

Adding to Richard's woes, messengers arrived warning that Philip had returned to France, where he was plotting with John to take Richard's Norman lands.

Well aware that he had come to the Holy Land to reconquer Jerusalem and that anything less would be regarded as a failure, Richard reluctantly committed himself to stay for another year. But dissension among the crusaders now broke out in earnest, primarily between Philip's and Richard's men. The French even went so far as to remove themselves from the rest of the camp, while the duke of Burgundy took to entertaining his followers with a foul song about the king, which soon spread throughout the entire army.[8]

By this time, the full heat of summer had arrived, drying up the water in the land. Word now came that Saladin had anticipated their arrival by polluting the streams around Jerusalem and destroying the cisterns outside the city's walls. Those among Richard's advisers who knew the land worried about the crusaders' prospects, especially with an army as small and divisive as theirs had become.

Richard agreed. He had no wish to lose an entire army, even a small one, beneath Jerusalem's walls. At length, with only a four-hour march between his warriors and the Holy City, he finally ordered a retreat.[9]

Retreat? All were stunned, even those who had most strongly disparaged their chances. After coming all this way and having suffered so much! To return to their homes in failure!

Saladin, too, was stunned—and understandably relieved. The Christian God may not have succored His warriors, but Allah had heard His children's prayers.

While the Saracens rejoiced, the crusaders morosely climbed a nearby hill from which they could see the Holy City in the distance. They gazed for a time and then dejectedly descended. God had not found them fit to save His Holy City. This would be as close as they would come to Jerusalem.

⚜

Both sides now jockeyed for position: Richard, to keep the crusader states alive and ready for another attempt on Jerusalem; Saladin, to make certain this would never happen.

After reinforcing Ascalon, Richard brought the remnants of his demoralized army back to Acre. Saladin immediately departed Jerusalem with a large army, marching rapidly until he reached Joppa, where he set his assault engines against the city's rebuilt walls in a style that would have done credit to Lionheart himself.

Surrounded and completely outnumbered, the Christian warriors who remained immediately called upon Richard for help. Arriving from Acre just in time, the king jumped into the waist-deep water and splashed ashore, his men close behind him. Within an hour they had cleared the harbor area of Saracens, and from there they retook the town.

After repairing Joppa's walls as best they could, Richard and his men set up camp outside the town to escape the stench of the unburied bodies left behind. In a desperate gamble, Saladin now decided to make the ultimate move. Early one morning, a raiding party crept into the Christian camp and tried to break into Richard's tent. They were spotted, and a fight immediately broke out.

Richard, hastily clad in little but his armor, led the way. He had only a few armed but equally unprepared knights, plus several horses and a modest number of infantry. Positioning his spearmen shield to shield, he set his crossbowmen in pairs immediately behind, loading and shooting nonstop. Rallying his men, he urged them to their utmost. They did as he demanded, resisting wave after wave of mounted attack. Remembering Arsuf, the Saracens stopped short and wheeled back, unwilling to engage.

Still vastly outnumbered, Richard and his handful of mounted men in turn charged, bursting through the Saracen host all the way to its rearguard, where the king suddenly found himself alone in a sea of hostile troops. At this, Lionheart wielded his sword so furiously that he cut a swath through enemy ranks. When the rest of his troops came thundering to the rescue, the enemy retreat became a rout.

But this victory, although sweet, was not enough to turn the tide. Following this legendary battle, Richard and his exhausted men fell severely ill. Beaten down by sickness, Richard now agreed to the inevitable truce.

In the end, he and his warriors managed to wrest only a narrow strip of coastline from the infidel, from Acre down to Joppa, plus the right to worship within the Holy City itself. Bitterly disappointed, Richard could not be brought to accept Saladin's invitation to visit the longed-for city. Conquest in Richard's mind was one thing; touring with one's enemy's permission, quite another. Instead, he resolutely turned his back on Palestine and set his course for home.

⟞⟡⟝

Darkness had already fallen that night in early October 1192 when Richard's galley spread its sails and slipped silently out to sea.[10] It had been impossible to hide the fact that the king was leaving; preparations for such a journey were difficult to disguise. And yet Richard's exact course and time of departure remained well concealed. Too many people in too many places sought to do the Plantagenet monarch harm.

Anticipating death or capture, Richard surrounded himself with Templars, whose fierce fighting and ironclad protection of pilgrims had won it healthy respect throughout the regions he was about to cross. The king additionally took care to disguise himself and his lay companions in

Templar surcoats of red cross on a white ground. Thus prepared, Lionheart and his small band set their course homeward.

It would take them the better part of two years.

Heading westward, Richard and his bold companions first touched land in Cyprus, now ruled by Richard's protégé Guy of Lusignan. About a month later, a vessel bearing a similar description arrived at Corfu, off the Albanian coast. Like Cyprus, Corfu offered safe harbor to anyone allied with Tancred or the English crown. From here, Richard simply had to make a dash for Sicily or the Papal States, and from there to his own lands.

He never made it. Bearing into wintry winds, Richard's galley battled its way toward safety, eventually limping into port near Marseilles (most probably in Pisa, where Richard acquired the ruby that later figures in the story). Characteristically, Lionheart never included Brindisi or Messina in his plans at all. Rather, trusting to boldness and surprise, he had set his sights on landing directly within reach of Plantagenet soil.

His daring almost paid off. Yet in another stroke of bad luck, an old enemy, Raymond of Toulouse, discovered his intent and set watch in every French seaport where the king could conceivably land. Everyone, including his enemies, now expected him to show up in the Papal States or Sicily. Instead, Richard reversed course for Corfu—probably with the intent of reaching the German holdings of his brother-in-law, Henry the Lion, where he would find refuge and safe passage home.

Taking yet again to the stormy seas, Richard once more approached the Adriatic, where he transferred to a galley (possibly a pirate ship) that he hired on the spot. Then he pressed northward along the eastern coast, until the winds and waves at last drove his broken ship ashore.

He and his band had shipwrecked in Istria, in lands held by vassals of Leopold of Austria—the touchy duke whose banner Richard's minions had once trampled in the dust.

It was not an auspicious sign.

⚜

The queens' journey had been considerably less perilous. Making their way directly westward through open sea, they landed first in Sicily and then slowly journeyed north through papal territory to Rome.

There, under Celestine's protection, they awaited Richard's arrival. Accompanied by Emperor Isaac's captive daughter and Bourguigne of Lusignan, the beautiful niece of the infamous Guy, the two queens passed their days, their anxiety growing. Crusading knights had been pouring out of the Holy Land for some time now, and the first had already reached their hearths and homes. Yet nothing at all had been heard from Richard, who was well overdue.[11]

While the two queens watched and waited, Richard and his band of warriors (including Baldwin of Béthune) found quarters in a small village. Here the king sent a messenger to the local lord requesting safe-conduct for the pilgrims under the Truce of God, accompanying his request with a large ruby set in a ring of gold. The messenger explained that the person requesting the safe-conduct was one Hugh, a merchant. But the count,[12] after thoughtfully examining the huge ruby, remarked, "He is not called Hugh, but King Richard." The count then added that, despite his vow to seize all pilgrims coming from Jerusalem, he would return the gift—"for the worthiness of the gift and also of the sender"—and grant the travelers freedom to proceed.[13]

Alarmed that their identities had been discovered, Richard and his men mounted horses in the midnight darkness and galloped from the village, heading north. Their fears were justified. Not only did the count send word to his brother, whose lands Lionheart was bound to cross, but he also set armed men along the road in wait. After a brief scuffle, in which several of Richard's knights were captured, the king escaped.[14]

The hunt was on.

❊ 9 ❊

A World of Enemies

$\mathscr{R}$acing through the darkness, Richard and his faithful colleagues found temporary shelter, but were quickly discovered by yet another armed gang sent to seize him. Lionheart escaped, but most of the rest of his company, including Baldwin of Béthune, did not.

Pushing themselves and their horses to the limit, Richard and his much-reduced retinue now pounded their way through the countryside, not stopping for food or rest for three days. At last, in a little village near Vienna, they collapsed in a dirty inn on the Danube's shores. Richard, who may not have completely recovered from the fever he had contracted in the Holy Land before departure, fell headfirst onto the first bedding he saw.

It was difficult enough under any circumstances to hide the presence of such a man. Yet it seems to have been one of Richard's courtiers who first aroused the locals' suspicions. When this young fellow went to exchange his master's Syrian gold pieces for coin of the realm, he behaved "in a haughty and pompous manner"[1] and poured out a small fortune in gold on the exchanger's table. At this, several of the citizenry cornered and questioned him. The young man hared back to the inn and implored Richard to be off, but the king was exhausted and could not move.

After that, one thing led very quickly to another, and Richard's fate now unfolded with grim precision. Four days before Christmas, he awoke from yet another of his many slumbers to hear the noise of armed guards, who had surrounded the inn. According to legend, Lionheart quickly made his way to the kitchen, where he pulled on a dirty apron and took his place by the fire, slowly turning the greasy spit.[2]

Unfortunately for Richard, a servant's garments could not disguise him. As the guards spotted this imposing man and made to arrest him,[3] he coolly faced them. He would surrender, he told them, to none other than the duke himself.

Leopold of Austria, who had returned to Vienna to celebrate Christmas, soon learned the amazing news. Hastening to the scene, he took the mighty Plantagenet into his own custody. Lionheart, dressed in a dirty scullion's apron! In his wildest dreams, Leopold could scarcely have asked for more.

⁂

Henry Hohenstaufen sat quietly on his intricately carved wooden throne—a gift from his father, the great Barbarossa. It had been a miserable year. Crowned Emperor Henry VI the previous April, he had headed south from Rome to conquer Sicily. By all accounts, this should have been an easy affair. But Naples had refused to surrender, which meant valuable time consumed in a siege. Worse yet, the Sicilians had cut the Pisan fleet to shreds, and the Genoese had straggled in too late to help. Suffering from disease and heat, his army had deserted in droves. He himself had fallen ill, and his wife was taken prisoner on her sickbed in Salerno.

There was nothing to be done for it, and so at last he struck camp and grimly retreated home. Once there, he found that his troubles had only begun. Bit by bit, and then in a flood, his enemies had joined against him, with Church and barons once more united in their most unholy bond. He had been in the thick of this rearguard battle when, shortly after Christmas, he received Duke Leopold's stunning news.[4]

Once again, Henry Hohenstaufen could contemplate conquest.

⁂

Soon the shattering news of Richard's capture shot across all Christendom. Along the frozen byways the word spread, from courts to market towns, and from castles to cottages. Richard, the king of crusaders, the most spectacular warrior East or West had ever seen—imprisoned in some dark, demonic dungeon!

People shook their heads in wonder and dismay. And they shook their fists, for this was a most heinous crime, not only against a warrior of unrivaled luster, but against the very Truce of God.[5]

Who would avenge him? Who, indeed, would rescue him? Who, for that matter, even knew his whereabouts or whether he still lived? For only Richard's most exalted enemies knew the answers to these questions, and for the moment, they were maddeningly silent.

The bishops of Ely, Salisbury, and Bath now converged on Germany, trying to pick up the trail, while the archbishop of Rouen sent the abbots of Boxley and Pont Robert to find the missing king. But while Richard's supporters labored under tears and sorrow, John did not bother to hide his glee. As soon as he heard the tidings, he took ship for Normandy and Paris, where he immediately did homage for Normandy and for Richard's other Continental territories ("and for England as well, as some said").[6] Agreeing to hand over the Norman Vexin, he capped off his performance by promising Philip that he would set aside his current wife (Isabelle of Gloucester) and marry the princess Alais.[7]

Philip, in turn, eagerly went to work to raid Richard's holdings, seizing all-important Gisors as well as several of its neighboring castles, all of which, in consideration of the current political climate, fell into his hands like overripe plums. Philip then marched to the Norman capital of Rouen, where he claimed both the city and the well-guarded Princess Alais.

Rouen's garrison, however, was by now commanded by Robert, earl of Leicester—the young man who had made such a name for himself in the Holy Land. Descended from the Beaumonts, who from the time of the Conqueror had held lands in both England and Normandy, Robert held important Norman properties, including the border castles of Pacy (on the river Eure) and Breteuil (on the Avre frontier). Scarcely disinterested in the outcome, he nevertheless seemed singularly unimpressed by Philip's army and twenty-four siege engines. When the king called for the city to surrender, Robert coolly told him that the gates were open and that he could enter whenever he liked. Philip, who was no fool, seems to have recognized how useful it would be for Richard's men to be able to offer up the French king in return for the imprisoned English one. He withdrew in bad temper, taking Robert's castle at Pacy as well as the important fortress of Ivry on his way home.

John, however, returned to England in a buoyant mood, prepared to put down any resistance and establish his own rule in Richard's place. After all, had not Richard's ancestor, Robert Curthose, disappeared into prison and stayed there?[8]

❦

While Western Christendom anguished over his fate, Richard quickly found himself the star prisoner of the muscular castle of Durenstein, guarded by the fiercest and most trustworthy soldiers under Leopold's command.[9]

Here he remained in isolation for a time, then was moved westward along the Danube to Ratisbon (now Regensburg) and Würzburg while emperor and vassal haggled over terms.[10] Henry Hohenstaufen may have been Leopold's suzerain, but Leopold was not about to release this extraordinary prisoner, even to the emperor, without just compensation for his pains.

Henry Hohenstaufen, of course, fully appreciated this particular prisoner's worth. With rebellion at high heat throughout imperial lands, he needed a miracle to survive. Richard had provided that miracle. Not that Henry placed much faith in miracles—he was inclined to give more credit to his own abilities than to divine intervention. Still, this particular Christmas gift was an astonishment.

In point of fact, it provided a most elegant solution to Henry Hohenstaufen's extensive problems. Richard was the linchpin in the wide network of anti-imperial alliances, as well as the greatest source of treasure Henry could hope to find. Not only would this prisoner provide a king's ransom, larger than any ever before seen, but he would also provide the key to taming Henry's opposition. Buoyed by such financial resources, and at last protected from the old threats at home, Henry could once again permit himself to dream imperial dreams.

What did it matter that this man was protected by the Truce of God?[11] Henry Hohenstaufen thought in terms of political necessity rather than of religious nicety. For as he clearly understood, a captured king was but a pawn.

At last Leopold and the emperor agreed on a sum that would nicely line the pockets of both duke and emperor and bring the entire Plantagenet kingdom to its knees.[12] Half of this sum was to go to the Austrian duke, to serve as a most magnificent dowry for the marriage of Richard's niece to Leopold's eldest son. In addition, Richard was to release Emperor Isaac and his daughter, provide personal aid to Henry Hohenstaufen in conquering Sicily, and turn over two hundred high-ranking hostages until the ransom's terms were met. Moreover, in nose-thumbing retaliation for the pope's excommunication of Leopold, the terms of Richard's release required him to obtain his captor's absolution.

Richard could not consent to all of these terms, "even though his life should be periled thereby,"[13] and so Henry now contrived a set of charges against his exalted prisoner from which Richard had to defend himself. That Richard would be an eloquent and commanding speaker, no one—least of all Richard—ever doubted. After all, this was Eleanor's son, the most shining product of her court at Poitiers. Still, the prospect was daunting. Everywhere Lionheart looked, he saw enemies, but the deadliest of all was Henry Hohenstaufen, and Henry Hohenstaufen held all the cards.

When the day came for Richard's defense, the emperor listened and watched as Lionheart launched into his performance, dismissing Henry's carefully constructed complaints about injuries done His Imperial Highness and Leopold of Austria, Isaac of Cyprus, and Conrad of Montferrat, not to mention His Royal Highness, Philip of France. Lionheart was in splendid form that day, and those in attendance broke into tears "for very joy."[14]

Swallowing his anger, Henry brought the English king to the dais beside him.[15] Richard, assuming the danger over, now promised to pay the hundred thousand marks for his liberation, as well as provide the emperor with fifty fully equipped galleys and twenty knights for a year. It was thus to his utmost surprise when, only a few days later, armed guards seized him and once again threw him into a dungeon cell—this time in the remote mountain stronghold of Triffels, where prisoners routinely disappeared forever. Philip of France had learned of the terms upon which Henry Hohenstaufen had settled and was unhappy about Richard's imminent release.

The emperor now had the French card to play.

❧

While John continued to stir up trouble in England, Philip proceeded with devastating effectiveness against Richard's Norman lands. Not only Gisors and Neaufles fell to him, but also the northeastern fortifications of Aumale and Eu, with the addition of Ivry and Pacy on the way home from his unsuccessful siege of Rouen. He had now broken the Norman frontier at three critical points, all of which led to Rouen.

Philip was thus not at all pleased to learn that Richard would soon be back in action, and the French king now offered a considerable bribe to persuade the emperor to hand Lionheart over to him, or at the very least keep Richard indefinitely imprisoned in Germany.[16]

As a consequence, Henry Hohenstaufen took the opportunity to toughen the terms for Richard's release. Under the threat of delivering

Richard to Philip, who could be expected to show no mercy, the emperor managed to ratchet up the ransom to a shattering 150,000 marks.[17] Just as significantly, he used Richard to obtain peace with the emperor's rebellious German lords, most especially with Henry the Lion himself—whose son and heir now married into the upper reaches of the Hohenstaufen family.[18]

Philip was not amused. But the emperor had not meant for him to be. Beneath all the fine talk, Henry Hohenstaufen was no more a friend of the French king than of the English one. While fully intending to keep either one from getting out of line, he also aimed at preventing either from curbing his own imperial dreams.

"The devil is loose," Philip wrote John, upon learning of Richard's imminent release.[19] Yet Philip immediately came to terms, for in order to halt Philip's incursions and break up the Capetian-Hohenstaufen alliance, Richard was willing to allow Philip to keep the lands he had taken. In addition, Lionheart promised Philip a payment of twenty thousand marks of silver, with the four great fortresses of Loches, Châtillon, Driencourt, and Arques transferred to French hands until the payments were made.

These were stiff terms, but they won Richard a temporary respite from Philip's marauding. As for the property he had lost, Lionheart could expect to settle matters more to his liking when once again in the saddle, leading an army.

❧

Late in June 1193, after Richard and the emperor at last came to terms, Berengaria and Joanna (along with Isaac's captive daughter and Guy de Lusignan's niece, Bourguigne) departed Rome for Pisa, Genoa, and Marseille. Raymond of Toulouse had at last agreed to provide safe conduct, and he even offered to send his son to escort the ladies safely to Poitou.

Joanna did not know it, but her own future would be decided in this fateful portion of the journey, for Raymond's son—Raymond the Younger—took one look at the beautiful Bourguigne and decided that his life was due for improvement. After setting aside his current wife and packing the startled woman off to a nunnery, he married Bourguigne before she even reached Poitou.

These events startled some others as well, most particularly those in the Plantagenet camp, for this marriage between the erratic and dangerous house of Toulouse and the incendiary house of Lusignan boded trouble. It therefore happened that when Raymond the Elder died, young Raymond came not only into his father's lands but into a head-spinning marriage with Joanna Plantagenet as well.[20]

Berengaria's path proved, quite typically, to be a quieter one. Having not provided the heir that Plantagenet policy required, she found herself relegated to playing second fiddle to her long-lived and forceful mother-in-law. Despite Berengaria's coronation, Eleanor most unquestionably was queen of England, and woe betide anyone—even Richard's wife—who presumed to think otherwise.[21]

⁂

With the terms for Richard's release at last settled, work began in earnest to collect the enormous ransom and provide the hostages against the day of reckoning. Not surprisingly, John Plantagenet had little interest in this effort, and Eleanor took charge, guiding and pushing the back-breaking effort to bring her son safely home.

During these same waning weeks of summer, Philip of France, searching for more reliable allies than the German emperor, wed Ingeborg, or Ingelburg, daughter (some say sister) of the Danish king.[22] That is, until after his wedding night, when Philip decided that the emperor's cousin Agnes—now promised to Henry the Lion's son—was perhaps a better choice. Sending Ingeborg packing, Philip pressed to make the other lady queen of France. Much to his surprise, he discovered that he had sadly underestimated the fighting spirit of either woman, for Ingeborg put up a fierce resistance, while Agnes, not wishing to share Ingeborg's fate, took matters into her own hands and secretly wed the Lion's cub.[23]

In the meanwhile, Richard's subjects, groaning under the heavy burden of a ransom meant to break their backs, bent themselves to the task. Collection proceeded with grinding slowness, but by autumn 1193, they had raised what Roger of Howden calls "the greater part,"[24] and the emperor agreed to release the king. At long last, the end of Richard's captivity seemed in sight. Armed with an impressive retinue of glittering nobility and heavily mailed guards, Eleanor anxiously pressed toward Speyer.[25]

Yet Henry still had one more card to play. Waiting until Eleanor's arrival, he expressed some last-minute qualms. Philip of France and John Plantagenet had between them offered yet another prodigious bribe if the emperor would keep Lionheart in captivity long enough for them to retrieve certain properties they believed due them, in recompense for all the injustices they claimed to have endured at Richard's hands.[26] The offer was but that—no solid silver had yet appeared from either man. And yet Henry Hohenstaufen was willing to give it due consideration, as yet another bargaining chip.

Not surprisingly, Richard now began to despair of ever being freed. But what Henry wanted, as it turned out, was for Richard to pay him homage as his liege lord—a courtesy that the emperor believed the king of England owed him. After consulting with Eleanor, Richard gave his consent, and the deed was done.[27] It was a simple enough gesture—removing the royal bonnet and presenting it to the emperor—but one that Henry seems to have vastly enjoyed. It was worth a hundred thousand marks to him, especially when he considered that this sum was still a paper offer from Richard's foes.

Henry looked about him and saw peace on all sides. He looked to Sicily and saw conquest. And he looked beyond and saw endless possibilities.

⚜

It was February 1194 when Richard left the emperor's abode a free man, and March when he arrived on England's shores. The sun shone so brightly upon his arrival that all deemed it a propitious sign.[28] The famed Lionheart had at long last returned.

Yet Richard did not linger long in England. After settling affairs in his island kingdom, he quickly departed for Normandy. Lent was over, and the fighting season had begun. He had some scores to settle and business of a military nature to transact.

Philip, he knew, would be waiting.

Part Four

❊ 10 ❊

Lionheart's Return

$\mathcal{I}$n late April 1194, Richard gathered a large transport fleet in Portsmouth, where his army mustered under stormy skies. Even under the best of circumstances, most denizens of the twelfth century did not enjoy the Channel crossing, and the gale winds that now ripped through the drenching darkness could only have reinforced a natural reluctance to sail forth on this highly unpredictable stretch of sea.

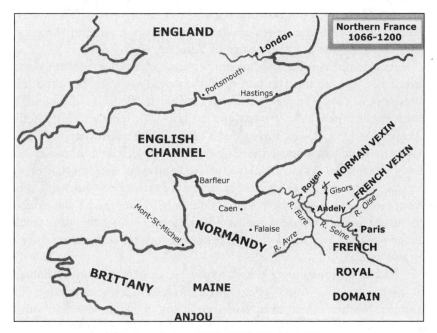

Northern France, 1066–1200. © J. McAuliffe

But while his men huddled in whatever shelter they could find, Richard eyed the tempest with impatience. He was not of timid stock. Despite memories of the White Ship, his father had crossed the Channel in the teeth of a raging gale en route to seizing England's crown. Fifty years before that, William Rufus—racing to the Continent to lift a siege in the county of Maine—had put to sea during equally memorable tempests.

Still, despite Richard's personal courage, he was not inclined to risk an army. So when he put to sea in the midst of howling winds and driving rain, it was from a particular sense of urgency. Philip of France had spent the previous year and a half chewing his way through Richard's properties, opening the way to Rouen. Rouen had held for the moment, but there was more than one way to skin an empire, and Philip had an ally in John, who had responded to the news of Richard's imminent release by hastily surrendering to Philip all claims to Normandy east of the Seine, together with essential territory along the frontier to the Seine's west.

Philip quite naturally leaped to claim John's concession before Richard could prevent him, invading through the Seine's western neighbor, the Eure River valley, where he easily snagged the important towns of Évreux and Vaudreuil. Adding insult to injury, he placed John in charge of Évreux, along with the formidable castles of Arques and Driencourt to the east. Then, as word came that Richard was sailing toward Normandy, Philip tried to squeeze in yet another prize—a quick siege of the great southeastern Norman fortress town of Verneuil, on the Avre.

As it happened, Philip's informers miscalculated, for violent storms forced Richard to return to port until the worst was over. But after ten interminable days, Lionheart at last set sail for Barfleur, on Normandy's northwestern tip. There, crowds greeted him with relief and joy, wildly cheering as he galloped through the bleak and beautiful lands of the northern Cotentin toward the Conqueror's city of Caen. Pressing on along Normandy's coast, he passed above windswept beaches that eight centuries later would enter history under the names of Omaha, Utah, Juno, Gold, and Sword. Bells rang wildly as he approached Caen, where he turned inland toward Lisieux. There, John—who had taken stock of the situation and decided to place his bets on Richard—came to beg forgiveness.

Richard magnanimously and somewhat contemptuously complied. In Richard's eyes, John was no threat. Indeed, Lionheart viewed his younger brother—then twenty-seven—as but a child who had most unfortunately allowed himself to be manipulated. Whether or not John resented the patronizing tone, he could only have been relieved at the interview's outcome. After all, Richard had unhesitatingly butchered almost three thousand hostages in Acre, and from his teens he had earned a solid reputation for cruelty. John escaped punishment not so much because of Richard's goodness or greatness of spirit, but because of this strong man's overwhelming confidence. Now that Lionheart had returned from the Holy Land and from imprisonment, he fully expected to keep his troublesome baby brother well in check.

Philip, however, was another matter. Perhaps it was their once-close friendship that added a particular intensity to the rivalry, but by this time there was no question that Richard of England and Philip of France were the most deadly of enemies. The roots of this enmity went deep, nurtured by more than a century of conflict between the English and the French crowns and given added edge by the easy dominance that William the Conqueror and his heirs had long enjoyed over their Capetian foes.

In large part, this was a function of raw power, for from the outset the Anglo-Norman kings had enjoyed far more territory and clout than their French overlords. Yet it was also testimony to the glory and dash of the Anglo-Normans, both on the battlefield and off. None of the Capetians until Philip could withstand the withering light of comparison with William the Conqueror, Henry I, Henry II, or even the much-reviled William Rufus. And when it came to personal courage and sheer flair, no one—especially not the lackluster Philip—could compete with Richard.

Overall, the Capetians' major virtue throughout the long years had been their sheer persistence and staying power. From Philip I on, they watched for small opportunities and took them, usually when their more flamboyant rivals began to throw the crockery at one another. So far, this had been a sufficiently effective policy to keep the Capetians in the game, but the role had little glamour or appeal—as Eleanor could readily testify. Eleanor's desertion of the one camp for the other in fact illustrated in starkest terms the Capetian failure to live up to twelfth-century expectations (most especially Eleanor's) for royalty, and this particular bit of family history rankled—not only with the long-suffering Louis VII, but with his son, who remembered the insult well.

Yet while the Capetians plodded on, they steadily kept at the job of building up their royal power and domain—perhaps not as imaginatively or as remarkably as the Conqueror or either of the Henrys, but sufficient to the purpose. As a result, the French royal domain—while still comparatively small—no longer was weak, and the clear power advantage that the Anglo-Norman monarchs once enjoyed over their rivals had gradually diminished. Philip entertained dreams of glory that would have seemed breathtaking to his ancestors, and (oblivious to the German emperors' claims) he actively cultivated legends promoting his family's links with Charlemagne.

Thus as Richard galloped southeast from Barfleur, the French king who awaited him not only was his deadly enemy but also was far stronger and more dangerous than any king of France that the dukes of Normandy and kings of England had yet confronted.

⚜

Verneuil, on the river Avre (a tiny stream marking Normandy's frontier to the immediate west of the Seine and the Eure), had from the outset been an important bastion. The still-visible earthworks and ramparts that Henry I gave it, along with a lengthy canal to ensure its water supply, made it a formidable fortification even three-quarters of a century after Beauclerk's death. By the time Richard reached Lisieux, Philip—who was no slouch at siege engines—had been furiously besieging Verneuil for almost three weeks.

Pressing on from Lisieux, Richard dined in Chambrais (now called Broglie), then swept south to L'Aigle, an important border town to the west of Verneuil.[1] Positioning himself in Tuboeuf while waiting for the main body of his own troops to catch up, he sent a contingency of knights and crossbowmen to relieve the beleaguered town, then took steps to cut the French supply lines. Instantly grasping that the besiegers were about to become the besieged, Philip quickly abandoned Verneuil. The following day, Richard entered in triumph. By saving Verneuil at this critical juncture, he had in effect saved Normandy.

John, who was eager to reassure Richard of his loyalty, had in the meantime hastened to Évreux. After insinuating himself into the French garrison by false protestations of friendship, he had every one of them seized and decapitated. In a particularly macabre touch, he had their heads jabbed onto pikes, which were then placed around the town. This episode, which seems entirely characteristic of the youngest Plantagenet, left Philip burning for revenge. Galloping the forty kilometers north to Évreux, he drove John from the city and brutally sacked it, then mopped up a small castle in the neighborhood of Rouen. Of far more importance, he also managed to capture Robert of Leicester, who had ventured forth to harry the French king and his men as they withdrew.

Richard in the meanwhile raced northward to take the castle of Beaumont-le-Roger—the pride of Robert of Meulan, a frontier lord who had gone over to Philip—before storming south to reestablish his authority in the Touraine and Poitou. His object in the Loire valley was the mighty fortress of Loches, one of four he had temporarily ceded to Philip and had subsequently lost, thanks to John's sweeping concessions. Relieving the siege forces of his brother-in-law and ally, Sancho of Navarre, Richard took the place in a single splendid assault.[2]

Richard now planned to sweep farther southward into Poitou and Aquitaine, to subdue the various rebellions that Philip had so successfully stirred up. But Philip, in a burst of bravado, followed his enemy into the Touraine, encountering Richard just outside the unfortified town of Vendôme.[3] Falling back on Fréteval, the French king sent a message to his rival, cockily informing him that he could expect a battle. Richard replied that he was ready. Moreover, if Philip failed to show up, he would come after him. At this, Philip turned and ran.

In hot pursuit, Richard caught up with Philip's rearguard, and soon the entire French army was fleeing before him. Yet Lionheart had little interest in Philip's men. Petty nobles be damned—he wanted the king! With white-hot memories of Philip's perfidy propelling him onward, Richard breathed out threats of slaughter as he galloped furiously on.

Thinking quickly, Philip eluded him. Slipping from the retreating mob, the French king piously entered a church not long before Richard stormed by. It was not until Lionheart reached the Norman border that he realized what must have happened. By this time, his own men had captured a host of prisoners and horses as well as Philip's entire baggage train, including arms, treasure, and an invaluable set of charters revealing who among Richard's Norman nobles had treacherously switched sides. A windfall, to be sure, but surely a disappointment to Lionheart, who for a few brief hours had tasted far sweeter possibilities.

☙❧

It is tempting to wonder what Philip's fate would have been had he in fact fallen into Richard's hands. In the heat of the moment, Lionheart had indeed sworn to have him, dead or alive, and it is possible that had his Angevin fury gotten the better of him, Richard might have slaughtered his royal prisoner on the spot.

Yet the moment quickly passed, and soon Richard found himself in an interminable slogging-match. Both sides were tenacious and strong, and although Philip was no equal for Richard in individual combat, he had patiently learned the art of siegecraft. He had also become—or at least had the good sense to hire—a military engineer of the first order, as his impressive addition to the Anglo-Norman bastion of Gisors clearly shows.

Gisors by this time was a century old, having its origins in an impressive motte (or man-made hill) piled high by William Rufus, who crowned it with a defensive donjon (tower, or keep). Rufus had the foresight—which his hapless brother Curthose had not—to envision this particular fortress as anchor to a series of castles forming a defensive line all the way down the river Epte to Vernon, thus creating a formidable barrier against incursion through the Vexin into the heart of Normandy. Quite specifically, Gisors was constructed to face the nearby French fortresses at Chaumont, Trie, and Boury, while the full stretch of Rufus's defenses stood at the ready to defend against French incursions anywhere along the line.

Supplementing already-existing fortifications at Vernon and Gisors' near-neighbor, Neaufles-Saint-Martin, William Rufus picked a vantage point above the Epte, about halfway between Gisors and the Seine, and crowned it with yet another fortified motte at Château-sur-Epte.[4] Half-

Château de Gisors, anchor of the Anglo-Norman Plantagenet defenses along the boundary between the Norman and the French Vexin. First constructed by William Rufus on an impressive motte, it was enlarged and strengthened by Henry I and Henry II. © J. McAuliffe

way between that point and the Seine, Rufus is credited with building yet another fortification at Baudemont, whose strategic location can still be appreciated, even if the fortress itself—now in ruins—cannot. In addition, sometime during the late eleventh or early twelfth century, a fortification at Dangu joined Neaufles-Saint-Martin and Gisors in defending that critical portion of the line.

Behind this bristling defense lay an equally purposeful secondary line, ranged between the Epte and the Norman Vexin's northern boundary, the river Andelle. Echeloned behind Gisors, the small towns of Hacqueville, Etrépagny, and Gamaches still exist, even if their fortifications do not, while two semicircular watchtowers along a northern section of wall serve to remind the twenty-first century of the extensive fortifications that defended the old town of Andely as early as 1119.[5]

Nor were the French sluggish about defending their side of the border. As Lemarignier has pointed out, Chaumont and Mantes from an early date anchored each end of the French line of defense, linked by the secondary fortresses of Trie, Boury, and Maudétour, and capably backed (just outside of Paris) by Pontoise. As in the Norman Vexin, the crown maintained key fortresses, but local families controlled a welter of other fortifications, including the ancient border fortresses on the Seine at Meulan and La Roche-Guyon.[6]

Gisors was a formidable fortress that had grown even more muscular with the passing years. By 1125, Henry I had surrounded the open space or bailey at the motte's base with a stone enceinte, or curtain wall. Henry II in turn reinforced this wall and built the present stone donjon, whose polygonal shape was a distinct remove from the older rectangular form that dotted the landscape, providing an interesting link with the newer circular towers that would soon be the latest thing in castle-building.[7]

Philip's addition to Gisors reflected the enormous importance he rightly placed on this key bastion. With considerable flair, he made his mark on this symbol of Anglo-Norman strength and pride, erecting in its southeastern corner a rectangular residence tower and large circular donjon of the latest style, linked by a strong curtain wall. This imposing complex offered yet another defense within Gisors' ring of already-stout defenses, but it also gave Philip the opportunity to place an unmistakable "Kilroy was here" on his enemies' walls.

Yet taunting gestures were the least of Richard's problems, for the challenge with which Philip confronted him in the summer of 1194 was indeed a grave one. Not only was the French monarch master of Gisors and the Norman Vexin, but he had also made huge gains in the Seine and Eure valleys, in addition to territory farther to the west and along Normandy's eastern and northeastern frontiers.

During the two months following Richard's return to the Continent in May, the English king had dramatically reasserted control over his lands, from the southern borders of Normandy to the Pyrenees, and had come within a hair of capturing Philip himself. Yet despite his essential save at Verneuil, Lionheart still had to pry Philip out of Normandy. And it was in Normandy—the old fighting grounds between the French and English monarchs—where Philip was the most deeply entrenched and the least inclined to give ground. In particular, Philip was determined to keep his gains in the touchy Vexin lands bordering his own, as well as those lands he had picked up along the Seine—that all-important link connecting Paris to the sea.

John's failure (while Richard was elsewhere) to retake the critical fortress of Vaudreuil, which had fallen to Philip only months before, showed the difficulty of Richard's task. He could not personally be everywhere, and in his absence, Philip had raced his troops to the scene and vanquished the foe with the kind of authority that made men sit up and take notice. Vaudreuil's location, practically at Rouen's gate, made it an especially vital property for all concerned, and in Richard's absence his representatives agreed to a truce before they could make an even worse mess of things. Richard himself seems to have been unhappy with the terms, which essentially agreed to the status quo,[8] but both sides—if not Lionheart himself—seemed ready for a rest. In any case, no one expected truces—least of all this one—to last.

❧

While Richard was engaged in winning back his lands in France, his world—from Western Europe to the Holy Land—continued to change at breathtaking pace. Saladin's unexpected death—only months after Richard's departure from Palestine—quickly led to chaos and strife among the Muslims, with Saladin's heirs going at one another's throats. In contrast, the Christians for once appeared downright statesmanlike. Upon Henry of Champagne's unfortunate death,[9] the beautiful Isabelle was once again wed for Jerusalem's sake—this time to Amaury (or Aymer) of Lusignan, who had inherited Cyprus from his recently deceased brother. The new king of Jerusalem thus held a most valuable double crown.

Ironically, the person who now stood to benefit most from this state of affairs was not Richard but Henry Hohenstaufen. Following Tancred of Sicily's most convenient death early in 1194, along with the highly profitable business of Richard's own release, the emperor had hands free and moneybags bulging for Sicilian conquest and beyond. Even as Philip and Richard settled into an uneasy truce, Henry marched into Apulia, seized Salerno, and by November had taken Sicily. Crowning everything, after nine years of childless marriage, his forty-one-year-old wife now gave birth to a son, the future Frederick II. All in all, Henry had every reason to call it a good year.

A good year for the emperor, however, meant a very bad year for the Church—especially for the papacy, which viewed with alarm Henry Hohenstaufen's territorial mop-up in Sicily and southern Italy. Philip's and Richard's total involvement in fighting one another meant that the pope could look for little help from either side—a considerable factor in prompting the papal legate, Melior, to urge the July 1194 truce between them.

Wheels spun within wheels, and although Philip's relations with the emperor may have fallen on hard times, Richard's—despite his recent captivity—had grown reasonably friendly. Yet for the moment, the papacy could expect little immediate help from either quarter. Nor could it expect much aid on behalf of Christendom, whose warfare with the infidel had received a decided setback on the Iberian Peninsula, just as opportunity for reconquest most surprisingly beckoned in the Holy Land.

What Richard thought of Henry Hohenstaufen's successes, we do not know, but we can well imagine his response to the unexpected news of Leopold of Austria's death. It was, after all, a gratifyingly unpleasant demise. All autumn, Leopold had been badgering Richard to pay up the rest of his ransom as well as to hand over young Eleanor, the king's niece, to wed Leopold's son. Thoroughly enjoying his newfound dominance, the duke had even threatened to kill off Richard's remaining hostages unless Lionheart immediately complied.

Understandably short of cash, Richard opted for placing his niece on the marriage block. He therefore bought appropriate clothes for her and her household as well as for the captive daughter of Isaac of Cyprus, who was to accompany her, and sent both young women eastward under the protection of the ever-loyal Baldwin of Béthune (who had been chosen by Leopold's other hostages to carry the irate duke's warnings back to the king).

For the moment, Leopold still held the upper hand. But a foot proved his undoing. One of his became gangrenous, and when Leopold's physicians proved reluctant to amputate, the duke himself was forced to do the deed. He died shortly thereafter, and suddenly his offenses against the royal pilgrim came home to roost. Now at long last the Church stepped forth to demand a righting of wrongs. The archbishop of Salzburg refused burial until the hostages Richard had given Leopold were released, the ransom silver he had paid was returned, and the remainder of the ransom remitted.[10]

During the relative calm of early 1195, to which this news could only have contributed, Richard dealt with some other unfinished business in his life, including his marriage. The nature of Richard's relationship with Berengaria has long puzzled historians, and it may have puzzled his contemporaries as well.

What exactly was the problem between the two? Berengaria may have been no beauty, but no one expected her to be. In any case, a quiet and prudent disposition, although perhaps not exciting, seems hardly sufficient to explain the wide berth that Richard consistently gave her. Incompatibility was no excuse when it came to the marriage bed (as Matilda and Geoffrey of Anjou clearly realized), and only a mismatch of truly gargantuan proportions would have warranted a breakup. Philip of France, for example, seems to have been thoroughly revolted by his second wife, the unfortunate Ingeborg of Denmark, but failed to convince the Church that this warranted a permanent separation from the lady.

There was of course the distinct possibility that Berengaria was barren. Given the dearth of opportunity she had to prove otherwise, this may seem a hasty conclusion. Yet if Richard had concluded that she was incapable of giving him an heir, then why did he not follow the time-honored course of divorcing her? After all, an heir to the throne was what royal marriage was about, and failure to produce at least one bouncing baby boy usually led the wife in question directly from the marriage bed to the nunnery.

It is true that there may have been other considerations. Berengaria's relatives, most especially her brother, had on occasion provided useful aid to Richard. Yet no one in those times considered any alliance—no matter how critical—as more important than the production of a legitimate male heir.

Had Richard been impotent, that would of course have mooted the entire issue. But early in life he is said to have produced an illegitimate son, Philip of Cognac, thus removing from history any question of his abilities, on the battlefield and off. Whether or not the question *should* have been removed is an interesting point, but unsolvable at this late date. Whatever the reason, by this time in his life Richard was behaving like a man who did not expect to produce offspring.

Ignoring precedent, he made no attempt to set Berengaria aside, but simply abandoned her. She seems to have suffered no humiliation of the sort that Eleanor endured from Henry, for Richard did not hasten to a mistress's arms. Indeed, Richard seems to have shown no particular interest in any woman. One in fact senses a certain embarrassment among the chroniclers on the subject and an effort—reinforced by nineteenth-century historians—to portray Lionheart as deeply in love with Berengaria, for whom (they say) he had formed an undying attachment at that fateful tournament in Pamplona, years before their marriage. Ambrose, for example, says that Richard "loved her much from the time that he was Count of Poitiers, and she had been his heart's desire."[11]

Whether or not Berengaria had been Richard's heart's desire during the many years between first sighting and actual marriage, the fires certainly did not seem to burn high once the couple actually wed. After his release from prison in early 1194, Richard did not so much as summon her to his side, even for his second coronation ceremony. Nor did he subsequently bother to visit her at her nearby residence in Le Mans.

This peculiar state of affairs has drawn new attention in recent years, and current wisdom has it that Richard the Lionheart must have been gay. Although John Gillingham makes the valid point that this "highly colored assertion which cannot be substantiated . . . tells us more about our own times than it does about the character of the man whom it ostensibly concerns,"[12] it nevertheless must be pointed out that it was not until recent times that such a conclusion could be seriously considered, let alone printed. Even in Richard's day, homosexuality was considered such a grave offense that its existence—evidently widespread among the clergy—was only hinted at. A king such as William Rufus took his reputation and perhaps even his life in his hands to live openly according to his sexual preferences (which he had prudently kept hidden during his father's lifetime), and a popular monarch such as Richard, who evidently cared deeply about the kind of image he was projecting upon history, would have shied from being so labeled.

Even so, there are several episodes in Richard's life that, although not conclusive, are at the very least thought provoking. By itself, his intense friendship with Philip of France would have meant little or nothing. But then, shortly before departing on crusade, Richard dramatically did penance in Messina for a sin in which he had lived and which he now most fervently abjured. Richard rarely did things by halves, and when he fell in abject penitence at the bishops' feet, he was stripped to the waist and bearing scourges.

Roger of Howden, who tells the tale, rejoices in the sinner's repentance and absolution, which from the medieval way of looking at things was the point of the story. But modern readers want to know more about the exact nature of the sin, and on this point neither Roger nor anyone else was forthcoming. All that the contemporary reader can glean is that it must have been a sizable one—far greater, certainly, than womanizing, which no one in those times seemed to get particularly worked up over.[13]

Richard, who evidently was preparing himself for his role as savior of Jerusalem, may well have kept his promise and led a reformed life throughout the crusade. Certainly he reflected prevalent Christian thought when he demanded celibacy from his crusading warriors, on the grounds that God would allow only the good and the pure to save His Holy City. Indeed, when these crusaders came home empty-handed, many believed that it was because they had strayed from their crusader vows.[14] But sometime after Richard's return from the Holy Land—possibly after his release from prison—he seems to have slipped again, for early in 1195 a holy man specifically warned him to consider what had befallen Sodom and leave off his unlawful behavior.[15]

Twelfth-century Christians may not necessarily have understood a reference to Sodom in today's explicit terms; the hermit could have been warning Richard of any private sin of significant proportions. Still, whatever it was that Richard was doing, it was sufficiently serious to prompt warnings of hellfire and damnation.[16]

Probably because Richard no longer was responsible for a holy crusade, he shrugged off the warning. That is, until Easter, when he became violently ill. Fearing for his life, he immediately began to make amends—feeding the poor and restoring holy vessels to those churches where his ransom-collectors had cleaned out everything of value. Perhaps of greatest significance, he chose this moment to reconcile with Berengaria.[17]

Nothing is said in any of the chronicles about how either husband or wife behaved on this first encounter in well over two years. Berengaria did not infuse any scene with drama, but perhaps her peace and calm benefited her seriously ill husband, for he soon began to mend. Similarly, we do not know how long she stayed. Soon Richard once again became most thoroughly immersed in affairs of war, and before long he would be holding forth from his favored spot in Andely, which quickly became his clubhouse. One simply cannot imagine Berengaria at Gaillard.

And yet, sometime after their April 1195 reconciliation, a French chronicler has the royal couple visiting Thorée, just south of Le Mans, where he says they bought land and built themselves a house.[18] This event, so cozily domestic and at odds with the rest of Lionheart's life, seems almost a figment of someone's imagination—and perhaps it was. We hear nothing further of Berengaria during the remainder of Richard's lifetime.

Despite the truce, it should come as no surprise that Richard and Philip continued to kick each other beneath the table. Neither was about to give way, for two kingdoms were at stake. Philip was thinking in terms of empire, and Richard already had one, if he could keep it. Everyone understood that the stakes were enormous.

Everyone understood as well that the real pressure points in this bitter conflict remained those lands around the Seine where the kings of France and England had for so long challenged one another. Philip had firmly taken hold of the Norman Vexin and several critical fortresses along the left bank of the Seine as well as along its sister waterway, the Eure. Gaillon, merely a loop in the river away from the Rock of Andely, remained securely in his hands, as did Vernon, an important river crossing at the mouth of the Epte, where Philip would soon replace the Conqueror's defenses with huge fortifications of his own.[19] Pacy-sur-Eure—a most satisfying conquest that Philip had seized from Robert of Leicester—still showed no signs of budging, while neighboring Ivry, a spectacular Norman fortification dating from the late tenth century, also remained solidly under Philip's control. Yet apart from these important holdings, a state of fluidity appears to have set in throughout these bitterly contested lands, and there are indications that Philip was holding on to many of his acquired properties by his fingernails.

In January 1195, for example, Richard briefly held court at Brionne, an impressive fortification overlooking the river Risle, between Beaumont-le-Roger and the Abbey of Bec-Hellouin. Presumably on this occasion Richard pitched his camp somewhere other than the castle itself, for Philip had done a thorough job of blasting his way through its walls en route to capturing the place the year before. Philip had destroyed the castle but had not retained control over it or its territory, and Richard— who did not rebuild it—seems to have been using this occasion as an opportunity to show the flag there.

Similarly, several days later Lionheart showed up in Vaudreuil, where his chancery boldly issued a charter. In June, Richard once again put in appearance at Vaudreuil. The significance of this, as one historian has pointed out, is that Philip still technically held this important bastion on the left bank of the Seine, within a stone's throw of Rouen. But the operative word is *technically*, for Richard must have established a sufficient military presence in the neighborhood to allow him to hold court there, at what amounted to Philip's very doorstep.[20] Any commander worth his salt would have recognized the realities of such a situation, and within a month, Philip had evacuated Vaudreuil, destroying it in his wake. This pattern seems to have been going on for some time, with Philip abandoning many of the castles he had seized when Richard was held prisoner—presumably because the French king no longer could hold them. As in the case of Vaudreuil, his preferred mode of exit was to destroy the place on his way out the door.

In the meantime, the emperor was busy stirring up as much trouble between the two monarchs as he could manage. While the papacy longed for peace in northern France, the emperor quite predictably saw the value of war there, especially if Richard were to emerge victorious. Henry Hohenstaufen was dreaming big dreams, and in his vision, Philip would come to acknowledge Henry's imperial overlordship, just as Richard had.[21]

Philip ducked and weaved, parleying for peace at one moment and slipping in a kick to the shins at another. The two kings met not far from Vaudreuil in mid-July 1195, each encamped on opposite sides of the Eure. This seems to have been the first time that they had met in person since Philip's departure from the Holy Land. The treaty of the previous July had been settled between the two kings' representatives, and (most fortunately for Philip) Richard had not caught up with him outside Fréteval. Philip now was thirty years old, but despite his growing power and maturity, he seems to have retained a certain awe for his older rival—as well he might, given Richard's larger-than-life personality and legendary reputation on the battlefield.

For his part, Richard had come to realize how dangerous—and elusive—Philip could be. Although Lionheart was hardly stupid, his straightforwardness nevertheless put him at a disadvantage when dealing with so slippery a fellow. This slippery element once again surfaced as the two kings parleyed outside of Vaudreuil, for as they went through the motions of negotiation, a huge crash from nearby abruptly informed Richard of what Philip was doing. Having concluded that he could no longer hold the place, Philip had set his engineers to work in undermining Vaudreuil's walls. The conference in which the two kings were engaged had done its job in occupying and distracting Richard while this business was going on.

Furious, Richard took off after Philip, swearing vengeance, while Philip bolted across the river, destroying the bridge behind him. Once again, Lionheart found himself staring after his elusive and rapidly retreating enemy. And then, with a firm grasp on the military realities, he gave up the chase and began to rebuild Vaudreuil.

❧

In the meantime, Richard and his mercenary henchman, Mercadier, had been pressing Philip hard to the south of Paris, in Berry and the Auvergne. This, as well as Henry Hohenstaufen's worrisome meddling, may have prompted the Vaudreuil parley, for discussions between the enemies continued even as they continued to bash away at one another. Although Clausewitz famously observed that modern warfare is merely the continuation of political policy by other means, the twelfth century seems to have reversed this dictum, at least where diplomacy was concerned. Opposing sides used these frequent diplomatic time-outs to catch their breath, evaluate their enemy's strength and determination, and reconfigure the chessboard to their advantage, all the while taking every opportunity to undermine the opposition's morale.

The stops and starts of this era's warfare may have originated in the rhythms of the feudal levy, which typically lasted forty days. Traditionally, in return for lands held, the feudal vassal owed his lord the service of an agreed-upon number of armed and mounted knights for forty days each year. In years gone by, this amount of military service had been sufficient to keep the fires of war burning throughout the length and breadth of Western Christendom during the entire fighting season, which generally began after Easter.

Yet by the late twelfth century, lords and kings such as Richard and Philip required service for far greater lengths of time than the feudal levy by itself made possible. The rise of towns and communal militias provided little direct help, for a town's carefully hammered out privileges often precluded anything other than outright defense. The burgesses of Andely, for example, were required to serve only on expeditions that left and returned on the same day. That left the lord with lengthy military requirements to bargain as best he could with his vassals, such as requiring fewer knights for longer periods of time. Ultimately, warring lords increasingly turned to hiring mercenary forces—that is, professional soldiers of humble origins who fought for pay.[22]

Money had in fact by this time become essential to warfare.[23] Paid soldiers were proving indispensable, not only in drawn-out conflicts such as the one in which Richard and Philip were engaged, but also in permanently garrisoning those fortresses of particular importance along volatile frontiers. Not all soldiers receiving pay were of humble origin, for as knights extended their military service, they too received money payment.

Wages for military service, however, were high. Six shillings per day, Angevin coinage, was not uncommon for a knight, while a mounted man-at-arms (not a knight) typically received two shillings and sixpence, and the common foot soldier, eight pence.[24] These wages were impressive, even if calculated in the money of Anjou—the copper-debased silver coinage used in Normandy at the time, valued at only a quarter of English sterling. When one realizes that a Norman during those years could buy a chicken for a penny and an entire ram for a shilling, even the foot soldier's wages were considerable. Yet with wages so high, even kings could not afford to maintain large permanent armies. The 890 men-at-arms serving on foot that Richard employed for eight days in Andely in 1197 or 1198, at the cost of more than three hundred pounds, would have set him back by almost fourteen thousand pounds per year had he chosen to maintain a force of this size year-round.[25]

Not surprisingly, then, even royal armies remained small—more likely several hundred men rather than the many thousands the chroniclers so enthusiastically speak of. And while a Lionheart or a Philip of France may have kept a permanent core of knights and men-at-arms about when in the thick of a long and drawn-out war, neither could have afforded to maintain an entire army on a permanent basis. Indeed, even with such enticing wages, many of the non-noble foot soldiers and men-at-arms, hailing from peasant stock, would have found other things to do come planting or harvest time.[26]

With factors such as these prompting them, in addition to the need to give at least an appearance of concern over the dire news of infidel conquests in Spain, the two kings soon followed their disastrous Vaudreuil meeting with yet another. This 1195 parley (we do not know the location) achieved a certain immortality by at long last concluding the unfinished business concerning Philip's unfortunate half-sister, Alais. Twenty-six years after her original betrothal to Richard, this unhappy princess at last stepped forth from her Norman captivity and rejoined her brother, the French king, who immediately married her off to a minor nobleman, William of Ponthieu.[27]

In addition, the two kings proposed a royal marriage of considerably more importance, between Philip's son and heir, young Louis, and Eleanor, Richard's niece (whose marriage to Leopold of Austria's son had fallen through following Leopold's death). The marriage terms called for Richard to give up all claims to the Norman Vexin, including the castles of Gisors, Neaufles, and Baudemont, in addition to nearby Vernon, Ivry, and Pacy, and bestow these upon Louis and Eleanor. In return, Philip was to give over to Richard all disputed territory in Angoulême as well as certain lands and castles he had taken during Richard's imprisonment, including the counties of Aumale and Eu, in northeastern Normandy, and the bastion at Arques. Neither king, despite solemn head-shaking over the beleaguered Christians on the Iberian Peninsula, offered to do anything about that unhappy situation, and no aid from either party made its way southward.

As for the treaty, no one seemed to take it seriously. Richard immediately put off ratification until he had heard what the emperor thought of it—an acknowledgment of his obligations to Henry Hohenstaufen as overlord that Lionheart as king of England certainly would not have made (despite his outstanding ransom bill and the unhappy lingering of certain hostages in Germany) unless he had found it to his advantage. Philip for his part immediately gave over Eu and Arques as Alais' dowry, thus wiping out any possibility of returning these contested properties to Richard, as the treaty called for.

Thus from the day of Alais' marriage, if not earlier, the proposed treaty between the two kings was effectively mooted, and the emperor's subsequent response only finished off an already-dead compact. Not surprisingly Henry Hohenstaufen objected, and even went so far as to remit seventeen thousand of the marks still due him, to help Richard recover all the lands he had lost to Philip while in prison. From Richard's point of view, this was a reasonable offer, but it infuriated Philip, who approached their subsequent November meeting at Verneuil in a black mood. According to Roger of Howden, the French king put off seeing Richard until he found the king of England on his very doorstep, demanding to meet.[28]

Their subsequent encounter fairly dripped with acid. Philip, surrounded by his ministers, disdained to speak. Instead, the bishop of Beauvais—an old enemy of Richard—condescendingly informed Lionheart that since he had failed to show up at the appointed hour, Philip considered him a faithless perjurer whom he now defied. At that, Richard stormed out, and the two kings returned to war.

Richard went after Arques, in northeast Normandy, while Philip destroyed Dieppe with Greek fire (which had made its way back to Europe from the Holy Land). And then presuming that he was keeping

Richard fully employed in Normandy, Philip swooped down on Issoudun, northeast of Poitiers. Amazingly, the castle held out and somehow got a message through to Richard at Vaudreuil, who dropped everything to come to the rescue.

Richard, like his father, had the ability to travel long distances in astonishingly short amounts of time, even with whole armies behind him. Now, covering more than 150 miles in little over three days, Lionheart appeared so unexpectedly before Issoudun's walls that Philip's men fell back before him, allowing him to enter. Philip, terrified by the sudden appearance of his old rival, asked permission for his army to leave without harm, but when Richard refused, he asked to talk terms. In a moment of quiet drama, the two kings met between the lines, on horseback and in full battle gear, while their followers stood back, watching and awaiting the outcome. After a brief, private conference, the two monarchs dismounted, took off their helmets, and exchanged a formal kiss of peace.

The outcome was yet another temporary truce, but one leading to a peace of some significance. The Treaty of Louviers, to which both kings agreed in early January 1196, clearly showed the steady military gains that Richard had made since his return to Normandy a year and a half before. The Norman Vexin (with the exception of Andely, which belonged to the archdiocese of Rouen) remained in Philip's hands, as well as the wedge of land between the Eure and the Seine (including Pacy and Ivry, along with nearby Nonancourt, up to Gaillon). Yet virtually all the rest of Normandy now was Richard's, as was Aquitaine and much of the disputed territory in between.

Yet this was only a brief resting point for Richard, a tallying of the records to date, for he could hardly afford to stop now. A mere glance at a map shows his difficulty. Despite Lionheart's many victories, Philip still was poised—on both sides of the Seine—at Rouen's very door. The loss of Rouen would be fatal, as both Richard and Philip well knew. Rouen was the great ducal city, the heart of Normandy, much as Paris was the center of Philip's own realms.

For three years, Philip had wormed his way up one route to Rouen, then another. With the Treaty of Louviers, both sides allowed the dust to settle and were taking stock, but only until the winter months were over and the spring campaign season could once again get under way. To defend Rouen and Normandy itself, Richard would have to win back all the remaining territory he had lost to Philip while in prison—most especially, the Norman Vexin.

Philip, who could read a map every bit as well as Richard, was just as ready for action once the fighting season again began.

It was equally clear that both monarchs had their eyes on one particular piece of property. For the Treaty of Louviers—made to be broken—most clearly stated that Andely "shall not be fortified."[29]

The Rock of Andely

*R*ichard Lionheart loved heights. All castle-builders do, but the fortress that this warrior and strategist built at Orival, high above the Seine upon the Rock of Fouet, bears particular consideration.

Little remains of the fortification itself, but the site was clearly the sort of spot that caught Lionheart's eye. Soaring skyward on limestone cliffs whose abrupt escarpments plummet downward, Orival was dangerously edgy and impervious to capture, with little room for enemy maneuver. Yet of even more importance than the particular conjunction of river and cliff was Orival's precise location, at the bend in the Seine just before Rouen. For Richard never forgot a castle's purpose.

He had studied castles from his boyhood and besieged them since his youth. Descended from great castle-builders, including William the Conqueror and the notorious Fulk the Black of Anjou, he had early come to appreciate not only the political and military importance of castles, but the opportunity they offered to leave a solid legacy—that is, if one's fortifications were sited, built, and defended sufficiently well to survive enemies and time.

At Gisors, he could admire the handiwork of William Rufus, Henry I, and Richard's own father, Henry II. At Caen, he could evaluate the mighty fortifications that Henry I added to the Conqueror's core. Verneuil owed its strong ramparts, which had so well resisted Philip, to this same Henry, who also left his mark on Falaise, Domfront, Nonancourt, and the great fortress of Arques, over which Richard and Philip now were fighting. Henry I had been a great castle-builder, in the tradition of his father, the Conqueror, who left a trail of castles in his wake. After all, the Normans had introduced the castle—"ditch and bank, palisade and motte"—to England.[1]

Nor was Richard's inheritance from his Norman ancestors alone. During the chaotic years around the millennium, Fulk the Black of Anjou had erected a great chain of more than a dozen castles, whose endurance and formidability remained a wonder, even after a span of almost two hundred years.[2]

The black count of Anjou, whose demonic temper had inspired legends as well as St. Bernard's pointed denunciation of the entire family ("From the devil they came, to the devil they will return"), knew what he was about. Despite an unsettling capacity for violence (he had his wife— whom he suspected of infidelity—burned at the stake), he nevertheless retained a clear grasp of the ends he sought and the means of achieving them. A warrior from the age of thirteen, Fulk spent more than half a century fighting his way to power, placing great castle keeps at critical points along his frontier and, step by inflammatory step, building up the power and greatness of his house over its enemies—most especially the archrival house of Blois.

This sense of vision propelled Fulk steadily onward in what, by medieval reckoning, amounted to a brilliant career. When, a century later, his direct descendant—young Henry of Anjou—seized the crown of England itself from Stephen of Blois, it could be said that Fulk the Black had finally achieved what he so ruthlessly and persistently sought all along.

Richard, of course, was of Angevin as well as Norman stock, and he never forgot it. He, too, had a vision, and as he thundered along the byways of Normandy or besieged high places in Aquitaine, he was retrieving and solidifying the far-flung empire that his father and forefathers had forged. There is no indication that Richard held more grandiose schemes. Philip could keep his own royal domains, so long as he refrained from interfering with Lionheart's.

The problem, of course, was that Philip did not view matters that way. And Philip had become an enemy of formidable proportions.

Yet Richard got to Andely first. The first record we have of him there is on March 25, 1196, soon after the Treaty of Louviers. According to the charter he issued on that date, Lionheart held court on the Isle of Andely, in the Seine.[3]

The Rock of Andely itself was off-limits. For that matter, so was the Isle of Andely. Not only did the Treaty of Louviers make this plain, but the archbishop of Rouen, whose property this was, felt quite strongly about the matter. The archbishop was already severely out-of-humor over

depredations that both kings had made on churches and Church properties throughout his lands. But Philip had done (and was continuing to
do) the most harm, and in any case, the archbishop had a long history of
extraordinary loyalty to Richard. As a consequence, this powerful churchman now placed an interdict on those lands belonging to Philip that lay
within Rouen's episcopal bounds.[4]

As a weapon, the interdict wielded tremendous force, for instead
of excommunicating merely the offending lord, it withdrew most sacra-
ments, including Christian burial, from that lord's entire district, thus
placing considerable community pressure on him to mend his ways. Although kings and lords—if sufficiently steely—could thumb their noses at
excommunication, most found an interdict difficult to ignore, at least for
any length of time. Philip, who already was in trouble with the Church
over his attempt to cast off his Danish wife, at first tried to intimidate his
foe by moving in on the ripe target of Andely and seizing the archbishop's
considerable possessions there. Very quickly, though, he seems to have
realized his mistake and turned conciliatory, offering to return everything
he had taken. With this, the archbishop agreed to undo what he had done.

Having failed in his attempt to move on Andely by force, Philip now
tried diplomacy. The French king soon began to court the archbishop, not
only promising him redress but inviting him to come for a friendly visit.
It was the latter point that Philip pressed with particular urgency. In fact,
after meeting in Pontoise, the archbishop returned to Paris with Philip to
talk not only of the upcoming papal inquiry into Philip's divorce, but of
Andely as well.

Richard, too, tried his hand at diplomacy, including sincere apologies
and promises of restitution. But in the face of Philip's inroads, Richard
seems to have decided that outright possession offered far more solid possibilities. Shortly after the archbishop lifted his interdict on the French
king, Richard began to hold court on the Isle of Andely—in March and
April, then again in May and June.

Still, the archbishop was not to be treated lightly, and Richard seems
to have proceeded with care, holding court on an offshore location and
refraining for the moment from fortifying the place. He must have shown
exceptional caution, for in July, the archbishop of Rouen wrote a friend
that his relations with both kings had significantly improved, and that all
was well.[5]

Yet despite greater warmth between Church and state, there was no
thaw in relations between Philip and Richard, who followed up the Treaty
of Louviers by immediately regrouping for their next confrontation. Philip

went fishing for allies and found some valuable ones in the northeast, including the new count of Flanders. He also took out an insurance policy on the succession by remarrying, this time wedding Agnes of Meran, who in time would add to Philip's pool of male heirs.[6] When Richard—perhaps giving thought to his own succession as well as to his control over Brittany—demanded that his young nephew, Arthur of Brittany, be placed in his wardship, the Breton nobles revolted, and Philip quickly stepped in and made the lad welcome at his court.

Richard took a brief time-out during April to subjugate the Breton lords, but his thoughts during this fierce encounter clearly remained on Philip. On April 15 he summoned all those English lords who owed him military service to be in Normandy by June 2, and to come ready for a long war with the French king.[7] This in turn corroborated Philip's assessment of the situation, for in June, almost immediately after sealing his alliance with the counts of Boulogne and Flanders, Philip swiftly moved to the northeast and laid siege to Aumale. In response, Richard took the castle of Nonancourt, on the Avre, and then marched his army to Aumale. Here, uncharacteristically, he failed to break Philip's hold, and after seven weeks of siege, the castle surrendered to Philip, who destroyed it.[8]

Even though John now seized Gamaches, in the heart of the Norman Vexin, Philip strikingly countered by retaking Nonancourt. Worse yet, Richard received a nasty wound in the knee from a crossbow while attempting to recapture Gaillon, and was out of action for a month.[9] It was now, on his sickbed and facing a galvanized opposition, that Richard took stock of the situation. It was clear that Philip had become an opponent of the first rank, requiring all of Richard's skill and attention. It was equally clear that only Richard could keep Philip in check, and that when the English king was absent from the field—whether on his sickbed or fighting battles in other parts of his domains—the war would not go well for him. He needed to devise a strategy that would allow him to focus his time and energies on that critical area where the struggle between the two monarchs would be decided—those old fighting-grounds between Paris and Rouen.

It therefore was no accident that Richard now took steps to come to permanent terms with Raymond, the troublesome count of Toulouse.[10] In the interest of protecting the Plantagenet southern flank from the sort of disruption that Raymond (prodded by Philip) so capably provided, Richard gave up his claim to Quercy—that rugged land north of Toulouse and east of Bordeaux, where Henry the Younger had died. Richard also proposed a marriage between the young count and Joanna Plantagenet, the widowed queen of Sicily. This represented a double windfall for Raymond, who soon married Joanna in Rouen and henceforth took out his aggressions against neighbors other than Richard.[11]

With his southern lands now reasonably secure, Richard could focus more single-mindedly on his Norman frontiers, which he began to fortify with a vengeance. The Rolls of the Norman Exchequer show that he immediately and strongly fortified Gamaches, to the tune of £400 that year and £900 the following. He spent more than £1,000 strengthening the walls of the northeastern frontier town of Eu, while he expended £80 on the small castle of Radepont, on the river Andelle. He beefed up Orival on the Seine, Lyons and Longchamp in the forest of Lyons, and Tillières and Courteilles on the Avre—Courteilles as a replacement for the lost fortresses of nearby Ivry and Nonancourt.

And above all, he now began to fortify the Rock of Andely.

❧

The Rock of Andely rises on the right bank of the Seine, almost directly opposite the farthest reach of a large peninsula that juts decisively from the opposite shore. This tongue of land, bounded by a watery loop that begins its abrupt northeastward curve just beyond Gaillon and returns with equal decision just beyond what now is called Les Andelys, is low and flat, amenable to cultivation. But its opposite bank, where river meets the high plateau, consists of sheer limestone bluffs, culminating in the Rock itself.

Once, eons before, the entire area undergirded a broad primordial sea, whose thick soup of crustaceans and microorganisms piled up a deep substratum of limestone that remained when the sea receded, leaving a river in its wake. Flowing across an imperceptibly tilted plain toward a now distant sea, this river—the Seine—followed a course shaped by the folds and faults of the limestone through which it carved its way, its waters outlining one peninsula after another in an alternating course of widely swinging curves as it meandered seaward, nearly doubling the distance it took to reach its goal.

Eons more passed, and the Ice Age's fierce winds left a thick layer of topsoil across the limestone plateau, while its receding glaciers flooded the limestone's faults and cracks, grinding out valleys that channeled their way to the Seine. The Epte and the Andelle, those small rivers bordering the Norman Vexin, flowed through two such broad valleys, while the tiny Gambon quietly trickled through yet another.

The Rock itself rises on the southern side of the Gambon. The original town of Andely—now Grand Andely, and in histories sometimes referred to as Old Andely—took root within the shelter of the Gambon valley, while a small hamlet of fishermen grew up at the Gambon's mouth, in what was to become Petit Andely. Between this small port and the town of Andely lay low but cultivatable land, with a road along one side connecting the two. Beyond the town, this narrow byway led to the old Roman road—now the N14—connecting Paris and Rouen via Saint-Denis.

Old Andely had been fortified since at least the early part of the twelfth century, for Orderic tells us that in 1119, the French burst in through the gates, occupied its stronghold, and temporarily took the town.[12] The little port of Andely, however, had no fortification, despite the fact that its command of the Seine made it an all-important source of revenue for the archdiocese of Rouen, which held the fief and the right to levy tolls on the river traffic that passed there. Not surprisingly, the archbishop kept a jealous watch over this profitable enterprise, and when Philip helped himself to Andely's lucrative revenues, he found an irate churchman in his path.[13]

Richard seems to have begun fortifying the river portions of Andely sometime in September 1196, immediately following Philip's conquest and destruction of Aumale. Soon the archbishop began to hear rumors and protested, but Richard decided to brazen it out. The Rock of Andely was far too critical a site to allow it to remain in Church hands, and Philip had already signaled his intentions. If Lionheart did not seize it, Philip undoubtedly would, and let the devil take the hindmost. Unfortunately, the devil was exactly what Archbishop Walter had in mind, for he laid all of Normandy under interdict as he packed up and departed for Rome, intent on winning a good blast of papal retribution on his behalf.

Of course Richard could play politics too, and he immediately sent off his own ecclesiastical team, headed by the bishop of Ely—no shrinking violet—to defend his action before the pope. William of Ely, Richard's contentious chancellor, died en route, but the others arrived at Rome in time to press their monarch's case before Pope Celestine III and his cardinals. Whether or not Richard's representatives liberally bribed the sacred college, as has been suggested,[14] they found a sympathetic audience for their argument that the French frontier, now located within a breath of Rouen, called for drastic measures of defense.[15]

Yet what to do about the archbishop of Rouen's just complaints? The issue went round and round until, under the pope's mediation, the archbishop agreed to accept a bonanza of other valuable properties in exchange for Andely. Well pleased, everyone at last departed for home.

On October 16, 1197, Richard officially received title to Andely and the Rock. Which was fortunate, because—not bothering to wait for the adjudication's outcome—he had already been building there for almost a year.

⚜

He began on the Isle of Andely, erecting royal dwellings and a tower surrounded by ditch and ramparts.[16] Having thus fortified the island, he linked it to both sides of the Seine—the bridge to the left bank passing through what then was a narrow island called Gardon.[17] Since according to the Treaty of Louviers, Philip's frontiers extended to a line that ran halfway between the fortresses of Gaillon and Vaudreuil, the Seine's left bank approaches to Andely occupied extremely vulnerable soil. Here, where bridge touched shore, Richard erected a barbican (towered fortification), while further upriver, he converted sleepy Tosny into a bristling fortress—having already fortified the Seine downriver at Porte-Joie.[18]

Yet the Isle of Andely was only the beginning—a portion of the outer circle in a series of concentric circles, each part integral to the whole. The bridge linking the Isle to the Seine's right bank quickly acquired the name "Between-the-Two-Islands," for Richard quickly perceived that the port of Andely, located on a little rise of land toward the mouth of the Gambon, had island properties as well. Bordered on the south by the Gambon and on the north by an even smaller stream, both of which fed into the Seine, all that remained to island this small hamlet was to flood the lowlands between it and the fortified town of Old Andely to the east, which Richard now did. The result was a wide pond, or *vivier*, which supplied fresh fish to the royal table while adding to Andely's intricate system of defenses.[19]

This man-made island, which in time became known as Petit Andely (thus creating, with its neighbor, the plural "Les Andelys"), had only three points of access: the bridge to the Seine's left bank, via the Isle, plus two bridges to the mainland, north and south—the northernmost named Makadé in honor of Mercadier, the brutal but effective leader of Richard's mercenaries. The king then set his army of builders to erect towers and battlements, taking special precautions with his bridge approaches, for Petit Andely was made to withstand the enemy at the base of the Rock itself.

꙳

Had the forces of Nature not gone to work with particular vengeance on the corner of limestone plateau to the south and east of where the Gambon meets the Seine, the cliffs here would have resembled those on the valley's other side—steeply scarped along their sides, but smooth and hilly on top, and thus relatively approachable from the plateau. But the Rock of Andely is different. It rises no higher than the others—indeed, for all its height, it does not rival the elevations to its rear. Yet here, Nature ground out a promontory separate from the others, divided from the plateau by deep ravines on either side and connected to the mainland by a steeply sloping isthmus. That, together with its sheer rock-face that plunges three hundred feet to the Seine, and almost as steeply to the Gambon, makes the Rock a military man's dream—or nightmare, depending upon whether he is called upon to attack or to defend.[20]

Richard completed his outer circle of defenses with an advance fortress at Cléry, on the plateau to the Rock's southeast, and a second advance fortress (called Boutavant) on an island in the Seine near Tosny. Taken together with Petit Andely and its Isle, as well as Tosny and

Château-Gaillard, from the north. © J. McAuliffe

Porte-Joie, these comprised an impressive and imaginative ring of outer defenses. Yet it was on the Rock itself where Richard showed his genius. Here, drawing upon a lifetime of military observation and experience, he created a masterwork that was virtually light-years ahead of any other Western European castle of its time.

The genius was not in its size, for the fortress Richard built upon the Rock was not unusually large. Instead, it was sleek and sophisticated, with the purity of form that so often accompanies a breakthrough in function. Indeed, this was a fortress that represented the most advanced engineering of its time. A century and a half before, a palisaded motte with surrounding ditch and embankment was enough to do the job, while the heavy square-rigged ramparts and keeps of Henry I's time had proven their utility down through Richard's day. But the increasing sophistication of warfare now called for something different. Siege engines had grown more powerful, and the crossbow—despite the Church's ban—had become the weapon of choice for the foot soldier as well as for castle defense.[21] Even more critically, the art of sapping had developed to such a degree that any castle builder worth his salt had to consider angles and blind areas from a totally new perspective.

Unlike his predecessors, who began with the line, Richard thought in terms of the curve. His massive donjon was circular, while the wall immediately surrounding it was elliptical, fitting neatly within an outer wall that, taken together with the advance works, was roughly the shape of a projectile. Not only was that inner wall elliptical in outline, but its course was scalloped in a series of close semicircles, while its vertical stretch—like that of the donjon it guarded—curved outward as it neared the ground.

None of this was haphazard. There is a precision to the intersection of line and curve that defines the rise of Richard's stonework throughout this fortification, just as there is a relationship governing the shape and proximity of the semicircles that escallop its innermost wall. Richard was thinking about dead spaces, where sappers and enemy crossbowmen could do their worst, undisturbed by defenders' projectiles. He knew how fast a team of determined sappers could work; after all, he had many a time led such an enterprise, and Philip had learned from the masters, including Richard himself. Lines and corners created havens for sappers and crossbowmen. Richard's circular donjon and scalloped elliptical inner wall eradicated such deadly retreats.

In designing his castle—for the records show no architect for Gaillard other than Lionheart himself—Richard also was thinking of assault engines, for here too he knew firsthand the damage that well-aimed and insistent battering could do. Although the catapults and slings of his time varied widely in power, accuracy, and rapidity of fire, in capable hands any of the lot could be devastating. Richard seems to have preferred the longer-ranged catapults, while Philip relied on shorter-range devices—lighter and less powerful, but far speedier and simpler to operate than Richard's cumbersome engines. It was difficult to argue with Richard's knockout blows, but in the long run Philip's series of sharp jabs could be just as effective, and Richard knew it. Not only did he equip his fortress with walls not less than eight feet thick, but the deep ditches with which he surrounded all three parts of the fortification, including the inner cita- del, were hewn into solid rock with perpendicular counterscarps on the outer side, to stymie an approaching enemy. Sloping scarps on the de- fenders' side not only gave added heft to the foundations, but also served to ricochet projectiles dropped or hurled upon them.

Richard's attention to such details was impressive, but it was his concept of this castle as a cohesive unit that put it in the forefront of its time. Utilizing to the ultimate the lofty site he had appropriated, he filled its long triangular shape with a three-part bastion directly pointed toward the isthmus—the only direction from which an enemy could conceivably advance. Here he erected a large triangularly shaped advance works, with the largest of its five towers, the Tower of Saint-Jacques, at its tip.

Behind this, and separated by a deep ditch, rose a concentric series of fortifications, with the stout ramparts of the outer wall providing the outermost defensive layer. Inside, behind its own ditch, rose the elliptical inner wall, and at the heart soared the donjon itself—circular in shape, but with an enormous reinforced *bec*, or beak, pointed directly toward the Tower of Saint-Jacques and the enemy beyond.

Continuing his magnificent use of the terrain, Richard backed his complex to the cliff's edge, from where he extended yet another line of fortifications down to the river and, from there—via a double stockade— across the Seine itself. Surrounded on all sides by cliff-face or ravines, and reinforced by deep ditches and high walls, this complex was layered like an onion, with its principal components—donjon *en bec* and Tower of Saint-Jacques—directly confronting the enemy and lined along a ridge that continued, via the narrow isthmus of land, up the steep hillside to the plateau.

This extraordinary fortress, first known as the Castle of the Rock, was not entirely without precedent. The nearby castle of La Roche- Guyon, built only a few years before, boasted a beaked donjon, while Henry I's fortress at Arques as well as Richard's own castle at Orival occupied sites similar to the Rock of Andely. Cherbourg had a scalloped wall of semicircular bastions that may have prompted Richard's consideration, while Gisors had an elliptical shell. More than this, the Holy Land in Richard's time was fairly littered with fortresses that summon up the image of Richard's Castle of the Rock, with their outwardly sloping bases, elliptical curtain walls, and formidable advance works. Most of all, these Middle Eastern bastions possessed the kind of concentric design that Richard incorporated on the Rock of Andely, with all parts integrally related to the whole. Richard had seen some of the most famous of these fortresses while on crusade, and unquestionably they made an impression.

Not that Richard was the only crusader to come home with building plans in his head. La Roche-Guyon, after all, was but one of several examples of Western European fortresses benefiting from Middle Eastern influences that had sprung up prior to the Castle of the Rock. The important point is how much more effectively than his rivals Richard applied what he had learned. La Roche-Guyon (which has been attributed to Philip) pales in comparison with Richard's fortress at Andely, not only in scale but in its limited vision and piecemeal approach to innovation.

Richard simply did it better.

∗∗∗

Richard also did it more flamboyantly. His Castle of the Rock was not only the most advanced European fortress of its age but also the most expensive. The cost came to more than £44,000 Angevin, which amounted to around £11,000 in English sterling—an extraordinary sum for a single fortification.[22] Yet this did not represent money carelessly spent, for though Richard was well accustomed to the perquisites of his rank, his expenditures on Andely were as solid as the rock on which he built. Except for plastering the chimney-pieces and the floors (at a total of £80, hardly an extravagance), he seems to have taken little interest in decoration or even comfort. The money spent on the Castle of the Rock was vast, but to the purpose. Richard, very simply, was intent upon fortifying Andely to the best of his abilities, and he did and spent what was necessary to do the job.

In the end, the results were boggling. Even the French were in awe of Richard's creation, although Philip expressed his envy in contempt. Within little more than a year (the year of 1197, with portions of 1196 and 1198 on either end), Lionheart quite literally moved mountains. This astonishing castle, though not the largest ever built, nevertheless was substantial, and the complex as a whole was enormous. By his decree, the king set in motion an army of workmen, from the hodmen and carriers who hauled water and mortar to the skilled workmen who shaped the timber and stone.

At the head of this army was the king, for unquestionably Richard's vision shaped this fortification in its entirety, from its ring of outer defenses to the shape and curve of its walls. Still, someone had to translate this vision into reality, and Richard must have delegated the task, much as he delegated the provisioning of his army. Most typically, this would have been the master mason or architect. Since no master mason or architect is listed in Andely's detailed building accounts, historians have assumed that Richard did the job. Yet while Richard may well have assumed the role of commander over the operation, he certainly did not concern himself with the architect's responsibility of translating the general into the particular, or with the coordination of all the elements necessary to produce the whole.[23]

The job of master mason or architect would have been a weighty responsibility in any large construction of the time, but it must have been especially so with Andely, where the king took such a direct interest in the outcome. Complicating the job, kingly interest meant kingly interference, and Richard's intense interest in his castle's progress undoubtedly caused stops and changes along the way.

Although undoubtedly frustrating, such a pattern was far from unexpected. There was an ad hoc quality to all medieval building operations, even one envisioned on so grand a scale as Andely. Cathedrals and castles alike were argued and reevaluated as they went up, sometimes surprisingly well into the process. The concept of a scaled blueprint was still a thing of the future, and although Richard's architect must have drawn up an overall plan and elevations (quite possibly dimensioned), this would not have been sufficient to guide the masons as they cut and placed the stone. Instead, these craftsmen regularly worked from full-scale two-dimensional templates for each rock, which the master mason set out on wood or parchment as his workers reached that portion of the project. To realize this kind of construction detail on an undertaking of such size, the master mason (or architect) would have bridged the gap between the highly general and the minutely particular with a series of full-scale drawings traced, section by section, on the plaster walls or even floors of a building provided for this purpose. From these, he could derive the templates for the individual stones.

What this meant was that, in practice, huge undertakings such as Andely were fraught with put-off decisions and construction details that no one had considered or even intended to consider until the last possible moment. Amazingly, Richard overcame the natural drag such a procedure would have on the overall time frame and pushed through completion, not in decades, but in little more than a year.

Sheer numbers of workmen would not have been enough to accomplish this prodigious feat, which called for a degree of efficiency quite uncharacteristic for its time. Richard got the results he wanted through superb organization and even more superb leadership. Although capable of great cruelty against his enemies, there is no evidence that he treated those under his command inhumanely. Instead of using fear and whips to drive and goad, there is every indication that he inspired men to do their best—not through words, for he was terse and to the point, but through deeds, summoning up hidden fires of determination and will.

He led his workers at Andely to the utmost, even as he had for so many years urged his warriors to the same end. The endless lines of carts and mule drivers; the army of men with pickaxes who cut the moats to a depth of forty feet from solid rock; the blacksmiths who worked the iron for the castle gates; and the carpenters who built the drawbridges that approached them—all knew they worked for Richard Lionheart, and all knew he needed each and every one of them to do his very best. If Lionheart asked it of them, men would gladly dare, risk, and give their all.

It is pertinent here to note that Lionheart regularly risked his life in battle on the assumption that men would not respect him as a king and leader if he failed to perform the very thing he called upon them to do. He took no needless risks with his troops, but when faced with daunting danger, he expected them to rise to the occasion, even as he did.

So while Richard undoubtedly listened, encouraged, and cajoled at Andely, reviving spirits just as he had outside the walls of Acre, would anyone have been surprised had he dismounted from his horse to help to heave a stone into place? After all, this was a man who had hauled heavy siege engines in the Holy Land and, wherever there was action, could be found in the thick of the fray. A strong man who did not mind a little dirt, and who well knew the value of fraternizing with his troops, Richard had never been arrogant or aloof. Nor, against every interest and inclination, would he have become so now.

First came the quarrymen. Heavy-booted and protected from the wind and rain by wrapped leg coverings and rough outer garments, belted to above the knee, they hoisted their picks and hammers high as they began their work—in winter, when the hours were short, as soon as they could see. From Lent until the autumn feast of the Archangel, they toiled for a few pence a day, picks and hammers clanging until day was done. Excepting time off for a midday meal and a brief afternoon break, they spent the long daylight hours forever pounding iron against stone, their only holidays for holy days or bad weather, for which they received no pay.[24]

Next came the roughmasons, who roughly hewed or dressed the stone with hammers and axes into standard lengths, widths, and breadths, while the hewers or freemasons[25] finished the rough blocks according to the master mason's templates. After this, the rough layers or (depending upon the complexity) more skilled setters put the finished product into place, with the help of scaffolding and a crude predecessor of the modern crane. Course by course, the inner and outer faces of the walls began to rise, filled with a thick and solid core of mortared rubble, largely flint—a core that would remain remarkably intact in Richard's Castle of the Rock, even after eight centuries.

The stone itself came from off-site quarries, transported wherever possible by water. Andely's location, overlooking a navigable river that wound its way through limestone, assured Richard of quarries within easy reach. There at the quarry site, a small army of masons—their caps fastened tightly beneath their chins—dressed and finished the newly won stone on the spot (an economical measure, as finished stone was lighter and cheaper to transport). A steady stream of ships and boats then slowly bore this limestone to Andely, bringing sand and timber as well, since anything cumbersome and heavy was cheaper to haul by water than by cart. It cost Richard £2,600 Angevin to quarry the stone for this entire fortification, and more than £9,000 to have the stone cut and laid. And while it set him back by a portion of £1,700 to have it shipped on the Seine,[26] this nevertheless represented a vast savings over having it carted in.

Yet the major savings, had Richard only known it, was in the cost of the labor itself, for his *bellum castrum* at Andely was built on the backs of workers making scarcely enough to feed themselves. This army of poorly paid laborers—the end-product of more than a century of climatic warming, longer growing seasons, and resulting population growth—provided a ready labor pool for building projects such as Andely. And it must have been a virtual army, for when one calculates the pittance that unskilled underworkmen received daily, as well as the shortness of the project's

Wood-carrier, illustrating Autumn. Early-thirteenth-century relief from the portal of the Coronation of the Virgin, the northern portal of the western façade of Notre-Dame de Paris, Paris, France. © J. McAuliffe

duration, the huge amounts recorded in the Rolls of the Norman Exchequer—such as the almost £10,000 Angevin paid to the hodmen and water carriers—had to have been divided among an enormous number of men. Add to these the lime-workers (more than £4,000), the workers who shoveled out and brought the sand (£1,500), the miners who cut the deep ditches and cellars from Andely's rock (£1,780), and the endless procession of carts and drivers (more than £4,000 worth), it is clear that the concentration of labor on this one spot for little over a single year must have been astounding.

Add to that the off-site workers, such as the quarrymen (£2,600) and the woodmen who felled and hewed the trees (more than £2,300), and the numbers of this huge workforce grow larger still. This does not even take into account the skilled workers such as masons, blacksmiths, carpenters, fletchers (who made the arrows and crossbow bolts), and bridge builders, in addition to guards and watchmen to protect the building site.[27]

The fact that the various types of carriers and hodmen are grouped under the category of "underworkmen" indicates that they were handled as a group by an overseer or master workman, who probably kept a sizable portion of the total for himself. Yet even when one assumes such practices throughout the entire operation, the vastness of the expenditures still speaks of multitudes of laborers. From late 1196 onward, the Rock of Andely and its companion sites must have resembled a vast anthill, and while Richard could only have rejoiced at the sight, Philip must have simmered.

We do not know for certain where Richard was from January through March 1197, while his ecclesiastical emissaries pressed on toward Rome. But given the stakes, it would be a safe bet that he spent these weeks at Andely, overseeing the extraordinary fortifications going up there. After all, so much depended on the Rock of Andely.

Defending Rouen was Richard's first objective, but neither Lionheart nor the castle he was summoning forth could rest easy in a static defensive mode. One look at Richard's Castle of the Rock was enough to convince all onlookers, including the king of France, that Lionheart would not be content to let the Norman Vexin remain in Philip's hands.[28] Formidably based in Andely, Richard would be able to harry Philip right down to the Epte—and beyond. Recognizing the danger, Philip now began the plans for a muscular new fortress of his own, named the Louvre, just outside the westernmost point of Paris's walls.

The frontiers of the Vexin throbbed in anticipation of war. As Richard's fortifications began to rise, the French ceaselessly prowled the periphery, probing for soft spots and looking for trouble. In turn, Richard brought in a troop of Welshmen—the twelfth-century equivalent of Hell's Angels—to keep the French at bay. Not surprisingly, the French found themselves at distinct disadvantage until, in a bloody encounter in the Vale of Andely, they managed to surround their foe and slaughter the entire lot. Infuriated by this unexpected development, Richard ordered three French prisoners in his dungeons to be dragged forth and hurled from the top of the Rock. Even more grimly, he had the remaining fifteen blinded and led by a one-eyed man back to the French king. Such a message was unmistakable, and Philip replied in kind, throwing three English prisoners in his possession off a similarly high rock and blinding fifteen others, with the wife of one of these unfortunates given the unhappy job of leading her husband and his colleagues back to Andely and the English king.

In such an overheated emotional climate, and with the entire duchy still under interdict, it was not surprising that men's fears took highly imaginative forms. In May, while Richard was supervising the work at Andely, it rained blood there—or at least the drops that came down were reported to have had an ominous red tinge.[29] Richard, who was not easily intimidated, seems not to have taken note, but others whispered uneasily and remembered.[30]

Signs and omens did not seem to shake Richard. The age was a superstitious one, but he had managed to retain his cool on a number of unsettling occasions—most notably at his father's funeral, when the dead king's body was reported to have oozed blood as Lionheart approached the bier. By comparison, whatever color of rain the heavens chose to send down did not especially disturb him.

Despite all obstacles, Richard's Castle of the Rock continued to rise, with carpenters fitting planed timbers together in tenon and mortise, while well-diggers chipped downward through solid rock. At the same time, miners hewed out vast storage caves that opened into the protected dry moat surrounding the inner curtain wall. As blacksmiths forged the iron for the castle gates that led successively from the advance works through the first and second set of walls, the beaked donjon was rising above the fray, its head crowned with a massive overhanging battlement of solid stone.

These workers climbed each day to the Rock from the burgeoning village of Petit Andely, which by now was partially walled and filled to the bursting point. The accounts show the money spent to build the bridge connecting Petit Andely with the shore beneath the Rock (£30), and they show as well that during this same time Richard spent £100 to build the mills of Petit Andely and provide them with millstones. His workers may not have had money to spare, but at least bread was plentiful.

Their lot was hard, but not as hard as that of some others in the vicinity. Tellingly, among the many expenses listed for building the Castle of the Rock is a small but poignant one: £10 of the king's alms for the lepers of Andely.

⚜

In Richard's day, when leprosy remained a grim presence, the responsibility of caring for these shunned unfortunates fell on local convents and monasteries, which in general took up the slack wherever private nursing of the sick or injured left off.[31] In making his modest donation, Richard was doing what was expected of him, providing a practical assist to the needy in the community. Yet far more important from the medieval point of view was the Church's assurance that such generosity would in some measure smooth the way to heaven for the king's immortal soul.

This kind of reasoning had for centuries operated as a powerful force on behalf of charitable giving throughout Christendom, largely because medieval men and women worried considerably about their immortal souls. Well they might, for life was brutal and success often came at a fearful price. Men like Fulk the Black alternated lives of almost criminal viciousness with bouts of repentance, during which good works such as pilgrimages or church-building temporarily filled their days. Similarly, a significant number of medieval males who had been anything but monk-like during the course of their careers—Henry the Younger comes to mind—found a deathbed of sackcloth and ashes particularly reassuring.[32]

Death provided the ultimate reckoning, but few of these warriors expected to die in their beds—a fact that added special urgency to the problem. Under these circumstances, many members of the blood-soaked nobility found that a liberal amount of good works—defined as financial support for a variety of ecclesiastical causes—provided a useful insurance policy, and brutal rulers such as the Conqueror or even Henry I built splendidly on behalf of the Church throughout their long careers.

Richard, however, did not appear to share their enthusiasm. Although paying reasonable attention to powerful ecclesiastics throughout his realm, he built castles rather than cathedrals and did not seem to feel the worse for it. Perhaps something of his father's attitude had rubbed off on him, for even before the Becket affair, Henry Plantagenet had taken little interest in religion. Indeed, when events compelled a one-on-one with his Maker, Henry tended to address Him in prayers that sounded remarkably like challenges. A certain cynicism ran through the family, culminating in Henry and Eleanor's youngest, John.

Yet despite a lack of religious fervor and a definite suspicion of ecclesiastical authority, Richard seems to have taken his religion reasonably seriously. Unlike his father, who conducted business during Mass, Richard paid attention to what was going on and occasionally even sang along with the choir. He had approached the crusade with considerable enthusiasm, not only as a warrior but as a warrior for Christ. And although his military reputation was no small matter to him, his fervor about saving Jerusalem seems to have been in earnest. Why else would he have scourged himself in such a fashion before his bishops in Messina?

Despite an evident relapse after his return home, Richard and the Almighty appear to have been on good terms by the time the Castle of the Rock got under way. Churchmen, of course, were a different matter, for like other rulers of his day, Richard had a distinct distaste for ecclesiastics and the politics they played—unless, of course, they played on his side.

Philip thought likewise, and the emperor—still under excommunication for Richard's imprisonment—completely agreed. The one act that bound the French and English monarchs together at the Treaty of Louviers was their attempt to keep the archbishop of Rouen in line. They both failed dismally, as the subsequent volley of interdicts clearly showed, but Lionheart did not confuse the politics of the situation with religion. Viewing his bout with the archbishop as a distinctly political dispute, Lionheart found the interdict distressing but not intimidating.[33] Until the interdict at last was lifted, he went about his castle-building without the slightest hesitation.

❧

At the same time, Richard's confrontations with his deadly enemy, Philip of France, continued. In April and May 1197, Lionheart struck along Normandy's eastern and northeastern frontier, raiding the dowry lands of the long-suffering princess Alais, and destroying a castle belonging to Philip of Dreux, the hated bishop of Beauvais. Filling Richard's cup to the brim, Mercadier now managed to capture the warlike bishop himself.

Despite the French king's protests, Richard had the bishop securely locked up in the tower of Rouen. Not only was Philip of Dreux the cousin of the French king, but he—along with the duke of Burgundy—had been a major troublemaker in the Holy Land, conniving with Conrad of Montferrat and stirring up much of the bickering and resentment that had torn Richard's crusading army asunder. When the French king protested, Richard scathingly replied that this particular churchman had clearly forfeited his ecclesiastical immunity. Indeed, the famous fighting bishop had been captured in full battle gear.[34]

The tide was turning, and Richard was not the only one to sense it. By midsummer, Richard had detached the count of Flanders from his French alliance and formed an alliance of his own with this well-placed neighbor to the northeast. Significantly, a number of border lords were present at the occasion and swore to uphold Richard's side of the bargain.

Philip tried to stem the tide, but while he was tied up in a lengthy siege at Dangu, Richard raided Philip's back yard in the area of Berry, where he seized several castles (some chroniclers say ten) belonging to the French king. At the same time, Baldwin, count of Flanders, besieged one of the western Flemish properties lost to France in recent years. Furious, Philip pursued Baldwin into enemy territory where, after Baldwin's men destroyed the surrounding bridges, Philip suddenly found himself entrapped in a maze of waterways. Cut off from his supply lines and unable to advance or retreat, the king of France was reduced to suing for mercy. In utter humiliation, he appealed to Baldwin as his liegeman not to dishonor the French crown.

He had in mind, of course, Richard's fate in Vienna.

Baldwin let Philip go, and the king of France slumped back to Paris.[35] The best he could make of matters was to agree to meet with Richard and Baldwin at a spot between his castle at Gaillon and Richard's behemoth going up at Andely, just a bend in the river away.

Philip's mood had not improved by the time he and Richard met, in mid-September. If they met on the Isle of the Three Kings, as has been speculated, it was no wonder, for this island—possibly the site of earlier meetings between Philip and both Henrys, Henry II and Henry the Younger—hugs the right bank of the Seine just beneath the Rock of Andely.

It is inconceivable that Philip had not already glimpsed Richard's castle going up from across the river, near Gaillon, but this would have been the closest he had come to the actual site. His courtiers were suitably awed, as Richard intended for them to be—after all, this ferocious war had never been limited to physical battles, and the mind games between these two monarchs had by this time reached a deadly pitch. Here, Richard in effect was telling Philip, is proof in stone and mortar of my superiority over you. *Here is the kind of man I am.*

Furious, Philip flung out his famous boast, that were this castle's walls of solid iron, he nonetheless could seize it. To which Richard irately retorted, "Were its walls of butter, I could and would defend it!"[36]

Not an especially auspicious beginning to a peace parley, which proceeded in predictably frigid fashion. The outcome was yet another truce—this one a lengthy one of sixteen months, to last until the Feast of St. Hilary in early January 1199. Since each party was to continue to hold what he held at the moment of negotiation, Richard could afford to be pleased with the outcome.

Still, despite Lionheart's considerable gains in the east and northeast, not to mention his conquests in Berry, the Vexin remained in Philip's hands.

⚜

While Richard and Philip were at each other's throats in northern France, Henry Hohenstaufen had his eye on world conquest. Not only had he occupied and subdued Sicily, but—with the help of his former prisoner, the king of England—he had also forged a series of alliances that quelled the fires back in Germany. With the death (1195) of his longtime foe Henry the Lion, he now could safely absent himself from the north and look eastward, toward the Holy Land and Byzantium. No one could accuse Henry Hohenstaufen of limited vision.

Lionheart's return to Normandy meant that both he and Philip were safely preoccupied for the moment and unlikely to interfere. Better yet, the young emperor had hit upon an ingenious plan for expansion eastward. With Saladin safely dead and his heirs squabbling with one another, it seemed an auspicious moment for yet another crusade. After all, who could object? Moving quickly, the emperor had already set plans in motion for such a crusade under his own most eminent leadership.

Henry Hohenstaufen was undoubtedly clever, but his rapid expansion of power was beginning to make people nervous—so much so that when he tried to reinstate the kind of hereditary succession that German emperors had once enjoyed, the German princes balked. A hereditary emperor, as they well knew, meant a far stronger imperial government, and this prospect took on special menace under an emperor of Henry Hohenstaufen's ambitions.

Not to be put off, Henry went to work on the opposition, negotiating and arm-twisting as he went. The stakes were high, and the pope—now virtually encircled by imperial lands—anxiously awaited the outcome. The young emperor seemed indomitable, another Alexander in the making.

And then in late September 1197, astonishing news swept Western Christendom: en route to the Holy Land, this young conqueror—this Alexander—had quite suddenly taken ill and most unexpectedly died. Death among the young was an everyday occurrence in medieval Europe, but nonetheless, the death of this particular young man came as a shock. Completely without warning, the young emperor who had so memorably manipulated Western Christendom's political chessboard had abruptly departed the game. "What shall it profit a man if he gain the whole world and lose his own soul?" Pope Celestine had warned him, but Henry had paid no heed.[37] Now he was dead.

Thus, just as Philip and Richard were completing their negotiations outside of Andely, the tectonic plates of Western Christendom's political relationships abruptly shifted. Now, instead of a powerful and virtually unstoppable emperor, there was merely that emperor's infant son. True, this infant (who would eventually make his own mark on history as the legendary Frederick II) had a hereditary claim to Sicily through his mother, and he was crowned king of Sicily soon after his father's death. Yet he had no hereditary right to the imperial crown, which in fact was up for grabs.

Even in kingdoms where the hereditary principle was well entrenched, the accession of a minor to the throne threw open the doors to infighting and strife. In Germany, where the princes had firmly rejected a hereditary principle for their emperor, it was far worse. Suddenly Henry Hohenstaufen's enemies were in full cry, led by Henry the Lion's friends and relations. Looking about for leadership (Henry the Lion had died two years earlier), they turned to the Lion's brother-in-law and traditional ally, Richard Lionheart, while in turn, the Hohenstaufens turned to their traditional ally, the king of France.

Looking for an adult to champion their cause, the Hohenstaufens quickly put forward the late emperor's younger brother, Philip of Swabia, while their opponents, at Richard's suggestion, turned to Henry the Lion's younger son, Otto of Brunswick. Otto's older brother was on crusade and unavailable for the honor, but more importantly, Otto had spent much of his youth (during his father's long exile) at the Plantagenet court. He was Richard's man, and Richard could count on him.

Thus as the year 1198 opened, Richard was clearly on top of his world. He had played kingmaker, to his considerable benefit, and had picked up a flurry of new alliances in the bargain, including not only a flock of German barons but a significant number of Philip's frontier vassals as well. In addition, the death of the aged pope, Celestine, now brought to the papal throne a vigorous young pope, Innocent III, who greatly admired Lionheart, was indignant over his imprisonment, and seemed fully prepared to confront the king of France over Ingeborg, the Danish wife whom Philip had so unceremoniously dumped.

Richard's preeminence in Western Christendom was now so marked that certain of the German magnates even proposed that Lionheart himself accept the imperial crown. The idea never came to anything, and Richard certainly did not encourage it, but it must have brought him considerable pleasure.

While, adding to his satisfaction, Lionheart's castle at Andely continued to rise.

✾ *12* ✾

The Treasure of Châlus

$\mathcal{O}$n February 28, 1198, Richard issued his first charter from "Château-Gaillard," his Castle of the Rock.[1] Although the fortification continued to be called the Castle of the Rock, or the Rock of Andely, Richard gave it its "Gaillard" nickname after he presented it to the world as his "fair daughter" and "yearling"—*Château-Gaillard* roughly meaning "strapping" or "saucy" castle.[2] Richard, who is said to have fathered a son (the illegitimate Philip of Cognac),[3] had no daughter, and he seemed to find it fitting to liken this extraordinary fortification to a sturdy and impudent young girl. For surely any daughter of Richard's lineage would have had just as much strength and spunk.

Perhaps as well, with the unsubtlety of the military jargon to which Richard was accustomed, the king of England was boasting that if those who witnessed this great feat found it amazing, they had seen nothing yet. For if Gaillard was merely Richard's daughter, this master castle-builder was surely capable of far more.

Indeed, although Richard does not seem to have had any additional castle plans in the works, he certainly had Philip on the run. By the end of August 1198, he had pulled together an impressive coalition of allies, including not only the newly crowned emperor but also a number of Philip's former vassals—a confederation Richard had been building for more than a year. In early September, war broke out again in earnest. Baldwin of Flanders struck first, successfully besieging the castle of Saint Omer and taking other nearby castles and towns. Protected by this second front to the northeast, Richard could now afford to move into the Vexin.

Recognizing the danger, Philip made a quick strike into the Norman Vexin, toward Gamaches (or Jumièges, in the chronicles), but Richard outmaneuvered him, capturing a number of French knights and forcing the French king to flee for his life back to Vernon. Tasting victory, Richard crossed the Epte by Dangu with a considerable army behind him. In one day he took the castles of Courcelles-lès-Gisors and Boury before retiring back across the river to Dangu.

As Philip could not help but noting, Richard was closing in on Gisors, for Courcelles and Boury, not to mention Dangu, lie on Gisors' doorstep. Setting off even more alarms, another force of Richard's men had recently captured Sérifontaine, just north of Gisors. Racing to the rescue of Courcelles, which he did not know had already fallen to Richard, Philip set off from Mantes with some three hundred knights plus a considerable number of men-at-arms. Richard concluded that the French king was heading for Dangu, to attack Lionheart's forces on the Norman side of the Epte. With this in mind, Richard left his main army at Dangu and recrossed the Epte with only a small band of reconnoiterers, not knowing that Philip was instead heading directly for Courcelles and Gisors. En route, Richard's and Philip's paths unexpectedly crossed.

Richard was always at his best when outnumbered, but here the risks were enormous. The king "put [his] life in peril, and [his] kingdom,"[4] yet at the moment this did not seem to faze him. With mighty yells, he and his small band burst upon the French, who fled like a flock of antelopes before a lion. Richard enjoyed every minute of it, chasing Philip and his men all the way to the gates of Gisors. There, the panicked French crowded and shoved their way through the gate in such numbers that the bridge broke beneath them, drowning twenty men in the water below. Even the French king, Richard later reported with relish, "had to drink of the river."[5]

All told, it was a great day for Lionheart—although it so easily could have been otherwise.

⁂

The war was not going well for Philip. He now set off to raid and burn along the left bank of the Seine, while Richard continued to make inroads into the Vexin. Still, Lionheart was unable to deal the final blow to this persistent foe. He simply did not have the resources with which to make war on a sufficiently grand scale. Château-Gaillard, although worth every penny, had drained his treasury, and he was scraping the bottom of the barrel in order to pay his troops, let alone his allies, who had been drawn to the Plantagenet banner by the promise of largess as well as by the assurance that they had picked the winning side.

One of the reasons Richard may have taken such risks in his recent encounter with Philip may well have been the prospect—still flitting across his mind—of capturing the French king. What sweet revenge! And what a ransom! But once again Philip slipped through his fingers, and Richard was left to find other ways to pay for this never-ending war.

Philip too was feeling the financial drain, as pressure from Richard increased on every side. In October, he offered to return all the Norman lands and castles he had taken—except for Gisors, whose fate he proposed be determined by combat. Earlier Richard would have jumped at such a proposal, especially if he were included among the warring champions. But now he had his allies to consider, and Philip clearly was trying to divide them. When Richard insisted that the count of Flanders and all the rest be included in the treaty, negotiations with Philip promptly broke down.

In addition to trying to peel away Richard's allies, Philip had the Church card to play. Although the papal legate who arrived in France in late December was interested in resolving Philip's ongoing marital difficulties, he was even more interested in resolving Plantagenet-Capetian differences. After all, there was a new crusade at hand, and it behooved all the parties to patch up their differences and come on board.

In Rome's view, this meant a compromise, and when the papal legate, Peter of Capua, met with Richard in early January, this was exactly the tack he took. Not surprisingly, Richard was obdurate. How could there be compromise on the lands in question, he fulminated, when Philip had most unjustly taken them at the very moment when Lionheart was on crusade? Indeed, Richard was not about to make any peace whatever so long as Philip held even a handful of Norman soil. It was bad enough, Richard hotly continued, that French malice had prevented him from recovering all of Jerusalem. Worse yet, he had been unjustly taken captive upon his return home, and what protection had the Church given him and his lands then?

It was a valid point, but Peter chose to ignore it, eventually wearing Richard down into accepting a five-year truce, on condition that Philip surrender all claims to the lands around the Norman castles he had taken. Given the difficulties in which Philip would soon find himself in those surrounded islands, minus their essential revenues, Lionheart at length consented.

At this point, Peter should have packed his bags and gone home, but he now made a major mistake in judgment. Philip of Dreux, the fighting bishop of Beauvais, still lay incarcerated in the tower of Rouen, and Richard did not intend to let the fellow go—not even for a hefty ransom. Not grasping the intensity of Richard's feelings on the subject, the papal legate now demanded that Lionheart release the captured bishop.

At this, Richard exploded. Did the pope think he was a fool? Philip of Dreux was captured as a knight, fully armed. On no account could the Church claim him as one of its own. When Peter protested, Richard cut him off. "Begone, you hypocrite!" he roared. "Begone, you traitor, you trickster and liar, before I thrash you within an inch of your life!"[6]

Taking the hint, the legate immediately fled, leaving the archbishop of Reims to work out the truce's details. But Richard was still in a foul mood when he and Philip subsequently met on a spot along the Seine, between Andely and Vernon. This parley between the two kings was the most hostile yet. Philip remained on horseback along the riverbank, while Richard kept to his boat, refusing to land. They agreed to a truce of five years, but the likelihood of its lasting even a few months seemed remote.

⚜

Truce or no truce, Philip was steadily losing ground, and Richard was set upon reconquest. All he needed to bring it off was a new infusion of silver.

Gold, of course, would do quite as well, and legend has it that not long after this, Richard received word of a magnificent treasure discovered in territory belonging to the lord of Châlus, in the Limousin.

When this news arrived, Richard was already making his way southward, with a sufficiently long stopover at his treasury, in the castle of Chinon, to assure him that his finances were indeed in need of a substantial boost. Farther to the south, the lords of Angoulême and Limoges were stirring up trouble, as usual, and Richard was headed in their direction when—according to legend—word of this wonderful treasure came his way. A poor plowman (some say a soldier) had unearthed a massive golden object, reported to be of a king and his family around a table. This wondrous discovery—which from the description could have been anything from golden statues to a gilded shield—belonged by rights to the viscount of Limoges, on whose lands it was discovered. But the viscount, Aimar of Limoges, had rebelled against Richard and shifted his alliance to Philip; under the circumstances, why should such a treasure go to him?

After all, Aimar and his half-brother, the count of Angoulême, were undoubtedly traitors and, as Richard typically viewed things, deserved to be treated as such.[7]

For centuries this story has served to explain the unfathomable, but now historians discredit it, arguing that Richard was heading south not in search of treasure, but with the simple intent of dealing with yet another uprising.[8] Of course, this meant destroying the castles of his rebellious subjects, and he started with Châlus, where he showed up in mid-March with a small band of mercenaries, promptly putting it under siege.

Perhaps Richard was after treasure. Perhaps he wanted to put the fear of God into the lawless viscount of Limoges and the count of Angoulême. Or perhaps he wanted both. We do not and cannot know. Certainly something was pulling Richard to this remote spot in a hurry during Lent, a time normally off-limits to war. Surely taking Aimar of Limoges in hand could have waited until after Easter. For that matter, of all the other castles in the Limousin that Richard could have besieged, why pick Châlus?

The place had no particular strategic value and definitely was beneath Richard's talents. It stood on a modest rise and consisted of little more than a walled farmhouse with a round tower keep. Inside, some forty people, including women, peered anxiously out the windows as the feared

Château de Châlus, where Richard Lionheart died. A small fortification consisting of a circular stone keep and a walled farmhouse. © J. McAuliffe

English king set his miners and crossbowmen to work. After three days of this, the small garrison—which included only two knights—offered to surrender if Lionheart would guarantee their safety. Even under far more challenging circumstances, Richard had never given his foes much slack. Here, too, he quite characteristically refused these terms, swearing that he would capture and hang the entire lot.

As this paltry crew fought on, dropping rocks on their besiegers and fighting back with anything they could find to supplement their dwindling arrow supply, Richard rode out one evening to survey the scene. As always, he did his own reconnoitering, but this time he did not bother with any armor except a buckler and iron headpiece. As he rode, he observed his sappers' work and used his crossbow to zing some well-placed bolts at any heads he saw pop up along the ramparts. All was well, and the only person putting up a defense seemed to be a lone figure on a tower bastion who had been shooting all day with a crossbow, while defending himself with a large frying pan. Afterward, the story went around that in some earlier confrontation, Richard had killed this man's father and brothers. But whether or not that was the case, this makeshift champion of Châlus had plenty of incentive to fight back. After all, Richard had promised to hang them all.

The arrow did not catch Richard entirely off guard. Hearing the characteristic sound of a missile streaking through air, he looked up and applauded the bowman, then ducked beneath his shield. But he ducked too late. The arrow struck his shoulder. Ironically, it had come from Lionheart's own armory; the determined bowman had retrieved it from a crevice when he ran out of arrows of his own.

Without a sound, Richard rode back to his quarters in the thickening twilight, where several of his men did their best to extract the arrow. Yet they only managed to break off its wooden shaft, leaving the iron barb deep within the flesh. This meant calling in a surgeon, who hacked away by torchlight until he could extract the deeply imbedded barb.

By itself, such a wound—although traumatic—was not necessarily fatal. The royal patient was in pain but not inclined toward alarm. It was only as the days passed and the wound grew gangrenous that Richard realized he was dying.

Confronting the inevitable, he sent for his mother, who raced from Fontevraud to be by his side. And then on April 6, 1199—twelve days after the fatal arrow found its target—Richard Lionheart met his end.

Nothing further was ever heard—except in legend—of the golden treasure of Châlus.

꧁꧂

It was not a good death. Not the sort, in any case, that a man like Richard would have wanted. The tragedy of Lionheart's death lay not only in its timing—the possibility that had he lived, he might have defeated Philip once and for all—but in its sheer ordinariness. To be killed at a siege of Châlus, of all places, and by a mere youth! How much better to have gone out in a surge of valor at Arsuf or at Joppa.

Richard of course realized this as well as anyone, and as he lay dying, he did what he could to immortalize the legend he had so well begun. He forgave his assailant. He hanged the rest of the garrison, as he had threatened, but forgave the boy and even gave him a gift of one hundred English shillings. Soon this single act of chivalry came to outweigh the other details of Châlus, and although Richard may have been giving special attention to his soul's welfare, he nevertheless could not have been unmindful of the scene's dramatic effect, as immortalized in years to come by troubadours and minstrels across the land.

Roger of Wendover tells us that Richard, with considerable contempt, ordered his intestines to be buried at Châlus, but he bequeathed his "invincible heart" to the church of Rouen.[9] Lastly, he ordered that his body be buried at the abbey church of Fontevraud, near the feet of his father, "whose destroyer he confessed himself to be."[10]

In death, if not in life, Richard sought forgiveness.

Part Five

❀ 13 ❀

Philip and John

$\mathcal{S}$o it had come to this. Philip and his father had played Henry Plantagenet against his sons, and the sons against each other. And now only
John remained.

On his deathbed, Richard declared John his successor. This had been
implicit since at least the autumn of 1197, in the wording of a treaty of alliance between John and Baldwin of Flanders. But now Richard intended
that John's role as his heir be made plain. There was no other choice.
Richard's nephew, Arthur of Brittany, was but a child and clearly was
under Philip's influence.[1]

It was not a happy decision. John had from an early age taken after
his older brother, Geoffrey, who—according to Giraldus—was eloquent
and astute, difficult to deceive but all too ready to deceive others. "His
[Geoffrey's] tongue is smoother than oil," Giraldus explained, in a much-
quoted passage, "for with wonderful industry he assumes all shapes, and
dissembles all his designs."[2] John may not have possessed the same eloquence, but he was every bit as bright as Geoffrey, and just as slippery.
The two brothers even resembled each other physically—short and dark,
unlike Richard or the younger Henry—and shared a penchant for foment-
ing trouble. To this unpleasant mix, John added a complete ruthlessness.

Despite a misspent youth, the youngest of the Plantagenets was no
mere libertine, having developed a hard edge and an appetite for power.
With his intelligence and ability, he possessed many of the ingredients
necessary for greatness, as his father must have recognized, for John had
always been Henry's favorite. Perhaps Henry even admired John's cun-
ning, for the old king had been a sly one himself. But then, John always

171

carried things to extremes. It was only on Henry's deathbed, as word of his youngest son's betrayal reached him, that the dying king finally realized what others had recognized all along.

Of course, there always was the possibility that a certain perverseness dictated Henry's choice, for Eleanor favored Richard and had little time for John. The colorful and dismaying Plantagenets had managed to concoct a particularly poisonous brew of intrafamily hate and conflict that bubbled up with special venom in Henry's and Eleanor's youngest child. John Lackland, as he was called, was born after all the family lands had been doled out to older brothers, and he early learned to resent the fact. Henry did what he could to amend this oversight, creating havoc in his relationships with his other sons while failing to satisfy his youngest. Not that John had any reason to expect an equal portion; as the youngest, he had no territorial rights whatever. Still, he felt entitled, and this led him down some dark and dangerous byways.

He betrayed his father, and he betrayed Richard. Yet with Richard's unexpected demise, there seemed little alternative. Richard, after all, had failed to father an heir.

So John now became king, and prepared to take on his family's traditional enemy and rival, the Capetian king. One could only pray.

⚜

Philip and John had never trusted one another. In 1193, when news of Richard's capture sent John flying to France, the youngest Plantagenet paid homage to Philip for Normandy. In return for Philip's recognition, he agreed to cede the Norman Vexin to the French crown. Yet the two had also agreed to a provision that allowed them to keep an eye on one another, like two scorpions in a bottle: neither was to make peace with the dreaded Lionheart without the other's consent.

Richard was equally wary of the combined talents of Philip and John. Although he had no fear of confronting John in the field—John was no warrior, and Richard held himself well able to beat any man alive—Lionheart nevertheless was apprehensive of the kind of back-door dealings of which his brother was capable, especially in league with Philip. Richard was of course right to be alarmed, for both Philip and John worked assiduously to keep him in captivity, offering a huge bribe to the emperor even as they worked to strip Richard of his lands and crown.

Yet now Lionheart was dead, and Philip and John were left to deal with one another. Upon hearing of Richard's demise, John (who most curiously was with his nephew Arthur at the time) dashed to secure the treasury at Chinon. Unaccountably, he failed to keep this rival to the throne in his own hands—an omission that Philip did not overlook. Acting quickly, Philip overran the frontiers of Normandy and Anjou, while young Arthur and his indomitable mother led a Breton force to the Plantagenets' ancestral city of Angers, which laid out the welcome mat. Soon a great assembly of barons from the lands along the Loire acknowledged Arthur rather than John as their liege lord and Richard's heir. It did not take much insight to perceive Philip's hand behind this uprising, and John was forced to flee.

He headed for Rouen, where the Normans swallowed their dislike and loyally supported Lionheart's chosen heir. Backed by Norman troops, John now reestablished his authority in Anjou before returning to Westminster for coronation. Yet Arthur once again eluded him, slipping away to Philip, who sent him to Paris for safekeeping. After quietly assessing the situation, Philip demanded that John turn over Anjou, Maine, and the Touraine, as well as Eleanor's lands of Poitou, to young Arthur. As for himself, Philip demanded the Norman Vexin.

This was not a modest request, and inevitably hostilities broke out between the two monarchs. Just as inevitably, the Church—still doing its best to calm troubled waters so that everyone could merrily depart on crusade—strongly intervened. Peter of Capua, the papal legate, was still around and had in fact expressed considerable displeasure at Philip's current marital arrangements (after repudiating Ingeborg, Philip had wed Agnes of Meran). This casual approach to divorce and remarriage did not sit well with the pope's legate, who threatened to place all of France under interdict unless the French king gave ground.

Philip was not about to give ground on Ingeborg, but by January 1200 was willing to consider a reasonable truce with John. In return for acknowledging John as Richard's rightful heir (to Normandy, Maine, Anjou, Touraine, and Aquitaine, as well as overlordship of Brittany), Philip got to keep the Norman Vexin except for Andely, which John retained. Philip also kept Évreux and its surrounding countryside, and agreed to seal the pact with an alliance of more than ordinary interest. His son and heir, young Louis, would wed John's niece—not Eleanor, Geoffrey's daughter, but a daughter of John's sister, Eleanor of Castile.

Queen Eleanor now traveled south to bring her granddaughter to her destiny. Surprisingly, the girl she selected was not the elder granddaughter, as everyone expected, but the younger. For some reason, Eleanor chose Bianca, or Blanche, and her judgment proved sound. In due course, this young girl would become one of France's greatest queens.

In May, Blanche of Castile wed her young prince in Port-Mort, just over the border into Normandy. Peter of Capua had made good his threat, leaving all of French royal domains most inconveniently under interdict. Philip, still at loggerheads with the Church, was banned from the ceremony, but Arthur was present and did homage to John for Brittany.

Both kings seemed reasonably satisfied with the outcome, and their peoples fervently hoped that peace had come at last.

⚜

It was a reasonable wish. Yet given the long history of hostility between the two dynasties, not to mention the characters of these two kings, peace for any length of time seemed unlikely. Philip was constitutionally unable to resist any opportunity for stirring up trouble in his rival's lands, even as John was constitutionally unable to avoid giving him the opportunity. And opportunity soon arose.

This time around, the cause was a woman, for John—unlike Richard—had a keenly appreciative eye for feminine beauty. Moreover, John—now thirty-three—still had no legitimate heir. Isabelle of Gloucester, his wife of twelve years, had borne him no children, and the next usual step would have been for John to divorce her on grounds of consanguinity. Unfortunately for John, a papal dispensation had been necessary to permit this marriage to begin with, making its dissolution trickier. Under the circumstances, how could John best get rid of Isabelle and acquire a new wife?

As it happened, his marriage's demise turned out to be the least troublesome part of the problem. John quickly found himself some Continental bishops willing to do the job, and wife number one had no objection to parting ways. Yet John was not yet out of the woods, for his eyes had lit upon the beauteous Isabelle of Angoulême. Unfortunately for him, this young beauty already was betrothed—to the heir of Lusignan, the infamous house that had roiled Aquitaine's political waters for as long as anyone could remember. Making John's choice even more dangerous, the damsel was of the same tribe that had done in Richard, or at least drawn him to Limoges through their treachery. Adémar, the incendiary count of Angoulême, was Isabelle's father.

The count of Angoulême and viscount of Limoges both had Richard's blood on their hands, and Hugh of Lusignan had recently wrested the county of La Marche from John, reportedly in exchange for Queen Eleanor herself, whom he had waylaid as she traveled south to Castile to pick up Blanche. The Plantagenets had never treated any of this bunch gently, and legend even has it that soon after Lionheart's untimely death, his son (the illegitimate Philip of Cognac) avenged him by dispatching the viscount of Limoges.[3] There is no evidence for this story, which may have put down roots simply because people wanted to believe it. Still, by the time John summoned the count of Angoulême and viscount of Limoges to perform their homage to him at Lusignan, the viscount of Richard's day had indeed died, leaving his heir to report to the new king. Since barely a year had elapsed since Richard's death, it seems quite possible that the pride of Limoges had departed this earth at the wrong end of a sword, or some other suitable weapon. But at whose hands, we do not know.

John's summons to these recalcitrant subjects, to pay homage to him at Lusignan, may have stirred up old resentments. Yet by the time of his arrival, changing circumstances—most especially the peace between the two kingdoms—assured a warmer welcome than he might earlier have expected.

The festivities upon the occasion were undoubtedly as magnificent as Count Hugh and his wife could make them, while the lustrous velvets, rich damasks, sumptuous brocades, and gold-threaded silks that bedecked this crowd undoubtedly glowed with the brightest of scarlet, periwinkle, and gold. Dress may have been simple in design, being essentially a layering of long and flowing tunics for men and women alike, but it hardly was muted. The king and his noble subjects would have flaunted color combinations that in vividness and sheer unexpectedness would have dazzled our own century.

Similarly, as Count Hugh led his royal guest toward the head table, he would have unleashed a procession of dishes that would boggle today's diner, whether in number, variety, or riotous conjunction of flavors. Medieval barons had an astonishing number of eating options, at least in the protein category.[4] Not only did the privileged few revel in abundance, but also in gastronomic adventure, for they ate their countless varieties of fish, fowl, and four-footed beasts served up in a kaleidoscope of flavor combinations.

In part, this was a natural outcome of ostentation, for a heavy hand with all manner of spices served as a not-so-subtle reminder of the host's wealth. Yet in the last analysis, medieval palates simply seem to have been conditioned to taste sensations quite different from our own. The surfeited members of the upper class enjoyed being surprised at mealtime, whether it was with brightly colored meat and gilded fowl, pastries containing all manner of surprises (including, yes, blackbirds), or food that mixed flavors in unusual ways. One historian has noted juxtapositions such as beef with pears, almonds, dates, and violets, and provides a stomach-churning recipe for meat pie that could have fed a village.[5]

It was during the course of such festivities in Lusignan that John's eye fell upon the reigning beauty, Isabelle of Angoulême, who had been betrothed at a tender age to the heir of Lusignan. Every instinct should have warned John to avoid this lovely lass, but wisdom and restraint were not on any list of virtues that he recognized. He certainly could argue that Hugh well deserved a comeuppance. Moreover, to John's way of thinking, marrying Count Adémar's daughter would make a staunch ally of the old codger, splitting up the dangerous alliance of Angoulême and Lusignan.

Adémar, as John anticipated, fairly drooled over the prospect of having his daughter become queen, and Isabelle, who was not lacking in ambition, does not seem to have objected. Playing his part, Adémar spirited her out of Hugh's clutches and restored her to his own. After that, it was a relatively simple matter to hand her over to the king, who married her forthwith and set out for Chinon and safety. Soon after—in October 1200—she was crowned queen at Westminster.

The Lusignans predictably reacted with shock and anger, demanding that Philip of France right their wrongs. But for the moment, Philip was too tied up in quarrels with the Church to respond. He had managed to extricate himself from interdict by agreeing to acknowledge Ingeborg as his lawful queen, but then promptly closeted her in virtual isolation in the royal castle of Étampes. Back in Paris, Agnes welcomed him with open arms and, in due course, gave birth to a son. Neither the Danes nor the Church, not to mention Ingeborg, were satisfied with this arrangement, and in the spring of 1201, Philip once again was forced to acknowledge Ingeborg, this time to the extent of bringing her home with him.

During these complications, he managed to maintain all outward appearance of cordial relations with John, even welcoming the English king and queen to his Paris abode before retiring to Fontainebleau, presumably with Agnes, who had not done well under her humiliating ordeal. Unable to bear up under her unexpected fall from wife and queen to mistress, and probably not recovered from her most recent childbirth, she departed this earth in midsummer 1201, leaving Philip with an unwanted wife and only one legitimate son. Frantic for the succession, he now badgered Rome to declare his children by Agnes legitimate.[6] Throughout that autumn and winter, as he waited for Rome's verdict, the Lusignans quietly simmered but did nothing to break the surreal calm.

In March 1202, word finally came. In the Church's eyes, Philip's children by Agnes—including that all-important second son—were legitimate. Without further ado, Philip promptly summoned John to Paris, as duke of Aquitaine and vassal of the French crown. At long last, the king of France was going to go after the sole survivor of Henry Plantagenet's difficult brood.

⚜

John had thought his troubles with Philip were over—or, at least, that he had gotten away with his abrupt marriage to the heiress of Angoulême. After spending eight reasonable months in England, where he behaved himself, he and Isabelle returned to the Continent, spending much of the summer in Paris as Philip's guests.

The weeks and months continued to pass pleasantly for him, filled with fêtes and other diversions, until quite suddenly Philip's summons burst upon him, for all the world like some chamber pot being emptied from an unseen window. Despite the formalities, John did not like the smell.

The actual charges said nothing about the beauteous Isabelle, but instead fastened on other injuries that John as duke and count had done to his vassals, the Lusignans, and to his own overlord, the king of France. John promptly replied that as king of England he could not be summoned to justice by a brother monarch. Philip retorted that it was not his problem that the duke also chanced to be a king. John—who had no intention of placing himself at the French king's mercy—avoided Paris like the plague. Soon Philip, having the pretext he needed, went to war.

After mopping up eastern Normandy to the very gates of Rouen, Philip knighted young Arthur, betrothed him to the infant French Princess Marie, and sent him off to attack Poitou. There, the young count of Brittany met up with the Lusignan brothers, who talked him into attacking Mirebeau, where Queen Eleanor had temporarily sought refuge. The Lusignans had no intention of letting such a valuable hostage slip from their grasp, and soon the dowager queen was under attack from troops led by her own grandson.

Although Eleanor managed to get word of her plight to John, no one expected much help from that quarter. Yet if given sufficient incentive, John was capable of surprising bursts of energy.

Upon receiving his mother's message, he immediately stirred himself into the kind of action that his father and older brother would have admired. Force-marching his troops by day and night, he covered the eighty miles from Le Mans in forty-eight hours, arriving in the early dawn before Arthur's men had even opened their eyes and scratched. In the ensuing brawl, John's troops emerged triumphant, with not a single one of their enemy allowed to escape. Among the many prisoners were the Lusignan brothers and, the biggest prize of all, Count Arthur himself.

Suddenly the tide had turned in John's favor—while Arthur, now locked up in the Conqueror's dungeons at Falaise, had every reason to fear the worst.

⚜

Word of this disaster reached Philip as he was on the brink of yet another successful siege on the eastern Norman frontier. Shattered by the news, he retired to rethink his strategy, while for the moment his rival seemed blessed by all the gods. Not only had John seen his worst enemies dragged back to Normandy lashed to oxcarts, but—in an unrelated adventure—he had also captured the viscount of Limoges. Adding to John's jubilation, the timely death of Isabelle's father now dropped all of Angoulême into the English king's waiting hands.

Yet despite appearances, the shadows had begun to lengthen on the last of Henry Plantagenet's sons. Years of warfare under Richard had drained the rich Plantagenet lands, and the prospect of yet more warfare under Richard's successor gave men pause. But in the final analysis, it was the kind of rule John provided that undermined his cause. Men spoke in whispers of the king's faithlessness and cruelty. He ruled with a heavy and arbitrary hand, treating his barons with contempt and allowing his mercenaries to ravage the people mercilessly. Throughout John's vast realms, men worried about their welfare and began to go over to Philip and to Philip's young ward, the count of Brittany.

As with any unknown, Arthur of Brittany held out the prospect of hope. Men could imagine him to be exactly what they wanted, and they imagined someone quite the opposite of John. Seeing defections on every side, John twisted and turned. At length he took steps to rid himself of his rival—first by having the youngster's eyes put out. When even Arthur's guards defended the young count from this outrage, the king tried another tack, promising to release Arthur and reinstate his Breton inheritance if only he would turn from Philip and pay homage to him.

At this, Arthur unwisely informed his uncle that he would only settle for all of Lionheart's domains, including England itself. Infuriated, John had the lad transferred from Falaise to the tower of Rouen, supposedly for safekeeping. Shortly after that, Arthur disappeared. Soon after Easter 1203, rumors began to spread that on Good Friday eve, Arthur died most horribly at John's own hand. Although these rumors do not jibe in all particulars, they share the elements of a drunken king, a murder, and a body—weighted with a rock—cast into the Seine.

What Arthur's actual end was, we do not know.

⚜

The problem, from Philip's standpoint, was that he had no positive proof that Arthur had even died, much less that John had killed him.[7] This uncertainty left the French king and Arthur's other numerous supporters in the lurch. If the young count still lived, then it behooved them to tread warily, so as not to put the lad in further danger. Taking full advantage of his enemies' uncertainty, John remained mum on the entire subject and waited for events to turn his way.

He was playing an increasingly desperate game. Despite lack of proof, most men suspected that Arthur no longer lived. Whether John himself was responsible for the count's demise, no one could say, but there was a readiness to believe that a murder had happened and that King John was personally responsible. This conviction lent solidity to rumor, which rapidly ate away at John's already-dwindling support. If Arthur no longer lived, men muttered, who among John's vassals could trust the king?

Unable to rely upon his own vassals, John for some time had been falling back upon mercenaries to supply the troops he needed. Yet the silver with which to pay them was becoming increasingly difficult to find. Not only had Richard's successor inherited a depleted treasury, but the barons who should have helped to fill it were defecting in ever-increasing numbers. Rumors of Arthur's murder only made matters worse, dramatically weakening John's already-tenuous hold. Recognizing a downward spiral, Philip quickly moved to take advantage.

In late April 1203, he struck, first moving down the Loire. He then swept into Normandy, with castles falling on every side. John did nothing to impede Philip's progress, and as it became clear that aid from the English king was not forthcoming, few had the willpower or the incentive to hold out against the French king. Throughout that spring and summer, the drumbeat of surrenders continued. As Philip approached Rouen, John's few remaining supporters pleaded with the king to do something about Philip's incursions, but John merely waved them away. "Let him do so," he told them. "Whatever he now seizes on I will one day recover."[8]

Perhaps John had in mind the complaint he had sent to Rome concerning Philip's long history of aggressions. Pope Innocent immediately sent envoys to arbitrate, but Philip curtly informed them that the Holy See had no business interfering in the dispute at hand.[9] John would have to rely upon his own resources.

Chief among these, of course, was the incomparable fortress of Gaillard at Andely. Despite John's fecklessness, Gaillard still remained inviolate—a magnificent barrier between Philip and Rouen. The place was impregnable—everyone knew it. Richard had planned it that way.

Yet now, solidly entrenched across the river from the Rock of Andely, Philip cast covetous eyes on Lionheart's beauty. If there was one castle in all creation he wanted, it was Gaillard.

Lionheart's Proud Daughter

For years, Philip had watched and learned from Richard, carefully crafting a type of warfare that best suited his own style. Lacking Lionheart's flamboyance and sheer enjoyment of personal combat, the young French monarch had gradually developed a method that, at its best, relied more heavily on brains than on brawn. Philip shone in siege warfare, and as the summer of 1203 drew to a close, he began to plot his way into Richard's fair Castle of the Rock, with all the care and connivance of which he was capable.

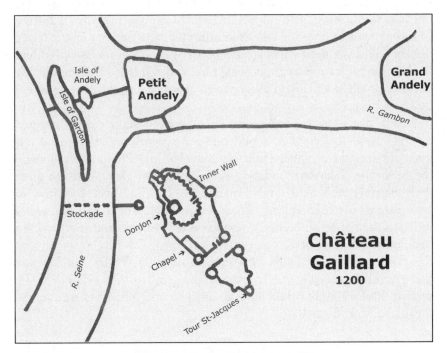

Château-Gaillard, 1200. © J. McAuliffe

No one better understood the obstacles facing him. Richard, for all his delight in thuggery, had not been short on brains, and Gaillard showed it. It was a most damnably clever arrangement, in which Nature and art complemented one another to an astonishing degree. Truly Richard had displayed his artful side at Andely, and the results still mocked Philip from their heights across the Seine.

Richard's successor was not short on brainpower, either, but he had grown remarkably short of followers—a fact that did not escape Philip's notice. Indeed, the French monarch had made good use of John's unfortunate inclination to foster mistrust, and on many an occasion had pushed the issue to his own advantage. John was not yet twisting in the wind in Normandy, but he was close to it. Yet so long as John had Gaillard, he was dangerous.

John's particular danger was his unpredictability. Although showily irreligious (he had refused to take Communion for years), he was superstitious, leading some to fear that he was under the influence of sorcery. Another way of looking at this is that as events in Normandy began to close in on him, John may have turned to soothsayers and fortunetellers. Even without such dark influences, the multiple hazards surrounding him would have been quite sufficient to explain his curious flitting from one spot to another, his alternating bouts of activity and extreme lethargy, and his departures at odd hours without so much as bidding his host adieu. John was afraid of capture, and rightly so. Surrounded by enemies on all sides, he no longer knew whom he could trust or where he could turn.

Still, despite what his enemies and worried supporters whispered behind his back, John had a perfectly good mind, and Philip did not make the mistake of underestimating him. Nor did Philip underestimate the men who defended Gaillard's walls. John had garrisoned the place with warriors who held no Norman lands and had little incentive to capitulate to the French king. Their commander, Roger de Lacy, was a well-regarded English baron of unquestioned courage and loyalty. John had nothing to fear there.

Thus as summer faded into autumn of 1203, Philip realized that there would be no easy way to capture the great fortress of Andely. To seize it, Philip simply would have to outthink and outwit its creator, the great Lionheart himself.

The quality of light reflected off the Seine takes on a particular glow in autumn, as the sun descends the northern skies toward its winter solstice. This glow, which shares certain properties with the last rays of sunset, envelops objects softly, illuminating them with an almost inner incandescence. As Philip gazed across the Seine that autumn at the object of his desire, the setting sun would have shimmered upward from the water to the castle high above, bathing cliff and fortress with a beckoning radiance.

Richard had called Gaillard his daughter—mockingly, to be sure, but perhaps with more truth than he cared to admit. This was the offspring that he proudly acknowledged to the world, his own flesh and blood. Richard now was gone, but Gaillard proudly lived on after him, as he had intended. His fair daughter remained a constant taunt to Philip, an affront of the highest order. But even more than this, she remained symbol and guardian of the empire that William the Conqueror and Henry II created. Richard had begotten her for this purpose, and Philip now had no choice but to make her his own.

As summer faded into autumn, Philip began by insinuating himself at the outermost point of Richard's far-flung complex—the flat peninsula opposite the Rock, which lay to the north of Philip's stronghold at Gaillon.[1] Here he encamped his men and set to work, first breaching the double stockade that Richard had erected across the river by sending in swimmers under cover of darkness to do the hazardous job. Although John's men had already burned the bridges linking Petit Andely and the Isle to the far shore, this no longer mattered. Now Philip could send his own boats through the breach, and he quickly threw together a pontoon bridge (protected by pontoon-supported towers) and sent a portion of his men across it to the other side.

With tremendous speed and two deft strokes, Philip had suddenly rearranged the entire chessboard, placing Petit Andely under direct siege and the Isle of Andely in a vise. In response, John also moved quickly, marching the largest body of troops he could muster up the left bank of the Seine by night, with the object of falling upon Philip's sleeping warriors on the peninsula. Supporting this operation, John launched a flotilla of boats out of Rouen, laden with troops with which to break up the French pontoon as well as with supplies for the beleaguered island. At the very least, John calculated, this double onslaught would cut off the French troops on the Seine's right bank from the main body on the left, while coming to the aid of the island garrison.

It was a clever plan—except for the fact that the Seine above Rouen is tidal, and John and his advisers had not properly calculated the mighty rush of river seaward on that particular night. John's land forces struck just before daybreak, as planned, but—unknown to them—the naval portion of this pincer movement had not yet arrived. With nothing to prevent them, the French fled from their attackers across the pontoon bridge, and virtually all managed to escape to safety on the Seine's far side. Worse yet, by the time the fleet struggled upstream to its appointed rendezvous, the French had regrouped, repaired and recrossed the pontoon bridge, and routed John's unsupported troops on the left bank. Badly outmanned, John's shipborne warriors put up a brave fight but, in the end, had to retreat with heavy losses.

Flush with victory, the French now set the island fortress on fire and seized the place. At this, the inhabitants of the fortified town fled for safety to the castle above, leaving the town gates flung open wide behind them.

Philip of France now set up camp at the very base of the Rock.

⚜

The next step, and by far the more difficult, was the Rock itself. Having taken the place's measure, Philip's first move was to invest, or lay siege to, the nearby fortress of Radepont—a small but extremely important fortification to the north of Andely, near where the road from Paris to Rouen crosses the river Andelle. Since Rollo's time, the Andelle had served as the northernmost boundary of the Norman Vexin and, after the Vexin fell to Philip, replaced the Epte as the dividing line between Normandy and the lands of the French crown. Much like the Epte, the Andelle is a small river occupying a glacially carved valley much too big for it. But the valley itself—if not the placid stream running through it—served as a kind of last-ditch defense before the gates of Rouen.

Well aware of Radepont's importance, Richard himself had taken great care to fortify the place. Philip, in fact, had failed to take Radepont only the year before. Now, to ensure against John's battered army making a reappearance, the French king marched rapidly northward to set up his siege engines. Within three weeks, Radepont's twenty knights, one hundred men-at-arms, and thirty crossbowmen surrendered.

With Radepont in his hands, Philip had now virtually encircled Gaillard and the Rock of Andely. But what next? Gaillard itself was impregnable. Everyone knew it, and having taken a good look at the place,

Philip was inclined to agree. Since assault seemed out of the question, the only other course was to starve the place out.

❦

Climbing the steep hillside out of Andely to the rise of land above the Rock, Philip's men now dug in for the long wait. As members of Gaillard's garrison peered out from their place of safety, the French established their entrenchments, well fortified by towers along the lines.[2] Although there was less danger of John appearing on the horizon behind them now that Radepont was taken and his army severely trounced, still it behooved Philip to be prepared. In any case, Gaillard's garrison—probably around three hundred men—was quite capable of mounting a counterattack.

Yet Philip was counting on those very numbers to work on his behalf. De Lacy had not only three hundred warriors to feed, but also those hundreds of civilians who had fled for their lives from Petit Andely below. Lionheart had prepared Gaillard for lengthy sieges by having his miners hew out an extensive network of well-fortified storage caves beneath it. If the records for the nearby town of Évreux are any indication, these caves would have been stuffed with food and supplies.[3] Gaillard, it was said, had enough storage capacity to outlast a yearlong siege. But the unwelcome introduction of Petit Andely's terrified residents added hundreds more mouths to feed. All Philip had to do was sit back and wait.

But de Lacy was no fool. As soon as he did some simple calculations, he decided to release a large number of the weakest and most aged among the civilians. These passed without incident through the siege lines and presumably returned to their homes in the village below. Concluding that this was the best solution to his problem, de Lacy now released all but those who could contribute to the castle's defense. On his orders, hundreds of men, women, and children now crossed the drawbridge linking Gaillard's advance works to the world beyond. Except that this time, instead of passing unmolested through the French lines, they unexpectedly encountered a barrage of arrows. Philip had heard of the previous release and royally upbraided his commander for his stupidity. Let these people go? Never! They were his secret weapon in the war of attrition he was conducting against Gaillard, and he was not about to let humanitarianism stand in the way.

Turning back in terror, this mob now fled to Gaillard. To their horror, they found the drawbridge raised and the gates firmly shut against them. These "useless mouths," as the unfortunates were called, were trapped, and in the terrible days and weeks ahead had no other course but to eke out a pitiful existence between the lines of the besieged and the besieger. Reduced to eating rodents and grass, and huddling together for warmth in the castle moats, they died in droves.

In January, when the garrison released its dogs (more "useless mouths"), the starving refugees tore these luckless beasts apart and ate them on the spot. Soon after, they set upon a stray chicken that wandered between the lines, devouring every raw morsel—feathers, intestines, and all. Not surprisingly, before it was all over, the "useless mouths" of Andely resorted to cannibalism.

At last, taking pity on these desperate souls, Philip gave the order to let them go and give them something to eat. But it was too late. By this time few remained, and the very act of eating was too much for their wracked bodies. Almost every one of them died immediately after taking the first real food they had tasted in months.

Philip's chaplain, Guillaume le Breton, conveniently blamed the tragedy on de Lacy and Gaillard's garrison, but succeeding centuries have recognized that there was plenty of blame to go around. In this bitter battle of wills between a king and his baronial opponent, it was the common people, as usual, who did the suffering.[4]

⸙

Throughout their long ordeal, the "useless mouths" of Andely must have dreamed of Lionheart appearing over the rise, leading an army to their rescue. Yet Lionheart was dead, and John had long since departed Normandy for the safety of England, leaving Gaillard to its own devices.

De Lacy was left to represent the interests of a king who did not seem particularly interested in the outcome, even though Gaillard remained the only real obstacle between Philip and complete victory over Normandy. Still, de Lacy had his pride, and he was not about to capitulate—especially not with a fortress such as this one under his command. His food supplies, although dwindling, could hold out for another year, while by contrast, Philip's besiegers, having stuck it out for almost six months at their king's command, had a worn and tattered air. Morale among the French had plummeted, and Philip was worried. Winter had taken its toll, and desertions were on the rise.

Thus it was an all-out gamble when Philip decided to attack—from the only place possible, that tongue of land connecting the hillside to the Rock. Sometime in mid-February, de Lacy's men looked out and saw the

French set up their protective hurdle-sheds and start to level this narrow strip of land. Despite the portable protection, it was dangerous as well as difficult work—within range of the great Tower of Saint-Jacques, the prow of Richard's awe-inspiring advance works. Bombarded by the first line of Gaillard's defenses, they struggled on, driven by a monarch who suddenly sensed the situation's possibilities.

Something had clearly summoned up more than Philip's usual dogged determination, and it seems probable that he had at last spotted a small but vital vulnerability in Gaillard's impervious-looking advance works—a place his great rival had failed to protect. Anxious for victory, Philip was about to make a drive for this soft spot. But first he had to position his siege engines and great siege tower on the unforgiving strip of land at Gaillard's threshold. There was no other choice but to rearrange the landscape to accommodate his equipment, and this he now did, driving his men with the thoroughgoing relentlessness of which he was capable.

When they at last finished, they had prepared the way for the French king's notorious catapults and slings to move within easy range of their prey. Philip was about to answer the challenge that Richard had issued barely five years before.

⚜

The most dramatic element of Philip's assault was the huge wheeled siege tower, which his men now rolled into place directly before the Tower of Saint-Jacques. From here, protected by sheaths of ox hide and iron, the French crossbowmen could shoot storms of arrows directly across at Gaillard's defenders, even while the men operating Philip's siege engines hurled stones, debris, and all manner of foul matter Gaillard's way. It was the first direct encounter between besieger and besieged, and it was intense, preoccupying the defenders while the real danger was quietly proceeding beneath their noses.

In fact, under the shelter of covered galleries, Philip's men were rapidly filling in the deep moat with sheaves of sticks, cartloads of gravel, and basketsful of dirt. As soon as the moat was sufficiently filled for ladders to be lowered down its perpendicular wall, Philip's sappers clambered down and began their work. Their objective was one that de Lacy certainly had not anticipated, for there beneath the great Tower of Saint-Jacques lay a dead angle, a sector that the flanking towers could not sufficiently cover and the defenders' missiles could not easily reach. There, after moving their ladders to the other side of the moat and climbing up the rocky escarpment, the sappers began to burrow into the limestone beneath the masonry.

They worked quickly, propping up their tunnel as they went. Hour after hour they hacked away in their underground lair as the sounds of war continued all around them. Steadily but urgently they carved away at the underpinning rock until they had excavated a hole that extended sufficiently far in the critical direction. And then, after setting fire to the scaffolding, they hastily departed. The fire devoured the wood, much as they expected, and the tunnel collapsed, bringing down a large part of the mighty Tower of Saint-Jacques with it.

Stunned by this development, de Lacy's men immediately fled to the safety of the castle proper, raising the drawbridge and lowering the heavy portcullis behind them.

Philip now was master of Gaillard's mighty advance works. But he had only cracked Gaillard's periphery. The famous red and gold banner of the Norman dukes still floated proudly above the castle keep.

⁂

While all this was going on, where was Roger de Lacy? Shying from risk, he had failed to rescue his men in the advance works when Philip attacked. Surely de Lacy could have driven away the sappers, either by an external sortie or a countermine, but he failed to do either. Instead, he holed up in his impregnable bastion and waited for the enemy to give up and go away.

It was a cautious and unimaginative response to Philip's challenge, and certainly not what Richard had in mind. The entire point of Gaillard was its connectedness, its ability to answer a challenge in one sector with a response from another. Instead, de Lacy chose to treat Gaillard as a box within a box, as a passive retreat rather than as an active defense.

Following this unexpected setback, the garrison withdrew to the main body of the fortress itself, while Philip was left cooling his heels on the outside. Unlike his attack on the advance works, where some clever engineering could rearrange the landscape to his liking, this next layer of fortification was so carefully positioned and moated on the Rock that it was virtually impossible to bring in the siege towers and engines to do their work. Still, Philip could take comfort in his progress to date, and most particularly in his enemy. However personally courageous de Lacy may have been, he had revealed himself as a less-than-formidable commander.

Clearly Philip had nothing to fear from de Lacy. The only trick would be how to breach this second set of walls.

❧

Philip admired ingenuity and in fact possessed a large helping of it himself. Yet in the end, the ingenuity that solved this particular puzzle belonged to several of his men. Understanding their monarch's determination to seize Gaillard, they began to explore by night, ferreting their way along the bottom of the deep dry moat that joined with cliff face to divide the heart of Richard's fortress from the world. Here, one night, they made an intriguing discovery.

Although nineteenth-century historians were loath to discuss the subject in any detail, referring delicately to an open window, the point of entry that Philip's men seem to have discovered was the outflow shaft of a latrine. For years there has been considerable confusion concerning this unmentionable facility's exact location, with some historians conferring the honor on the basement of a chapel that John had only recently erected along the southeastern wall. This of course shifted any blame for what subsequently happened to the original architect's less popular younger brother, but nevertheless did not solve the location problem, for this building's ruins show no sign of having harbored a twelfth-century loo. Instead, the square tower farther down the wall (which the nineteenth-century architect Viollet-le-Duc insisted on depicting as round) contains three obvious candidates in its lower level, the outflow of the nearest being just barely accessible from the cliff face.[5] Here a doughty young man named Pierre de Bogis edged his way along the cliff and then, so to speak, took the plunge.[6]

This dauntless young man's work had only just begun. After penetrating Gaillard's walls in this creative fashion, he helped his four companions in after him—possibly through the window that subsequently entered history. Other soldiers quickly followed, and the noise at last aroused the garrison. But instead of running Bogis and his companions to ground, de Lacy's men seem to have considered themselves outnumbered and responded by setting fire to the buildings of the outer courtyard. Then they ingloriously retreated across the last bridge, where they barricaded themselves behind Richard's ingeniously designed inner curtain wall.

Bogis and company only had to wait for the worst of the flames to die down before they rushed to the gate and lowered the drawbridge. Much to Philip's gratification, the French then marched inside.

Two down and two to go, for although Philip had successfully navigated Gaillard's outer ring of defenses, the formidable citadel with its awe-inspiring donjon still lay inviolate at the core.

Richard's elliptical wall, with its careful elimination of dead angles, represented a challenge of the first order, as did the donjon itself, with its overhanging crown of solid stone. Yet Philip was well pleased with the progress made so far and was more than ready to tackle the impossible. Especially since, with his careful eye, he had noticed yet another flaw in Richard's design. Unlike the drawbridge leading into the advance works, or even the drawbridge connecting the advance works with the main body of the fortress, the bridge into the inner citadel was immovable, cut from a thin wedge of "living rock" that remained after the dry moat around it had been hacked away. Moreover, even though this bridge inclined upward to the stout citadel gate, the defensive works surrounding this gate could not completely cover the area beneath the bridge itself.

Recognizing an opportunity for sappers when he saw one, Philip immediately wheeled his siege engines into place—a difficult feat, given the lay of the land at this particular junction. Then he set his sappers to work. Protected by the solid stone of the bridge itself, as well as by French archers now posted along the top of the outer curtain wall, they began to burrow beneath the heavy masonry surrounding the gate.

It never should have come to this, for any commander with even the faintest understanding of the vast resources at his disposal would not have allowed such a crisis to come to pass. Roger de Lacy was a good man and a brave one, but of the old school, which looked upon a castle as a pile of rocks. Trusting to the thickness of Gaillard's walls, he saw his only challenge as that of outlasting Philip's blockade. It had never occurred to him to use Gaillard in the way Richard had intended—as a structure whose possibilities were only limited by its commander's ingenuity.

Yet with Philip's sappers at the very door, it was useless to play the waiting game any longer. De Lacy set his own sappers to work to construct a countermine. Unfortunately, even this was too late, for the multiple tunnels beneath the masonry now fatally weakened it from below, while Philip's catapults continued to pound from above. Unable to resist any longer, the gate-tower split open and collapsed.

Pouring in through the breach, the French caught their enemies in the open. De Lacy and his men had not even managed to occupy the great tower keep, which would play no role whatever in Gaillard's final defense. De Lacy and his men fought bravely, but it was no use. They had never understood how to defend Gaillard, and in the end—badly outnumbered—they had no alternative but to surrender.

⚜

A tremor shot through medieval Christendom on March 6, 1204, as the proud banner of the Norman dukes slowly descended from Gaillard's great tower keep and the royal standard of France rose in its place. It had taken Philip many months, but in the end he had done the impossible. By wile and by force, this exceptional monarch had at last met Richard Lionheart's final challenge.

Lionheart's fair daughter, the pride of the Plantagenet empire, was his. And all of Normandy would soon follow.

After almost three centuries, Rouen and all of Normandy now belonged to the kings of France.

Epilogue

꧁꧂

"*Fortune*," Orderic wrote, "is like a turning wheel. One moment she suddenly lifts a man up, the next throws him down."[1]

With Gaillard's fall, the wheel of fate—a staple of medieval thought—had turned, raising up Philip Capet and bringing down the Plantagenets' far-flung empire with a mighty crash. Roger of Wendover tells us that when informed of Gaillard's fall, King John sent a message informing his overseas barons "that they were to expect no assistance from him." The outcome was stunning. With "all kinds of defence failing in those provinces, the whole of Normandy, Tours, Anjou, and Poictou [*sic*], with the cities, castles and other possessions . . . fell to the dominion of the king of the French."[2]

Although the Plantagenets would for a time retain portions of Eleanor's lands below the Loire, they and their successors increasingly operated as kings of England rather than of a cross-Channel empire. Philip would go down in history as Philip Augustus, the great conqueror, while John, to most men's way of thinking, would best be forgotten.

As for Normandy, many of its nobles—who owned lands on both sides of the Channel—decamped for England, and Philip made sure that those who remained understood where power now lay. But Normandy did not merely change sovereigns. Absorbed into the kingdom of France, it quickly lost the privileged position it had once held under England's kings. Even Normandy's ducal title retained little of its previous luster. Philip disdained to claim the title for himself, and certainly was not interested in bestowing it upon another. Subsequent French kings occasionally conferred the title on family members, but it was England's monarchs who would continue to value it, ruling as duke of Normandy over the tiny Channel Islands, which originally were part of Normandy and to this day remain dependencies of the British Crown.

For several centuries, England's monarchs also continued to claim all of mainland Normandy, in addition to the rest of their former French possessions. They attempted to win these back during the Hundred Years' War, and the two nations tangled in recurring hostilities until the end of the Napoleonic Wars in 1815. Despite Europe's relative peace during the nineteenth century, this long-standing enmity did not really begin to abate until World War I, when British and French together fought the Germans on French soil.

But it was World War II that truly brought this long and blood-soaked history to a close. Cross-Channel rivalries continue, and may do so for all time, but when the Allies crossed the Channel to the beaches of Normandy, this second Norman invasion came *from* England, with liberation as its goal. As a recent commemorative plaque in Saint-Clair-sur-Epte puts it: "To the Normans, whose victorious daring linked the destinies of the French and the English."

As for Gaillard, this twelfth-century fortress continued for many years to offer a rugged challenge to would-be attackers. During the Hundred Years' War, more than two centuries after Gaillard's birth, Lionheart's bold fortification changed hands several times, but only after lengthy sieges.

Despite the introduction of gunpowder, Gaillard remained an active fortress until the late sixteenth century, when—during the course of fierce civil and religious warfare—it held out under siege for an impressive two years. But once under Henri IV's control, it fell on hard times. The king agreed with local authorities that Gaillard should be destroyed, to prevent it from harboring armed bandits or falling into rebel hands. Nearby convents now received permission to go to work on the venerable castle, removing its stones to repair their own religious buildings. This demolition continued during the reign of Louis XIII and Louis' all-powerful minister, Cardinal Richelieu, who was responsible for razing countless castles throughout France. With its towering donjon decapitated and other critical portions dismantled, Lionheart's splendid fortress began its slow and irreversible decline.

The seventeenth and eighteenth centuries forgot Gaillard, but nineteenth-century romantics rediscovered it, drawn to its brooding ruins. More recent visitors—pounded by a century of totalitarianism, terrorism, and war—tend to see a fortress flexing its muscles rather than a castle in the moonlight. Yet even the most cynical may find there is something about the place that moves them—whether it is Gaillard's direct link to the past, or the clean, almost contemporary starkness of its lines.

Normandy has undertaken a massive restoration effort, but Gaillard will never completely recover from all those centuries of deliberate destruction and neglect. Yet more than a millennium after Rollo trod this soil and eight centuries after Lionheart set to work here, Château-Gaillard still dominates its chalky cliff above the Seine—crowning Andely's heights and linking our century with that distant age when the royal houses of England and France began their mighty struggle for dominance.

Key People

❧❦❧

Abbot Suger (ca. 1081–1151): Abbot of Saint-Denis, biographer of Louis VI, and counselor to Louis VI and Louis VII of France. Served as a regent of France during Louis VII's absence while on the Second Crusade.

Adele of Champagne (ca. 1140–1206): Third wife of Louis VII of France and mother of Louis' only son and heir, the future Philip II. Her brother Henry I of Champagne was married to Marie, the daughter of Louis VII of France and Eleanor of Aquitaine; her brother Theobald V of Blois was married to Marie's sister Alix.

Adémar, or **Aymar (Aimar), count of Angoulême:** Father of Isabelle of Angoulême and half-brother of Aimar V of Limoges.

Agnes of Meran: Called Marie by some chroniclers. Daughter of the German duke of Genest or (according to some chroniclers) the duke of Moravia and Bavaria. Third wife of Philip II of France, whose marriage (and the legitimacy of her children by Philip) was disputed by Philip's second wife, Ingeborg of Denmark, and by Ingeborg's supporters, including the pope.

Aimar V of Limoges, viscount of Limoges: Lord of Châlus, where Richard Lionheart died.

Alais of France (1160–1220): Second daughter of Louis VII of France and Constance of Castile. Betrothed as a child to Richard Lionheart, she remained unwed for years, subject to rumors that Richard's father, Henry II of England, had made her his mistress and that she had borne him a child. Eventually her half-brother, Philip II of France, arranged for her return to France and her marriage to the count of Ponthieu.

Arthur I, duke of Brittany (1187–1203): The posthumous son of Geoffrey of Brittany, and grandson of Henry II of England. Regarded as Richard Lionheart's heir until Arthur came under the influence of Philip of France. Captured by John, Arthur disappeared; it was rumored that he was murdered by John himself.

Baldwin de Béthune, count of Aumale: Devoted follower of Richard Lionheart, who accompanied Richard on his ill-fated journey from the Holy Land and served as a hostage for the remainder of Richard's ransom after Richard's departure from prison.

Berengaria of Navarre (d. 1230): Wed Richard Lionheart in 1191. Married him in Cyprus, en route to the Third Crusade. She died without issue.

Bertran de Born (last half of twelfth century): Baron from the Limousin and a major troubadour, especially on the subject of warfare. Sided with Henry the Younger in Henry's struggles with his father and, later, with Richard Lionheart.

Blanche of Castile (1188–1252): Queen of France (consort to Louis VIII) and granddaughter of Eleanor of Aquitaine and Henry II of England. Her marriage to Louis marked an important attempt at peace between the French and English crowns.

Bourguigne of Lusignan: Niece of Guy of Lusignan and, after her return from the Holy Land, wife of Raymond VI of Toulouse. Later set aside by Raymond, who married Joanna Plantagenet.

Conrad, marquis of Montferrat: Contender with Guy of Lusignan for the crown of king of Jerusalem. Killed in 1192, shortly after he was chosen king of Jerusalem.

Eleanor of Aquitaine (1122–1204): Duchess of Aquitaine, countess of Poitou, queen of France (as wife of Louis VII), and queen of England (as wife of Henry II). Mother of King Richard I and King John.

Eleanor Plantagenet (1162–1214): Second daughter of Henry II of England and Eleanor of Aquitaine. Married Alfonso VIII of Castile. Mother of Bianca, or Blanche of Castile, who married the future Louis VIII, son and heir of Philip Augustus.

Eustace (d. 1153): Son and heir of Stephen of Blois. His death made it possible for Matilda's son (Henry I's grandson) to become king of England, as Henry II.

Frederick Barbarossa (1122–1190): Ruled the Holy Roman Empire as Emperor Frederick I, from 1155 until his death en route to the Holy Land on the Third Crusade. His reign was marked by struggles with the Church, the Lombards, and the German nobility, chief among whom was Duke Henry the Lion.

Geoffrey II, duke of Brittany (1158–1186): Fourth son of Henry II of England and Eleanor of Aquitaine. Allied with Philip Augustus against Henry II. Geoffrey died in Paris. His son, Arthur, was born posthumously.

Geoffrey of Anjou (1113–1151): Count of Anjou, Touraine, and Maine; duke of Normandy by conquest. Wed to Matilda, daughter and heir of Henry I. Father of Henry II and founder of the Plantagenet line.

Giraldus Cambrensis, or Gerald of Wales (ca. 1146–ca. 1223): Chronicler; royal clerk and chaplain to Henry II of England.

Guy of Lusignan: King of the crusader state of Jerusalem (1186–1194), as husband of Sibylle of Jerusalem, who had succeeded to the throne. Guy refused to give up the crown after Sibylle's death, even though the succession had passed to Sibylle's younger sister, Isabelle, and to Isabelle's husband, Conrad of Montferrat. Eventually Conrad won the crown, and Guy accepted the crown of Cyprus.

Henri I of France (1008–1060): Grandson of Hugh Capet; ruled France from 1031 to 1060. Came to the aid of young Duke William of Normandy (who became William the Conqueror) at the battle of Val-ès-Dunes.

Henry Hohenstaufen (1165–1197): Ruled the Holy Roman Empire as Emperor Henry VI, from 1191 until his death. Conquered Sicily and imprisoned Richard Lionheart, who was en route home from the Third Crusade, for an enormous ransom. Henry's unexpected death left an infant heir, who became Emperor Frederick II.

Henry I of England (1068 or 1069–1135): Youngest son of William the Conqueror. Seized the English crown in 1100 upon the death of his brother, William Rufus (William II), and ruled until his own death in 1135. Left no legitimate male heir, leading to almost two decades of civil war in England between the contestants to the throne: Henry's daughter, Matilda, and Henry's nephew, Stephen of Blois.

Henry II of England (1133–1189): Son of Geoffrey of Anjou and Matilda of England; grandson of Henry I. Ruled England from 1154 to 1189. First of the royal Plantagenet dynasty.

Henry the Lion (1129–1195): Duke of Saxony and Bavaria; wed Matilda Plantagenet (his second wife). Stripped of his lands and exiled by Emperor Frederick Barbarossa, Henry and Matilda fled to the court of her father, Henry II of England. In 1189, upon the departure of Frederick Barbarossa for the Holy Land, Henry returned to fight for his lands.

Henry the Younger (1155–1183): Also known as the Young King and, before his coronation, as Prince Henry. Second of the five sons of

Henry II of England and Eleanor of Aquitaine, and first among those who survived infancy. Crowned during his father's lifetime and wed to Marguerite of France, daughter of Louis VII of France and Constance of Castile. Died while at war with his father and younger brother, Richard Lionheart.

Henry, count of Champagne: Grandson of Eleanor of Aquitaine and Louis VII; king of Jerusalem following the death of Conrad of Montferrat.

Hugh Capet (938 or 939–996): First king of France (987–996) and founder of the Capetian dynasty.

Ingeborg of Denmark: Second wife of Philip II of France, who tried to have the marriage annulled, leading to years of dispute between Philip and the Church.

Isaac Comnenus: Ruler of Cyprus before Richard Lionheart conquered it in 1191, en route to the Holy Land.

Isabelle of Angoulême (1188–1246): Second wife of King John of England. Originally betrothed to Hugh of Lusignan. Her marriage led to resumed conflict between John and Philip Augustus. After John's death she married Hugh of Lusignan (Hugh X), bearing him nine children.

Joanna Plantagenet (1165–1199): Youngest daughter of Henry II of England and Eleanor of Aquitaine. Wed William II of Sicily, becoming Sicily's queen. Following William's death, she was rescued from imprisonment by her brother, Richard Lionheart, and accompanied Richard's bride, Berengaria, on the Third Crusade. She later married Raymond VI of Toulouse. Died in childbirth after a daring escape from her husband's minions.

John of England (1166 or 1167–1216): Youngest son of Henry II of England and heir of his older brother, Richard Lionheart. Ruled England from 1199 to 1216.

Leopold V, duke of Austria (1157–1194): Took Richard Lionheart prisoner when he was en route home from the Third Crusade.

Louis VI of France, or **Louis the Fat** (1081–1137): Son of Philip I; ruled France from 1108 to 1137. Abbot Suger served as his adviser and biographer.

Louis VII of France (1120–1180): Son of Louis VI; ruled France from 1137 to 1180. Wed Eleanor of Aquitaine (1137); the marriage was annulled after fifteen years, two daughters, and no male heirs. Next he married Constance of Castile, who bore him two daughters (Marguerite and Alais) and died in 1160. Louis promptly married Adele of Champagne, who in 1165 bore him a son and heir, the future Philip II.

Louis VIII of France (1187–1226): Son and heir of Philip II; he ruled France from 1223 to 1226. Married Blanche of Castile (1200), granddaughter of Eleanor of Aquitaine and Henry II of England.

Marguerite of France (1157–1197): Eldest daughter of Louis VII of France and Constance of Castile, and twice a queen. Wed as an infant to Henry the Younger (eldest surviving son of Henry II and Eleanor of Aquitaine), she brought the contested territory of the Norman Vexin as her dowry. Became queen when her young husband was crowned during his father's lifetime. After his death she married King Béla III of Hungary. Following Béla's death she set out on pilgrimage for the Holy Land, where she died.

Matilda of England (1102–1167): Daughter and heir of Henry I of England. Married at a young age to Emperor Henry V, she was widowed and then married Geoffrey of Anjou, by whom she had three sons, the eldest of whom became Henry II of England. Upon the death of her brother (Henry I's only legitimate son, William Aetheling), her father made her his heir. But her cousin, Stephen of Blois, seized the crown before she could claim it. She remained at war with Stephen, both in England and in Normandy, throughout his long and turbulent reign.

Matilda Plantagenet (1156–1189): Eldest daughter of Henry II of England and Eleanor of Aquitaine. Married Henry the Lion, duke of Saxony and Bavaria. She and her husband were forced to flee from Germany to her father's court during Duke Henry's exile at the hands of Emperor Frederick Barbarossa.

Mercadier: Soldier from Provence. Leader of Richard Lionheart's mercenaries and right-hand man to Lionheart.

Otto of Brunswick: Younger son of Henry the Lion, nephew of Richard Lionheart, and rival to Philip of Swabia for the imperial crown following the death of Emperor Henry VI. Became Emperor Otto IV, but for years faced opposition from Philip of Swabia.

Philip I of France (1052–1108): Son of Henri I of France; ruled France from 1060 to 1108, during the reigns of William the Conqueror, William II of England, and Henry I of England, all of whom were also duke of Normandy.

Philip II of France (1165–1223): Only son of Louis VII. Ruled France from 1180 to 1223. Also known as Philip Augustus.

Philip of Dreux, bishop of Beauvais: Known as the "fighting bishop"; longtime antagonist of Richard Lionheart. Eventually captured in battle by Richard's chief mercenary, Mercadier. Philip Augustus protested, but Richard retorted that as a warrior, the bishop clearly had forfeited his ecclesiastical immunity.

Philip of Swabia: Younger brother of Emperor Henry VI; the Hohenstaufens' candidate for emperor following Henry's death. Ultimately unsuccessful, he continued for years to fight for the crown.

Pope Innocent III: Elected to the papacy in 1198, where he exerted tremendous power and influence until his death in 1216.

Richard Lionheart (1157–1199): Second surviving son of Henry II of England. Ruled England (1189–1199) as Richard I. Died without legitimate issue.

Robert Curthose (1054–1134): Eldest surviving son of William the Conqueror. Became duke of Normandy after the death of his father in 1187. In 1106, Robert's younger brother, Henry (who had ruled England as Henry I since 1100), defeated Robert's army at the Battle of Tinchebray, imprisoned Robert for life, and claimed Normandy as a possession of the English crown.

Robert, earl of Leicester: As a teenager, made a name for himself on the Third Crusade. Continued to support Richard Lionheart in Normandy until his own capture.

Roger de Lacy: Baron of Pontefract and commander of King John's garrison at Château-Gaillard.

Rollo (ca. 846–ca. 931): Viking leader and first ruler of what became known as Normandy.

Rosamond Clifford (1150–ca. 1176): Henry II's mistress.

Saladin (ca. 1138–1193): The great leader of the Muslim and Arab opposition to the crusader states and to the Third Crusade.

St. Bernard of Clairvaux (1090–1153): Abbot of Clairvaux and leader of the austere and reform-minded Cistercian monastic order, who played a leading role in combating heresy, preaching the Second Crusade, and ending schism within the Church. A major figure in the growth of the cult of the Virgin.

Stephen of Blois: Nephew of Henry I of England. Claimed the English crown upon Henry's death. Stephen's reign (from 1135 until his death in 1154) was marked by civil war and anarchy, during which Henry I's daughter, Matilda, and her husband, Geoffrey of Anjou, fought Stephen for the crown.

Tancred (1138–1194): Count of Lecce; king of Sicily from 1189–1194. Unwilling host to the crusading armies of Richard Lionheart and Philip Augustus en route to the Holy Land.

Walter Map (1140–ca. 1210): Man of letters and member of Henry II's court.

William Aetheling (ca. 1103–1120): The sole legitimate son of Henry I of England. Drowned on the White Ship in 1120.

William Clito: Son of Robert Curthose, nephew of Henry I of England, and—until his untimely death in 1128—contender for the English crown and duchy of Normandy.

William II of Sicily (1155–1189): Last in the line of Norman kings of Sicily. Wed to Joanna Plantagenet, he died childless, leaving his rich kingdom up for grabs. Tancred grabbed first, but Henry Hohenstaufen (as Emperor Henry VI) soon conquered Sicily, becoming its king.

William Marshal (1146–1219): Legendary knight and faithful protector of Henry the Younger, Henry II, and Richard Lionheart, as well as King John and young Henry III. Rewarded by the monarchs he so loyally served, he became rich and powerful, ending his life as earl of Pembroke.

William Rufus (1056?–1100): Second son of William the Conqueror, who ruled England as William II (1087–1100) following the Conqueror's death. Killed in what was either an assassination or a hunting accident.

William the Conqueror (1027 or 1028–1087): Descendant of Rollo the Viking and bastard son of Duke Robert I of Normandy. Ruled Normandy as duke from 1035; conquered England in 1066, where he ruled as William I (1066–1087).

Chronology

911 Rollo the Viking is defeated by the Franks in battle. Soon after, in Saint-Clair-sur-Epte, he agrees to peace in return for land surrounding Rouen. In the decades that follow, Rollo and his son, William Longsword, extend their holdings to what becomes known as Normandy.

987 Hugh Capet becomes king of France, establishing the Capetian line.

1027 or
1028 William, illegitimate son of Robert of Normandy, is born. Robert subsequently inherits the ducal title and departs on pilgrimage for Jerusalem, leaving William, an illegitimate seven-year-old, to claim the title.

1047 Battle of Val-ès-Dunes, in which Henri I of France comes to the aid of young William, duke of Normandy, in defeating rebel Norman barons who have challenged William's claim to the ducal title.

1053 William, now established as duke of Normandy, weds the high-born Matilda of Flanders.

1060 Henri I of France dies, leaving his young son as Philip I of France.

1066 William, duke of Normandy, invades England and seizes the crown.

1087   William, duke of Normandy and king of England, confronts the French in the Vexin, sacks Mantes, and subsequently dies.

His second surviving son, William Rufus, becomes William II of England.

1100   Death of William Rufus in the New Forest. The Conqueror's youngest son, Henry, seizes the crown as Henry I.

1106   Henry I defeats in battle and imprisons his elder brother, Robert Curthose (the Conqueror's only other surviving son).

1108   Death of Philip I of France; his son becomes Louis VI of France.

1120   Death at sea (on the White Ship) of William Aetheling, the only legitimate son of Henry I of England. In the absence of legitimate male heirs, Henry names his daughter, Matilda, as his heir.

1128   Matilda, daughter of Henry I of England and widow of the German emperor, weds Geoffrey of Anjou, who soon becomes count of Anjou (establishing the Plantagenet line).

Death of Robert Curthose's only son, William Clito (marking the end of William Clito's claim to Normandy and England).

1135   Death of Henry I of England. When his daughter, Matilda, is unable to secure the crown, England descends into almost two decades of civil war between her supporters and those of her cousin, Stephen of Blois.

1137   Death of Louis VI of France. His eldest surviving son, who has just married Eleanor of Aquitaine, becomes Louis VII.

1151   Geoffrey of Anjou and his eighteen-year-old-son Henry arrive at the French court to claim (successfully) the duchy of Normandy on Henry's behalf. Death of Geoffrey shortly thereafter.

1152   Louis VII of France and Queen Eleanor divorce; soon after, Eleanor marries Geoffrey's son, now Duke Henry of Normandy and contender for the crown of England.

1153   Death of Eustace, son and heir of Stephen of Blois and contender (with Duke Henry of Normandy) for the English crown.

1154	Henry becomes Henry II of England. He already is duke of Normandy, count of Anjou, and count of Maine. Aquitaine and Poitou significantly round out his empire through his queen, Eleanor of Aquitaine.
1155	Birth of Henry, second son of Eleanor and Henry II of England.
1157	Birth of Richard Lionheart, third son of Eleanor and Henry II of England.
1158	Birth of Geoffrey, fourth son of Eleanor and Henry II of England.
1160?	Marriage of Marguerite of France (age two) and Prince Henry of England (age five), with the Norman Vexin as Marguerite's dowry.
1165	Birth of Philip (eventually Philip II of France), only son of Louis VII of France.
1166?	Affair begins between Henry II and Rosamond Clifford, ending with her death in 1177.
1166 or early **1167**	Birth of John, last child of Eleanor and Henry II of England.
1168	Henry the Lion, duke of Saxony and Bavaria, weds Matilda, the eldest daughter (born in 1156) of Eleanor and Henry II of England.
1169	At Montmirail, Henry II announces his intention of dividing his realm between his three eldest surviving sons (Henry, Richard, and Geoffrey), while Louis VII agrees to betroth his youngest daughter, Alais, to Richard.
1170	Prince Henry is crowned king during his father's (Henry II's) lifetime; he is henceforth known as Henry the Young King, or Henry the Younger.
1173	Warfare between Henry II and Louis VII, in which Henry's queen, Eleanor, and his three eldest surviving sons (Henry the Younger, Richard, and Geoffrey) ally with Henry's enemy, the king of France. After Henry II's victory, Eleanor becomes his prisoner until his death in 1189.

1177   Emperor Frederick Barbarossa unexpectedly makes peace with his longtime enemy, the Church.

Joanna Plantagenet (born in 1165 to Eleanor and Henry II of England) weds William II of Sicily.

1179   Coronation of young Philip of France; illness of Louis VII.

1180   Death of Louis VII of France; Philip's reign (as Philip II) officially begins. Philip weds Isabelle of Hainaut during this same year.

1182   After losing his lands (at the hands of Emperor Frederick Barbarossa), Duke Henry the Lion is exiled from Germany, fleeing to the court of his father-in-law, Henry II of England.

1183   Death of Henry the Younger, while rebelling against his father.

1186   Death of Geoffrey, son of Henry II, in Paris. This leaves Henry II with two surviving sons, Richard Lionheart and John. A son, Arthur, is born posthumously to Geoffrey.

1187   A son, Louis (the future Louis VIII), is born to Philip of France.

Saladin conquers the kingdom of Jerusalem, excepting Tyre.

1188   In response to escalating disputes between the two monarchs, Henry II renounces his vassal's allegiance to Philip and goes to war. Richard Lionheart does homage to Philip.

1189   Richard Lionheart joins Philip of France in fighting Richard's father, Henry II of England. Death of Henry II; Richard Lionheart becomes King Richard I; Eleanor emerges from prison.

News arrives of the fall of Jerusalem to Saladin. After Henry II's death and Richard's coronation, Richard and Philip agree to set off on crusade together—a plan that is temporarily set back by the death of Philip's wife, Isabelle.

Emperor Frederick Barbarossa departs on crusade.

Duke Henry the Lion returns to Saxony, where he reclaims his lands.

King William II of Sicily dies, leaving no children. William's aunt (and heir) is married to Henry Hohenstaufen, who is

Emperor Frederick Barbarossa's son and heir. William's widow is Joanna, Richard Lionheart's youngest sister.

Guy of Lusignan, king of Jerusalem, attempts to besiege the city of Acre and is surrounded by Saladin's forces. The crusaders hang on through two desperate winters.

1190   Philip and Richard meet with their respective armies in Vézelay to launch the Third Crusade. Philip arrives in Sicily before Richard and ingratiates himself with Sicily's new ruler, Tancred, who has imprisoned Joanna. Richard sacks Messina, prompting Tancred to provide Lionheart with a fortune in gold and to release Joanna. In turn, Richard recognizes Tancred's claim to Sicily and agrees to betroth Tancred's infant daughter to Richard's nephew (and Geoffrey's son), Arthur of Brittany.

Frederick Barbarossa drowns en route to the Holy Land, leaving his son and heir, Henry Hohenstaufen, in his place.

Henry of Champagne (Eleanor's grandson) arrives in the Holy Land, with troops and siege engines. Joins Guy of Lusignan's siege of Acre.

Eleanor (determined that Richard not marry Philip's sister, Alais) crosses the Alps in midwinter to deliver a bride for Richard—Princess Berengaria of Navarre.

1191   Site of King Arthur's tomb said to have been found at Glastonbury.

Eleanor and Berengaria encounter Henry Hohenstaufen in Lombardy, en route to Rome and his coronation (as Emperor Henry VI). The women arrive in Sicily following the departure of Philip, who is incensed over Tancred's alliance with Richard as well as with Richard's impending marriage to Berengaria.

Henry Hohenstaufen is crowned emperor in Rome. He besieges Naples but returns after an epidemic decimates his army.

Marriage of Richard and Berengaria in Cyprus following Richard's successful invasion of the island. Guy of Lusignan arrives, desperate for Richard's support in retaining the crown of Jerusalem.

Richard arrives in Acre and relieves the beleaguered forces there. Acre soon falls to the crusaders, but Richard antagonizes Leopold of Austria as well as Philip of France.

Philip returns to France. Richard butchers Saladin's garrison and then leads the crusaders down the coast, en route to Jerusalem. The Battle of Arsuf.

Richard moves his forces closer to Jerusalem, while Saladin withdraws into Jerusalem itself. Winter leaves the crusaders mercilessly exposed.

1192   Richard retreats to Ascalon. Desertions—and tensions between the French and the English—increase.

Conrad of Montferrat is chosen king of Jerusalem and is assassinated shortly after.

Word reaches Richard that Philip has returned to France and is plotting with John to take Richard's Norman lands.

Richard at last orders a retreat and agrees to a truce with Saladin. He then departs by sea for home.

After shipwreck, Richard finds himself in lands held by vassals of Leopold of Austria. Hunted down by his enemies, he is captured outside of Vienna and imprisoned by Leopold. Unopposed, Philip helps himself to Richard's lands, while John works to establish himself as king in Richard's place.

1193   Emperor Henry VI (Henry Hohenstaufen) takes control of the royal prisoner and demands an astronomical ransom for his release. John continues to stir up trouble in England and courts Philip's support for his claim to the English crown, while Philip continues to seize Richard's lands. By autumn, Richard's subjects have collected the greater part of the ransom (which Henry plans to use to pay for his own conquest of southern Italy).

Death of Saladin in early 1193, not long after Richard's departure.

Philip repudiates his second wife, Ingeborg of Denmark, who refuses to accept the repudiation.

1194   Richard finally is freed and departs for England. He gathers an army and sails for Normandy, where he relieves a critical siege and sends Philip flying. John comes to beg forgiveness, which Richard grants. By now, Philip and Richard are deadly enemies. Richard comes within a hair of capturing Philip, but Philip manages to elude him. Although Richard wins back a great portion of his lands, Philip still is deeply entrenched in Normandy.

Death of Tancred of Sicily. Emperor Henry VI (Henry Hohenstaufen) comes to an accord with the German duke Henry the Lion. Emperor Henry then captures Sicily. After many years of childlessness, Emperor Henry's wife gives birth to an heir, the future Emperor Frederick II.

Death of Leopold, duke of Austria.

1195   Reconciliation between Richard and Berengaria.

Death of Duke Henry the Lion.

Princess Alais of France is at last released, twenty-six years after her original betrothal to Richard. Philip immediately marries her off to a minor nobleman, William of Ponthieu.

Fighting continues between Richard and Philip, culminating in Richard's dramatic rescue of the castle of Issoudun. The Treaty of Louviers follows (in early 1196).

1196   The Treaty of Louviers, agreed to by Richard and Philip, shows the steady military gains that Richard has made since his return to Normandy in 1194. Yet Philip is still a threat there.

Soon after the treaty has been agreed upon, Richard holds court on the Isle of Andely, despite the treaty's provision that Andely "shall not be fortified."

Philip marries Agnes of Meran; welcomes Richard's nephew, Arthur of Brittany, to his court; and successfully besieges the Norman castle at Aumale.

After Philip's conquest of Aumale, Richard begins to fortify the river portions of Andely. In retribution, the archbishop of Rouen places Normandy under interdict and departs for Rome to plead his cause. Richard sends off his own ecclesiastical team to defend his action.

Joanna Plantagenet marries Raymond of Toulouse as part of an agreement between Richard and Raymond.

Emperor Henry VI (Henry Hohenstaufen) is rebuffed by the German princes, who block his bid to make the imperial crown hereditary.

1197   In late 1196 or early 1197, Richard starts to build his magnificent castle on the Rock of Andely.

Richard and Philip's military confrontations continue. Richard captures Philip of Dreux, the fighting bishop of Beauvais, and forms an alliance with Baldwin of Flanders, who captures Philip but allows his safe return to Paris.

The two kings meet near Andely. Here, Philip utters his boast that he could seize this castle even if its walls were made of iron (leading Richard to boast that he would be able to defend it against all comers). They agree to another truce, to last until early 1199. The terms show Richard's continued gains, although the all-important Vexin remains in Philip's hands.

The unexpected death of Emperor Henry VI (Henry Hohenstaufen) leaves his infant son (the future Emperor Frederick II) with no hereditary right to the imperial throne, although he is crowned King of Sicily. The Hohenstaufens and Philip of France support Philip of Swabia (Henry Hohenstaufen's younger brother) as the new emperor; their opponents, including Richard, support Duke Henry the Lion's son, Otto of Brunswick, who is Richard's nephew.

In October, after the archbishop agrees to an exchange of lands, Richard officially receives title to Andely and its Rock. But he has already been building there for a year.

1198   Innocent III comes to the papal throne and works to secure the imperial crown for Otto of Brunswick. He also champions the cause of Ingeborg of Denmark versus Philip of France.

Richard issues his first charter from Château-Gaillard in February. By late August, he has pulled together an impressive coalition of allies, including the newly crowned emperor, Otto IV (Otto of Brunswick).

1199   Warfare continues between Richard and Philip, with Philip steadily losing ground. Then Richard shockingly dies at Châlus. At his request, he is buried with his father at the Abbey of Fontevraud.

John becomes king of England. Soon warfare breaks out between him and Philip, who at the same time is battling the pope to retain his marriage to Agnes of Meran.

1200   Truce between John and Philip, according to which John keeps his Continental lands (with the exception of the Norman Vexin and other Norman properties) and Philip's son and heir, Louis, marries John's niece, Blanche of Castile. Everyone hopes that peace has come at last.

John sets aside his first wife to marry Isabelle of Angoulême, already betrothed to the heir of Lusignan. The Lusignans demand that Philip of France right their wrongs, but at present Philip is tied up in quarrels with the Church over his marriage to Agnes of Meran, who has borne him a son.

1201   The Church forces Philip to acknowledge Ingeborg. Philip welcomes John and his new queen to Paris. Agnes dies. Philip does nothing about John while awaiting Rome's verdict on the legitimacy of his son by Agnes.

1202   Philip learns that the pope has legitimized his two children by Agnes. Philip now summons John to Paris to account for injuries done to John's vassals (the Lusignans) and to his own overlord, the king of France. This leads to war, in which Philip quickly gains the advantage, although the tide turns when John unexpectedly rescues his mother, Queen Eleanor, at Mirebeau and captures Arthur of Brittany. John now inherits Angoulême.

1203   Arthur disappears, fate unknown, although it is widely rumored that John has murdered him. Philip strikes in Normandy, but Château-Gaillard still blocks his path to Rouen.

Philip encamps his men across the Seine from Gaillard, sets up a pontoon bridge, and establishes his troops on the Isle of Andely. John fails to block him. The residents of Petit Andely flee to Château-Gaillard. Philip puts Gaillard under siege. Gaillard's commander, Roger de Lacy, releases many of the refugees as "useless mouths," who are caught between the lines and reduced to starvation.

1204   Philip succeeds in assaulting and crippling Gaillard's advance works (the Tower of Saint-Jacques) and takes the next layer of fortification by stealth. After successfully targeting the drawbridge to the innermost citadel, Philip takes Gaillard on March 6, 1204. Soon Rouen and all of Normandy follow, along with other major portions of the Angevin empire.

During the years that follow, the English fail to retake their lost territories, while Gaillard remains an active fortress until the late sixteenth century, when it is dismantled and falls into ruin.

Notes

⚜

INTRODUCTION

1. As told by Giraldus Cambrensis, *De Principis Instructione Liber*, ed. George F. Warner, in *Giraldi Cambrensis Opera* (London: Eyre & Spottiswoode, 1891), 8:289–90.

1. MERLIN'S PROPHECY

Selected sources for this and subsequent chapters are listed, by chapter, in the approximate order in which they informed the text: Geoffrey of Monmouth, "The Prophecies of Merlin," in *History of the Kings of Britain* [henceforth cited as Geoffrey of Monmouth, "The Prophecies of Merlin"], trans. Sebastian Evans (London: J. M. Dent, 1928); *The Autobiography of Giraldus Cambrensis* [henceforth cited as Giraldus, *Autobiography*], ed. and trans. H. E. Butler (London: Jonathan Cape, 1937); Ralph of Coggeshall, *Chronicon Anglicanum*, ed. Joseph Stevenson (London: Longman, 1875); John of Glastonbury, *The Chronicle of Glastonbury Abbey: An Edition, Translation, and Study of John of Glastonbury's* Cronica sive Antiquitates Glastoniensis Ecclesie, ed. James P. Carley, trans. David Townsend (London: Boydell Press, 1985); Leslie Alcock, *Arthur's Britain: History and Archeology, AD 367–634* (London: Allen Lane/Penguin Press, 1971); Étienne de Rouen, *Draco normanicus*, in *Chronicles of the Reigns of Stephen, Henry II, and Richard I*, ed. Richard Howlett (London: Eyre & Spottiswoode, 1889); Ralph de Diceto, *Opera Historica: The Historical Works of Master Ralph de Diceto, Dean of London* [henceforth cited as Ralph de Diceto], ed. William Stubbs, 2 vols. (London: Longman, 1876); *The Historical Works of Giraldus Cambrensis* [henceforth cited as Giraldus, *Historical Works*], ed. and trans. Thomas Forester (London: Henry G. Bohn, 1863); Roger of Wendover [formerly attributed to Matthew Paris], *Roger of Wendover's* Flowers of History: *Comprising the History of England from the Descent of the Saxons to A.D. 1235* [henceforth cited as Roger of

Wendover], 2 vols., trans. J. A. Giles (London: Henry G. Bohn, 1849); John Gillingham, *Richard I* (New Haven, CT: Yale University Press, 1999); John Gillingham, *Richard the Lionheart* (New York: Times Books, 1978); Jean Flori, *Richard the Lionheart: King and Knight*, trans. Jean Birrell (Edinburgh: Edinburgh University Press, 2006); Jean Flori, *Eleanor of Aquitaine: Queen and Rebel*, trans. Olive Classe (Edinburgh: Edinburgh University Press, 2007); Amy Kelly, *Eleanor of Aquitaine and the Four Kings* (Cambridge, MA: Harvard University Press, 1978 [first published 1950]); Jane Martindale, "Eleanor of Aquitaine," in *Richard Coeur de Lion in History and Myth*, ed. Janet L. Nelson (London: Centre for Late Antique and Medieval Studies, King's College, 1992); William Marshal, *History of William Marshal* [henceforth cited as *History of William Marshal*], ed. A. J. Holden, trans. S. Gregory, historical notes D. Crouch, vol. 1 (London: Anglo-Norman Text Society, 2002); Robert de Monte [also known as Robert de Torigni], *The Chronicles of Robert de Monte* [henceforth cited as Robert de Monte], trans. Joseph Stevenson (Lampeter, UK: Llanerch Publishers, 1991 [first published 1856]); W. L. Warren, *Henry II* (London: Eyre Methuen, 1973); Christopher Harper-Bill and Nicholas Vincent, *Henry II: New Interpretations* (Woodbridge, UK: Boydell Press, 2007); Jim Bradbury, *Philip Augustus: King of France, 1180–1223* (London: Longman, 1998); Walter Map, *De Nugis Curialium* [henceforth cited as Walter Map], ed. and trans. M. R. James, rev. C. N. L. Brooke and R. A. B. Mynors (Oxford, UK: Clarendon Press, 1983); Andreas Capellanus, *The Art of Courtly Love*, ed. and trans. John Jay Parry (New York: Columbia University Press, 1990); Bertran de Born, *The Poems of the Troubadour Bertran de Born*, ed. William D. Paden Jr., Tilde Sankovitch, and Patricia H. Stäblein (Berkeley: University of California Press, 1986); Lionel Landon, *The Itinerary of King Richard I* (London: J. W. Ruddock & Sons, 1935); Rigord, *La vie de Philippe II Auguste* [henceforth cited as Rigord], trans. from Latin by François Guizot (Clermont-Ferrand, France: Paléo, 2003); Roger of Howden [also known as Roger of Hoveden], *The Annals of Roger de Hoveden, Comprising the History of England and of Other Countries of Europe from A.D. 732 to A.D. 1201* [henceforth cited as Roger of Howden], trans. Henry T. Riley, 2 vols. (London: Henry G. Bohn, 1853); David C. Douglas and George W. Greenaway, eds., *English Historical Documents, 1042–1189* (New York: Oxford University Press, 1953); John Gillingham, "Some Legends of Richard the Lionheart: Their Development and Their Influence," in *Richard Coeur de Lion in History and Myth*, ed. Janet L. Nelson (London: Centre for Late Antique and Medieval Studies, King's College, 1992); John Gillingham, *The Angevin Empire*, 2nd ed. (London: Arnold; New York: Oxford University Press, 2001).

1. The full citation reads: "This shall the Eagle of the broken covenant gild over, and the Eagle shall rejoice in her third nesting." Geoffrey of Monmouth, "The Prophecies of Merlin," 176.

2. Giraldus, *Autobiography*, 119. The exact wording on the cross is disputed. Ralph of Coggeshall does not mention Guenevere (*Chronicon Anglicanum*, 36).

3. Unfortunately, this tomb did not survive the Reformation, when its bones were scattered about, lost forever. As for the inscribed lead cross, it was last seen around 1542, while the two mysterious stone monuments flanking the original burial spot were last noted in 1777. See *The Chronicle of Glastonbury Abbey*, 183, 245–46. On the

stone monuments (called pyramids), see 276–77, n47. On the fate of the tomb and lead cross, see Alcock, *Arthur's Britain*, 74–75.

4. See de Rouen, "Draco normanicus," in *Chronicles of the Reigns of Stephen, Henry II, and Richard I*, 2:600, for an interpretation of one particular prophecy.

Merlin, unlike Arthur, was an entirely fictional character, a legendary prophet and wizard who combined both Christian and pagan traditions. Geoffrey of Monmouth appears to have borrowed freely from legend in his "The Prophecies of Merlin," which he began as an independent work but then incorporated into his *History of the Kings of Britain*. Despite disclaimers to the contrary, he most likely made up the rest. The result was a highly obscure series of prophecies that most people took seriously, in particular when it came to Henry II and his family. See William Stubbs's comment in his introduction to Ralph de Diceto, 1:lvi–lvii.

Interestingly, Henry himself appears to have placed little credence in Merlin. According to Giraldus Cambrensis, Henry readily challenged one especially dire prophecy without ill effect, and then remarked, "Who now will have any faith in that liar, Merlin?" See Giraldus, *Historical Works*, 238–39.

5. The chroniclers Roger of Wendover and Ralph de Diceto both interpreted the "Eagle of the broken covenant" prophecy as referring to Eleanor and Richard Lionheart. Roger of Wendover, 2:77–78; Ralph de Diceto, 2:67.

6. Eleanor's two daughters by Louis were Marie and Alix; her five sons by Henry were William (who died in infancy), Henry, Richard, Geoffrey, and John; her three daughters by Henry were Matilda, Eleanor, and Joanna.

7. Crowning young Henry was not a good idea, according to William Marshal, in whose care Henry II had placed his eldest son: "The King did not act wisely when he forced all his barons to pay homage to his son." *History of William Marshal*, 99.

8. According to Robert de Monte, the tipping point came when "the elder king Henry . . . removed from his son's council, and from attending upon him, Asculf de St. Hilary, and some other young knights." At this, the younger Henry "left his father in anger . . . and went to the king of France" (117). This chronicler also adds that "no landed inheritance had as yet been assigned him, although he had an annual allowance from his father . . . , but this was little to satisfy the largeness of his heart" (146).

9. William Marshal observed that the young king "spent lavishly, for he was aiming at those heights which a king, and son of a king, should rise to, if he wishes to attain such high eminence." Henry II, however, "thought to himself that his son was far too lavish," and "there were many who advised [the young king] to turn against his father, and use force to reduce him . . . to doing all his son's desires and wishes" (*History of William Marshal*, 101–103).

10. See chapter 5, note 11.

11. Based upon Giraldus, *Autobiography*, 37–38.

12. Although W. L. Warren argues, based on an 1169 letter of John of Salisbury, that Alais was dowerless (*Henry II*, 145n2).

13. Warren, *Henry II*, 121.

14. Flori concludes that "between 1168 and 1173 she came near to wielding real power. But the handicap of her gender and the failure of her rebellion soon put it out of reach" (*Eleanor of Aquitaine*, 279).

15. Giraldus, *Historical Works*, 252. On the episode of the bishopric, see Giraldus, *Autobiography*, 59–60. Eventually Giraldus responded to a summons from Henry and became the king's clerk, probably around 1184 (Giraldus, *Autobiography*, 81).

16. Walter Map, 479. Map seems to have served Henry during the 1170s and was a friend of Giraldus Cambrensis.

17. According to Andreas, on May 1, 1174, Marie of Champagne [Eleanor's daughter by Louis VII] gave the following verdict: "We declare and we hold as firmly established that love cannot exert its powers between two people who are married to each other. For lovers give each other everything freely, under no compulsion of necessity, but married people are in duty bound to give in to each other's desires and deny themselves to each other in nothing" (Andreas Capellanus, *The Art of Courtly Love*, 106–7). According to Andreas, Queen Eleanor readily agreed that "love can exert no power between husband and wife" (Andreas Capellanus, *The Art of Courtly Love*, 175).

18. Landon cites the *Chronicle of Meaux* as well as the author of the *Gesta Regis Henrici Secundi* and Giraldus Cambrensis as sources for this story (*Itinerary of King Richard I*, Appendix H, 228).

19. Landon, *Itinerary of Richard I*, Appendix H, 228.

20. Walter Map tells this story (*De Nugis Curialium*, 226). Another version of the story appears in the same source on page 453.

21. Rigord (20–22) focuses on the adventure—getting lost in the forest while hunting—that led to Philip's illness, while Roger of Howden is more interested in Louis' visit to Canterbury (1:516–18). Robert de Monte (132–33, 135) gives a briefer version of both.

22. Giraldus, *Historical Works*, 250–51.

23. Giraldus, *Historical Works*, 162–63.

24. Roger of Howden says he died "from bruises which he had received from the hoofs of horses at a tournament," and was buried in the cathedral of that city [Notre-Dame de Paris]. Rigord says that he became ill (82). Geoffrey's son, Arthur, was born after Geoffrey's death.

25. After the death of King Béla, Marguerite "assumed the cross and set out for Jerusalem, and remained in Acre, in the land of Jerusalem, in the service of God, until the end of her life." She died in 1197 (Roger of Howden, 2:394, 409).

26. See note 12.

27. Giraldus, *Historical Works*, 163.

28. Philip's wall, constructed between the 1180s and 1210, replaced a wall of Roman origins that merely encircled the Ile de la Cité. This new wall, reinforced upstream by a chain across the river and downstream by the Louvre fortress, stood more than thirty feet high and had more than seventy towers along its length, reinforced by a ditch on its outer side. Remnants of this wall (which defended both the Right Bank and the Left Bank) can still be seen near the Panthéon (Rue Clovis at Rue du Cardinal-Lemoine) and in the Marais (along the Rue des Jardins-Saint-Paul), as well as in several more obscure locations. The enclosed area, although representing a quantum leap in size from the area Paris had occupied for centuries, nevertheless seems minuscule by today's standards.

29. Louis, born in 1187.

30. John Gillingham, who strongly disagrees with those who hold that Richard was homosexual, gives a good summary of the issue's historiography in *Richard I*, 84, 263–66, and *Richard the Lionheart*, 298.

31. Roger of Howden says that "at night [they] had not separate chambers," which may have meant the same thing (2:64).

32. According to Roger of Howden, "The king of England, not forgetful of the injuries which the king, his son, had done to him in return for a similar promotion, made answer that he would on no account do so" (2:99). According to Roger of Wendover, Henry refused to agree to these demands "in the existing state of things, lest he should be said to have done so by constraint and not of his own free will" (2:72).

33. Rigord, 108–9; Roger of Howden, 2:98–99. Although according to Roger of Wendover, Richard did homage to Philip "for the whole territory of his father which belonged to the crown of France, saving the tenure to his father as long as he lived, and saving the allegiance due to his father" (2:72–73).

34. Roger of Howden, 2:106–7.

35. Warren, *Henry II*, 622–23.

36. William Marshal tells of personally stopping Richard Lionheart from pursuing and capturing (and possibly killing) Henry, his father (*History of William Marshal*, 447–51).

37. Roger of Howden, 2:110–11; Roger of Wendover, 2:76.

38. Roger of Wendover, 2:76; *History of William Marshal*, 463–67; Roger of Howden, 2:111; Gerald of Wales [Giraldus Cambrensis], in Douglas and Greenaway, *English Historical Documents, 1042–1189*, 384–85.

39. Roger of Wendover, 2:76; Roger of Howden, 2:11. Yet William Marshal, who was there, gives a much less dramatic account: "He [Richard] stood before the body for some time, without moving, and then he moved up to the head of the body, where he immediately lost himself again in deep thought, saying not a word of ill or good" (*History of William Marshal*, 473).

2. TURNING POINT

Selected sources for this chapter: Robert de Monte; Karl Jordan, *Henry the Lion: A Biography*, trans. P. S. Falla (Oxford, UK: Clarendon Press, 1986); Peter Munz, *Frederick Barbarossa: A Study in Medieval Politics* (London: Eyre & Spottiswoode, 1969); Geoffrey Barraclough, *The Origins of Modern Germany* (Oxford, UK: Basil Blackwell, 1966).

1. Robert de Monte gives these details, 145.

3. ROLLO THE VIKING

Selected sources for this chapter: David C. Douglas, "Rollo of Normandy," *English Historical Review* 57 (October 1942): 417–36; David Bates, *Normandy before 1066*

(London: Longman, 1982); Dudo of Saint-Quentin, *History of the Normans*, trans. Eric Christiansen (Woodbridge, UK: Boydell Press, 1998); Rigord; Daniel Power, *The Norman Frontier in the Twelfth and Early Thirteenth Centuries* (Cambridge, UK: Cambridge University Press, 2004); Elizabeth M. Hallam, *Capetian France, 987–1328* (New York: Longman, 1980); Jim Bradbury, *The Capetians: Kings of France, 987–1328* (London: Hambledon Continuum, 2007); John Le Patourel, *The Norman Empire* (Oxford, UK: Clarendon Press, 1976); David C. Douglas, *William the Conqueror: The Norman Impact upon England* (Berkeley: University of California Press, 1964); Eleanor Searle, *Predatory Kinship and the Creation of Norman Power, 840–1066* (Berkeley: University of California Press, 1988); William of Poitiers [Gulielmus Pictaviensis], *The Gesta Guillelmi of William of Poitiers* [henceforth cited as William of Poitiers], ed. and trans. R. H. C. Davis and Marjorie Chibnall (Oxford, UK: Clarendon Press, 1998); Frank Stenton, ed., *The Bayeux Tapestry: A Comprehensive Survey* (London: Phaidon, 1957); David C. Douglas, *The Norman Achievement, 1050–1100* (London: Eyre & Spotteswoode, 1969); Lewis Thorpe, *The Bayeux Tapestry and the Norman Invasion* (London: Folio Society, 1973); Jim Bradbury, *The Battle of Hastings* (Stroud, UK: Sutton, 1998); Orderic Vitalis, *The Ecclesiastical History of Orderic Vitalis* [henceforth cited as Orderic], ed. and trans. Marjorie Chibnall, 6 vols. (Oxford, UK: Clarendon Press, 1969); Suger, Abbot of Saint Denis, *The Deeds of Louis the Fat* [henceforth cited as Suger], ed. and trans. Richard Cusimano and John Moorhead (Washington, DC: Catholic University of America Press, 1992); William of Malmesbury, *William of Malmesbury's Chronicle of the Kings of England* [henceforth cited as William of Malmesbury], ed. and trans. J. A. Giles (London: Henry G. Bohn, 1968 [first published 1847]); R. H. C. Davis, *The Normans and Their Myth* (London: Thames and Hudson, 1976); John Le Patourel, "Guernsey and Jersey in the Middle Ages," in *Feudal Empires: Norman and Plantagenet* (London: Hambledon Press, 1984); Charles Homer Haskins, *The Normans in European History* (Boston: Houghton Mifflin, 1915); Georges Duby, *France in the Middle Ages: From Hugh Capet to Joan of Arc*, trans. Juliet Vale (Oxford, UK: Blackwell, 1991); Jean-François Lemarignier, *Recherches sur l'hommage en marche et les frontières féodales* (Lille, France: Bibliothéque Universitaire, 1945); Douglas and Greenaway, *English Historical Documents*; William of Newburgh, *The History of William of Newburgh* [henceforth cited as William of Newburgh], trans. Joseph Stevenson (Lampeter, UK: Llanerch Publishers, 1996 [first published 1856]); Eadmer, *Eadmer's History of Recent Events in England* [henceforth cited as Eadmer], trans. Geoffrey Bosanquet (London: Cresset Press, 1964).

1. Dudo's translator, Eric Christiansen, notes that Dudo "is not a reliable source for the early history of the Normans; nor did he know of any; nor do we." Dudo of Saint-Quentin, *History of the Normans*, xv. See Dudo's account of the events at Saint-Clair-sur-Epte, 46–50.

2. Although the derivation may be clear to English speakers, it would not necessarily be obvious to the French, for whom "man of the north" is "un homme du nord" or "un homme du septentrion." The twelfth-century French chronicler Rigord explained to his readers that Normandy (*Normandie* in French), formerly known as Neustria, received its name because "in their barbaric tongue, they gave themselves

the name of *Normann*, which means man of the north, because they had indeed come from the north, which in their language is expressed by the word *nort,* just as *mann* means man" (Rigord, 74).

3. Hugh Capet's name is a mystery, but may have referred to the cloak, or cape, of St. Martin, the most important relic of the abbey of Saint-Martin at Tours, over which Hugh served as lay abbot (see Hallam, *Capetian France*, Appendix I, 330–31). Despite the limited domains over which he effectively ruled, Hugh Capet—who replaced the last of the Carolingians (the descendants of Charlemagne) in the west—is generally reckoned as the first king of France.

4. John Le Patourel discusses this point in *The Norman Empire*, 5–8.

5. See Douglas, *William the Conqueror*, Appendix A, 379–82. In a more recent addition to the debate, Eleanor Searle discounts the tradition that Arlette's father was a tanner and, citing the twelfth-century Norman chronicler Orderic Vitalis, contends that Fulbert must have been a member of Robert's household. Searle, *Predatory Kinship and the Creation of Norman Power*, 154. Note that "Arlette" appears to be an updating of the original "Herleve."

6. Unlike the events surrounding the origins of Normandy, the story of William's rise to power and kingship, including the Battle of Hastings, received a solid (although understandably biased) contemporary account from William of Poitiers, one of Duke William's chaplains. See *The Gesta Guillelmi of William of Poitiers*, ed. and trans. R. H. C. Davis and Marjorie Chibnall.

7. This can clearly be seen in Stenton, *The Bayeux Tapestry*, plate 39.

8. A contemporary chronicler such as Richer of Rheims could as late as 996 disparagingly refer to the then ruler of Normandy as a pirate chief, and Viking raiders turned up in Rouen as late as 1014. Still, by the eleventh century there is a certain tone of embarrassment among Normans about their Viking roots and an eagerness to define themselves in terms of the Frankish, or French, society into which they aspired to meld. When, a century after Richer, a contemporary chronicler has Bohemund, son of Robert Guiscard, rather stridently proclaim to his fellow Normans in Italy, "Are we not Franks? Did not our fathers come from France?" he is merely saying what all good Normans by that time wanted to hear—much like the scion of a latter-day robber baron emphasizing his genteel connections on the distaff side. Richer and Bohemund quoted in Douglas, *The Norman Achievement*, 24–26.

9. As early as William Longsword's time, the Norse of Rouen spoke French, and one had to go to outlying districts such as Bayeux to find the Scandinavian tongue spoken.

10. See *The Bayeux Tapestry and the Norman Invasion*, plates 69–71, 74.

11. Orderic, 5:25.

12. "Being warlike descendants of the Danes, the Normans are ignorant of the ways of peace and serve it unwillingly," Abbot Suger noted, from the twelfth-century French perspective (Suger, 70). Writing at about the same time, William of Malmesbury wrote: "The Normans are a race inured to war, and hardly live without it, fierce in rushing against the enemy; and where strength fails of success, ready to use stratagem, or to corrupt by bribery." They "envy their equals, wish to excel their superiors, and plunder their subjects" (William of Malmesbury, 280).

13. For a reassessment, see Davis, *The Normans and Their Myth*, and Bates, *Normandy before 1066*. See also Le Patourel, "Guernsey and Jersey in the Middle Ages," in *Feudal Empires*, pt. 4:444, and Le Patourel, *The Norman Empire*, 288.

14. Haskins, *The Normans in European History*, 50–51. Eleanor Searle does find evidence that Normandy's earliest Norse chieftains maintained the purity of their bloodline through multiple wives and by limiting the succession to one male heir, born of a Scandinavian woman (*Predatory Kinship*, chapter 7). But intermarriage with the Franks had taken place from the outset, and by the end of the tenth century, the practice that Searle notes (if, indeed, it had ever been widespread) was already breaking down.

15. For background on this important power shift in the French Vexin, see Lemarignier, *Recherches sur l'hommage en marche et les frontières féodales*, 42–43. Basically, the lord of the Vexin had retired to a monastery without first providing for an heir.

16. Orderic, 4:75.

17. Orderic asserts that Henri I had granted William's father the French portion of the Vexin in return for the duke's aid in helping Henri retain his crown (4:75, 77). Marjorie Chibnall notes, though, that there is no proof that this ever happened (Orderic, 4:xxxii).

18. "An account of the death and character of William the Conqueror, written by a monk of Caen," in Douglas and Greenaway, *English Historical Documents*, 280.

19. William of Newburgh called him "this ferocious prince" (402).

20. Orderic, 4:79.

21. William of Malmesbury gives the story of the pommel ripping into William's stomach (William of Malmesbury, 310). Orderic and others merely write of the Conqueror's fatal illness, without mentioning any specific injury (Orderic, 4:79).

22. "An account of the death and character of William the Conqueror, written by a monk of Caen," in Douglas and Greenaway, *English Historical Documents*, 279–80; Orderic, 4:81.

23. Corroborating versions appear in the chronicles of Eadmer (26) and William of Malmesbury (311), the latter in a way that redounds to the credit of William's youngest son, Henry; but Orderic has the fullest account (Orderic, 4:105–9).

4. FATHERS AND SONS

Selected sources for this chapter: Charles Wendell David, *Robert Curthose, Duke of Normandy* (Cambridge, MA: Harvard University Press, 1920); Florence of Worcester, *The Chronicle of Florence of Worcester* [henceforth cited as Florence of Worcester], ed. and trans. Thomas Forester (London: Henry G. Bohn, 1854); Suger; Orderic; Andrew W. Lewis, *Royal Succession in Capetian France: Studies on Familial Order and the State* (Cambridge, MA: Harvard University Press, 1981); Duby, *France in the Middle Ages*; William of Malmesbury; Robert Fawtier, *The Capetian Kings of France: Monarchy and Nation (987–1328)*, trans. Lionel Butler and R. J. Adam (London: Macmillan, 1960); W. L. Warren, "The Death of William Rufus," *History Today*

9 (January 1959): 22–29; Duncan Grinnell-Milne, *The Killing of William Rufus: An Investigation in the New Forest* (Newton Abbot, UK: David & Charles, 1968); F. H. M. Parker, "The Forest Laws and the Death of William Rufus," *English Historical Review* 27 (January 1912): 26–38; Frank Barlow, *William Rufus* (Berkeley: University of California Press, 1983); Walter Map; Sumner McKnight Crosby, *The Royal Abbey of Saint-Denis: From Its Beginnings to the Death of Suger, 475–1151* (New Haven, CT: Yale University Press, 1987); Jean Dunabin, *France in the Making, 843–1180* (New York: Oxford University Press, 1985).

1. See David, *Robert Curthose*, 39n100.

2. Suger, 27.

3. Orderic notes that Philip "entrusted the administration of the whole kingdom to him" (4:265). This probably was an exaggeration, although according to Andrew W. Lewis, Louis seems to have played "a very active role in the royal government" from 1100 on (*Royal Succession in Capetian France*, 51). Given the times, this would have been primarily a military role, with Louis representing Capetian interests in the field (Duby, *France in the Middle Ages*, 119).

4. Of these, William of Malmesbury was probably the most insulting: "The French king, inactive, and surfeited with daily gluttony, came hiccupping, through repletion, to the war: but, as he was making great professions, . . . the king of England met him by the way; with which his resolution being borne down, he unbuckled his armour, and went back to his gormandizing" (William of Malmesbury, 331).

5. See Duby, *France in the Middle Ages*, 121, and Fawtier, *The Capetian Kings of France*, 17, 19.

6. Suger, 63.

7. Although William Rufus's death was officially treated as an accident, it may not have been. See Warren, "The Death of William Rufus," and Grinnell-Milne, *The Killing of William Rufus*. An earlier article, by F. H. M. Parker, links the reputed origins of New Forest with a possible cover-up of conspiracy to murder William Rufus ("The Forest Laws and the Death of William Rufus").

8. Quote and description from William of Malmesbury, 446–47.

9. The sobriquet "Beauclerk" seems to have surfaced well after Henry's death, as did "clericus," from which it probably derived. According to Frank Barlow, "there is nothing to suggest that it was a pet name in the family or had any contemporary currency, and is best forgotten" (*William Rufus*, 13).

10. Robert died in captivity just months before Henry's own death.

11. Clovis was buried here, with Ste. Geneviève by his side, and after her sainthood both the church and its abbey were dedicated to her. Replaced by the Panthéon, no trace of the first church or of its royal inhabitant remains. Ste. Geneviève's relics were destroyed at the height of the Revolution, but her sarcophagus stone has been preserved in a shrine within the neighboring church of Saint-Étienne-du-Mont.

12. Of these, perhaps the most dangerous was the count of Meulan. Powerfully based in Normandy and England (where he was earl of Leicester) as well as in the French Vexin, the count additionally held the lordship of Le Monceau-Saint-Gervais, from where he was perfectly capable of sacking the Cité, should he be so inclined (see Duby, *France in the Middle Ages*, 128). When Louis was young (according to the

almost-contemporary account of Walter Map), he "was unable to go outside the gates of Paris to the third milestone without the leave or escort of the neighbouring princes, and not one of them either kept or feared his orders" (Walter Map, 443).

13. According to ninth-century legend, the Romans martyred St. Denis on Montmartre, or Hill of Martyrs, giving it its name. After decapitation (so goes the legend), the bishop picked up his severed head and walked the several miles northward to his chosen place of burial, which in time became the site of his abbey. Despite legend, Sumner McKnight Crosby has found conclusive evidence that St. Denis was martyred near his gravesite and buried under the present abbey church (*The Royal Abbey of Saint-Denis*, 5).

14. A faded copy of this banner is currently displayed in the church (now basilica) of Saint-Denis.

15. Crosby points out that it was not until the advent of Louis IX that the Abbey of Saint-Denis received the monarch's full acknowledgment of his vassalage: "In 1248 he went to Saint-Denis with his eldest son to place four pieces of Byzantine gold on the altar as a symbol of the feudal head-tax paid to a sovereign lord. He departed on his crusade as a Knight of Saint-Denis, and on his return repeated the symbolic act, giving twenty-eight pieces of gold to the abbey—four for each year that he was absent." This was the first and last time a French monarch performed this ceremonial submission, and the moment "may be looked on as the climax of the monks' efforts to make their saint the true sovereign of the French monarchy" (*Royal Abbey of Saint-Denis*, 12).

16. Suger, 27.

17. Suger, 111.

18. Only four of these (Louis, Henry, Robert, and Peter) appear to have survived to adulthood. Henry is credited with as many as twenty illegitimate offspring, but only one legitimate son and daughter.

19. As told by William of Malmesbury, 455. See also Orderic (6:295–301), who has many details.

20. William of Malmesbury, 456.

5. THE VIRGIN AND THE QUEEN

Selected sources for this chapter: Suger; William of Malmesbury; Marjorie Chibnall, *The Empress Matilda: Queen Consort, Queen Mother, and Lady of the English* (Oxford, UK: Blackwell, 1991); Jim Bradbury, *Stephen and Matilda: The Civil War of 1139–53* (Stroud, UK: Sutton, 1996); William of Newburgh; Lewis, *Royal Succession in Capetian France*; Flori, *Eleanor of Aquitaine*; Kelly, *Eleanor of Aquitaine*; Bernart de Ventadorn, *Songs*, ed. and trans. Stephen G. Nichols Jr. (Chapel Hill: University of North Carolina Press, 1962); Eileen Edna Power, *Medieval Women*, ed. M. M. Postan (Cambridge, UK: Cambridge University Press, 1975); Georges Duby, *William Marshal: The Flower of Chivalry*, trans. Richard Howard (New York: Pantheon Books, 1985); Penny Schine Gold, *The Lady and the Virgin* (Chicago: University of Chicago Press, 1985); *Gesta Stephani*, or *Deeds of Stephen* [henceforth cited as *Deeds of Stephen*], ed. and trans. K. R. Potter (London: Thomas Nelson, 1955); R. H. C. Davis, *King Stephen, 1135–1154*, 3rd ed. (New York: Longman, 1990); Orderic; Henry of Huntingdon, *The Chronicle of Henry of Huntingdon* [henceforth cited as Henry of Huntingdon], ed. and trans. Thomas Forester (London: Henry G. Bohn, 1859); Warren, *Henry II*; Harper-Bill and Vincent, ed., *Henry II*; Power, *The Norman Frontier in the Twelfth and Early Thirteenth Centuries*; Gillingham, *Angevin Empire*; Kate Norgate, *England under the Angevin Kings*, 2 vols. (New York: Haskell House, 1969 [first published 1887]); F. M. Powicke, *The Loss of Normandy 1189–1204* (Manchester, UK: University Press, 1913); Landon, *Itinerary of Richard I*; Flori, *Richard the Lionheart*; Lemarignier, *Recherches sur l'hommage en marche et les frontières féodales*; Giraldus Cambrensis, *De Principis Instructione Liber*; Walter Map; H. J. R. Murray, *A History of Chess* (Oxford, UK: Clarendon Press, 1913); Roger of Wendover.

1. Matilda and Geoffrey were betrothed in 1127 and married a year later, once arrangements had been made to establish Geoffrey as count of Anjou during his father's lifetime (his father, Fulk, had already left for Jerusalem, where he married the king's daughter and eventually ruled in his own right). At age fourteen, Geoffrey had reached his majority and was eligible for marriage.

2. Henry I lived to see the birth of his second grandson as well (Geoffrey, born in 1134). A third grandson, William, was born in 1136, after Henry I's death.

3. "He was a man of fervent devotion towards God," comments William of Newburgh, "and of singular lenity towards his subjects, and likewise one who highly venerated men in holy orders. He was, however, more easily led away than became a prince" (516).

4. At age eleven, young Louis was too young to take a role in government, as was also the case with his older brother, who was only four at the time of his consecration and thirteen at the time of his death. In this instance, making the son co-king was not "an equal partnership" but "a means of assuring the automatic succession of the heir without disorder" (Lewis, *Royal Succession in Capetian France*, 56–57).

5. Quoted in Power, *Medieval Women*, 36. The Duchess of Brunswick lived and died at the end of the Middle Ages rather than in the twelfth century, but the life of the medieval lady had changed little during the intervening years.

6. Other *chansons de geste* featured women more prominently, but these female characters played entirely subservient roles. See Gold, *The Lady and the Virgin*, especially 4–5, 37, 42.

7. Upon her death in 1167, Matilda was indeed buried in the Abbey of Bec-Hellouin, but centuries later her body was transferred to Rouen Cathedral.

8. Nicholas of Mont Saint-Jacques, quoted in Chibnall, *Empress Matilda*, 204. The anonymous author of the *Gesta Stephani*, or *Deeds of Stephen*, was particularly hostile to Matilda. An ardent supporter of Stephen, he clearly held Matilda to blame for England's subsequent two decades of strife. Had she behaved like a proper woman, he strongly implied, she would have immediately conceded the crown to the man and left England in peace.

9. Orderic, 6:445.

10. Matilda had no money to spare, and so—according to the story—Henry audaciously applied to King Stephen himself for aid. Stephen, who probably was glad for

an opportunity to send Henry back to Normandy, may well have responded favorably. This story, reported in the *Deeds of Stephen*, has been challenged, but recent research has reinforced its plausibility (see 135–37, especially 135n1).

11. "How much of the Vexin was conceded [at this time] by Geoffrey and how much by Henry in 1151 is not clear from the sources," comments Henry II's biographer, W. L. Warren (*Henry II*, 32n1). Warren concludes that Geoffrey handed over the key fortress of Gisors at the time of his homage in 1144, and the rest in 1151 in return for Louis' recognition of young Henry as duke (32, 71). Norgate agrees, in her classic *England under the Angevin Kings*, 1:342–43. However, both R. H. C. Davis (*King Stephen*, 75) and F. M. Powicke (*The Loss of Normandy*, 128n2) state that Geoffrey granted Louis the entire Norman Vexin in 1144. Power agrees, stating, "It is easier to believe that Louis received the whole Norman Vexin in 1144 (when Geoffrey was in no position to refuse the king's demands and needed recognition) than in 1149 or 1150, when the count of Anjou was more firmly established in the duchy and his relations with his royal lord were rapidly deteriorating" (*The Norman Frontier in the Twelfth and Early Thirteenth Centuries*, 392n23). Interestingly, Landon, citing the Rouen Chronicle, proposes that Geoffrey did not capture Rouen and the duchy until after Louis departed on crusade in 1147 (*Itinerary of Richard I*, Appendix H, 219n6). If Landon is right, Geoffrey never did homage to Louis for Normandy at all, which left the entire issue of recognition for a later date—at which point Geoffrey no longer was claiming Normandy on his own behalf, but on behalf of his son. See Lemarignier, *Recherches sur l'hommage en marche et les frontières féodales*, 45n53, for a discussion of the problem.

12. See note 11.

13. Giraldus Cambrensis, *De Principis Instructione Liber*, 8:309.

14. Eustace's death in 1153 removed a major obstacle between Henry and the English throne. William of Newburgh comments, "The French, indeed, pined with envy, but were unable to arrest the duke's progress" (442).

15. Giraldus Cambrensis reported this rumor with considerable relish (*De Principis Instructione Liber*, 8:300). According to the gossipy Walter Map, who by the 1170s was a royal clerk in Henry II's household, Eleanor "cast her unchaste eyes" on Henry "and married him, even though she was secretly reputed to have shared the couch of Louis with [Henry's] father Geoffrey" (475–77; see also xvi).

16. Matilda's epitaph, according to Roger of Wendover (2:58):
Great was her birth, her husband greater, greatest was her son,
Here lieth Henry's daughter, wife, and mother, all in one!

6. THE GOLDEN TABLE OF SICILY

Selected sources for this chapter: For the account of the Third Crusade, I have drawn chiefly from the chronicle of the Norman poet and minstrel Ambrose (or Ambroise), an eyewitness (one of his translators has referred to him as a "war correspondent"). I primarily used the prose translation, "The History of the Holy War," in *Three Old French Chronicles of the Crusades* [henceforth cited as Ambrose], ed. and trans. Edward Noble Stone (Seattle: University of Washington Press, 1939), but I referred to the verse translation as well—*The Crusade of Richard Lion-heart,* trans. Merton Jerome Hubert, notes and documentation John L. LaMonte (New York: Columbia University Press, 1941). Additional sources for this chapter include Richard of Devizes, *The Chronicle of Richard of Devizes of the Time of King Richard the First* [henceforth cited as Richard of Devizes], ed. and trans. John T. Appleby (London: Thomas Nelson, 1963); Roger of Howden; Roger of Wendover; Rigord; William of Malmesbury; Giraldus, *Historical Works*; William of Newburgh; Gillingham, *Richard I*; Flori, *Richard the Lionheart*; Bradbury, *Philip Augustus*; Flori, *Eleanor of Aquitaine*; Peter Spufford, "Financial Markets and Money Movements in the Medieval Occident," in *Semana de Estudios Medievales: Viajeros, peregrinos, mercaderes en al occidente medieval* 18 (1991): 202–10; T. A. Archer, *The Crusade of Richard I, 1189–92* (New York: G. P. Putnam's, 1889); *Magni Rotuli Scaccarii Normanniae sub Regibus Angliae* [henceforth cited as Stapleton, *Rolls of the Norman Exchequer*], ed. and trans. Thomas Stapleton, 2 vols. (London: London Antiquarian Society, 1840–1844); Landon, *Itinerary of Richard I*; Powicke, *Loss of Normandy.*

1. Roger of Howden notes that immediately following Henry's death, Richard refused Philip's request for Gisors, and in fact paid Philip a considerable sum to regain everything that he and Philip had taken from Henry during the war (2:112).

2. Roger of Wendover says he received it at Vézelay (2:94).

3. Rigord, 113–14.

4. They sewed these to their clothing.

5. A *terrini* was a gold coin weighing about a gram. See Richard of Devizes, 17n3.

6. Roger of Howden has all the details, including the terms of the treaty and Richard's letter informing the pope (2:163–69).

7. A tidbit from William of Malmesbury, 447.

8. William of Malmesbury, 308, 341, 446; Giraldus, *Historical Works*, 161–63, 250–53.

9. As for Eleanor's virtue, the chronicler could not let this kind of compliment pass without reminding the reader, with the literary equivalent of a wink, of the reputation Eleanor earned as a younger woman while on the Second Crusade (Richard of Devizes, 25–26).

10. Ambrose, 26. William of Newburgh adds that she was "a lady of distinguished beauty and modesty" (586).

11. This typically irreverent observation came from Richard of Devizes (25), who never saw Berengaria but who seems to have based his account of the crusade, up to Sicily, on an eyewitness who apparently caught a glimpse of the princess.

12. Roger of Howden tells this episode in some detail (2:194–95).

13. About two and a half tons of silver. When Godefroy of Bouillon had to sell his family lands in 1096 in order to pay his way to the First Crusade, the buyer paid thirteen hundred marks of silver—amounting to more than a quarter ton—plus three marks (more than half a kilo) of gold. See Spufford, "Financial Markets and Money Movements in the Medieval Occident," 202. Archer says that a twelfth-century mark

("not a coin, but a money of account") weighed two-thirds of a pound (*Crusade of Richard I*, 371). The Roman pound, however, weighed twelve rather than sixteen ounces. According to Stapleton, by the late twelfth century the mark contained eight ounces of silver and had replaced the twelve-ounce livre (which had become debased) as a standard of reckoning. An equivalency given within the rolls of the Norman Exchequer for 1198 has £3,226 Angevin (one-fourth the value of pounds sterling) as equal to 1,210 marks (introduction to Stapleton, *Rolls of the Norman Exchequer*, 2: xiii, xvii). This works out to a mark with two-thirds the value of a pound sterling and containing eight ounces of silver.

14. Rigord gives the treaty's terms (125–130).

15. See Landon, *Itinerary of Richard I*, Appendix H, 228–32, and Powicke, *Loss of Normandy*, 126–29, for lengthy assessments of the problem.

16. Rigord, 125.

7. TO JERUSALEM!

Selected sources for this chapter: Roger of Howden; William of Newburgh; Richard of Devizes; Gillingham, *Richard I*; Flori, *Richard the Lionheart*; Bradbury, *Philip Augustus*; Flori, *Eleanor of Aquitaine*; Kelly, *Eleanor of Aquitaine*; Ambrose; Sidney Painter, "The Third Crusade: Richard the Lionhearted and Philip Augustus," in *A History of the Crusades*, ed. Kenneth M. Setton, vol. 2 (Madison: University of Wisconsin Press, 1969); Giraldus, *Historical Works*; Rigord; Roger of Wendover; William Marshall; Walter Map; James A. Brundage, *Richard Lion Heart* (New York: Scribner, 1974); Anna Comnena, *The Alexiad*, trans. E. R. A. Sewter (London: Penguin, 1969).

1. Eleanor probably arrived in Rome in time to be present at Pope Celestine III's consecration.

2. William of Newburgh tells us that before she left, Joanna sold to Tancred "the very ample property of her noble husband" [her hard-won inheritance] "in order that she might be able to accompany her brother, and had, by these means, vastly increased his treasures" (586).

3. Richard of Devizes gives considerable detail about the ships and their order of departure (15, 28, 35).

4. Ambrose, 40–41.

5. Ambrose, 41.

6. Roger of Howden, 2:127–28. By the time of Philip's arrival, Genoese held the north end of the line, where it touched the sea. Next came the Knights of the Hospital, followed by Conrad of Montferrat and a number of French bands, each commanded by its own lord. Next were the English, under Bishop Hubert of Salisbury, and the Flemings, under the seneschal of Flanders. Guy of Lusignan held the next section, along with his brothers and those barons of the kingdom of Jerusalem who still followed his banner. Next to them stood the Templars and the band of James of Avesnes (a Fleming), followed by the Danes, the Frisians, and the sadly reduced band of Germans, under the leadership of Barbarossa's son, Duke Frederick of Swa-

bia. Last, and holding down the southern side of the line where it touched the sea, were the Pisans. Thus, although Conrad of Montferrat, Guy of Lusignan, Henry of Champagne, and Frederick of Swabia were important, "no one man stood forth as a dominant and effective leader." This force, however formidable, was "less an army than a conglomeration of armed bands." Painter, "The Third Crusade: Richard the Lionhearted and Philip Augustus," 2:65.

7. As noted by Giraldus, *Historical Works*, 160.

8. Accounts vary. Roger of Howden says that Saladin sent Richard pears, plums, and an "abundance of other fruits of his country, besides other little presents" (2:209).

9. Certainly implied, if not directly stated, in Rigord, 140.

10. Richard of Devizes, 42. William of Newburgh similarly noted that Richard's "surpassing glory . . . had already begun to vex the king of France, and he [Philip] could with difficulty conceal the venomous workings of his soul on beholding himself far inferior in strength and resources" (589).

11. Roger of Wendover adds this important detail (107).

12. This sum appears in Roger of Howden, 2:214; Roger of Wendover gives the sum as seven thousand gold pieces (104).

13. Ambrose says it was 2,700 (79), but Richard himself estimated the number at about 2,600 (see Richard's letter to the abbot of Clairval [Clairvaux], in Roger of Howden, 2:222). In his letter to the abbot, Richard added that he held off from killing some of his more high-ranking prisoners, in order to use them to recover the Holy Cross as well as certain Christian captives that Saladin held. Whatever the exact number of Saracen captives killed, though, it was a lot.

14. Philip also bent the ear of the pope on the subject, although William of New-burgh reports that the "still more subtle pontiff" saw through him (595). Roger of Howden says that "neither our lord the pope nor the cardinals put any faith in his words, knowing that they proceeded rather from envy than from any bad conduct on the part of the king of England" (2:256). Newburgh adds, "It was commonly reported among the French, by certain inventors of falsehood, hereby thinking to palliate their king's return, that the king of England, by insidiously and wickedly seeking his life, had compelled him to depart prematurely, in opposition to his intention" (593).

15. Yet another fascinating detail reported by eyewitness Ambrose, 80.

16. All agreed on the necessity for providing special protection for the mounted warriors and their horses, and not only because of the warriors' social class. Both horse and rider represented a large investment in time as well as money. Twelfth-century knights spent years in training for warfare, and once of age did little else. The best kept in shape with the kind of rigor any contemporary athlete would understand. Once mounted, their exercises became more difficult, demanding special training for horse and rider alike. This was especially the case with the charge, the tactic for which the French were famous. Although this shock tactic with couched lance required strength, it also called for considerable dexterity on the part of both horse and warrior. The horse that carried its rider into battle had to be sufficiently strong, unflinching, and maneuverable to do the job. Such destriers, as they were called, were worth a fortune—about thirty times the cost of an ordinary horse—and could make the difference between victory and defeat.

17. William Marshal gives a lively contemporary account of the hazards of being outfitted in such fashion. He tells of having to go to a blacksmith and lay his head down on the forge in order to allow the smith to extract him from his helmet, which had been crushed during a tournament: "It was no laughing matter, far from it," he tells the reader, "for the smith, with his hammers, wrenches and pincers, was going about the task of tearing off his [Marshal's] helmet and cutting through the metal strips, which were quite staved in, smashed and battered. The helmet was so tight around his neck that it was freed with great difficulty" (William Marshal, 159).

18. According to Ambrose, "Loath and slothful were the folk to go; for most delightful was the city, with its good wines and damsels fair, of whom were some that were most beautiful. With wine and women had they much traffic and took their pleasure foolishly withal, so that in the city was much unseemliness and so much sin and so much wantonness that good men were sore ashamed of that which the rest did" (81).

19. The only women who came with the troops, according to Ambrose, were the charwomen and washerwomen, "who washed heads and linen and were as deft as monkeys in removing fleas" (81). Still, it's hard to believe that all the barmaids and prostitutes remained in Acre.

20. Ambrose refers to it as "the Dragon" (87).

21. Philip may have brought around 650 knights and 1,300 squires, but may not have brought any infantry with him—which normally would have numbered approximately three or four times the number of knights and squires. Richard is supposed to have had some 800 men with him, but according to Sidney Painter, that number is "probably high" ("The Third Crusade," 2:57–58).

22. This is the figure given for the army as it approached Saladin's larger forces (given as three hundred thousand) at Arsuf (Ambrose, 87).

23. By Richard's day, the military activities of the Knights of the Hospital, or Hospitalers (the Order of the Hospital of St. John of Jerusalem) had overtaken their original mission of caring for poor pilgrims, and the Hospitalers had become fierce military rivals of the Knights of the Temple, or Templars. For a contemporary assessment of both orders, see Walter Map, 67–69.

24. See, for example, Brundage, *Richard Lion Heart*, 139.

25. Brundage, *Richard Lion Heart*, 139.

26. Ambrose notes that they were "so tightly ranged that, had ye tossed an apple, ye had not failed to hit or beast or man" (87).

27. Ambrose, 88.

28. Ambrose, 87.

29. Terce, one of the canonical hours, or daily progression of prayer services, took place at around 9 a.m.

30. Comnena, *The Alexiad*, 416.

8. THE LION AT BAY

Selected sources for this chapter: Ambrose; Peter W. Edbury, *The Conquest of Jerusalem: Sources in Translation* (Hants, UK: Scolar Press, 1996); Landon, *Itinerary of*

Richard I; Gillingham, *Richard I*; Flori, *Richard the Lionheart*; Bradbury, *Philip Augustus*; Roger of Howden; William Marshal; William of Newburgh; Bernard Lewis, *The Assassins: A Radical Sect in Islam* (New York: Oxford University Press, 1967); Walter Map; Roger of Wendover.

1. For three weeks in July and August, Berengaria and Richard had occupied the same quarters in Acre—although Lionheart's long convalescence may not have contributed much in the way of marital bliss. Soon after he sufficiently recuperated, he set up camp outside Acre's walls. On August 6, 1191, in a letter to William Longchamp, bishop of Ely (his chancellor in England), Richard reported that he was restored to full health (Edbury, *The Conquest of Jerusalem*, 178–79). A week later, on August 14, he pitched camp outside Acre (see Landon, *Itinerary of Richard I*, 53).

2. See Richard's letter of October 1, 1191, to N. [otherwise unidentified], in Roger of Howden, 2:221.

3. See Richard's letter to the abbot of Clairval [Clairvaux], in Roger of Howden, 2:223–24). This also was written on October 1, 1191, not long after Arsuf. In it, Richard told the abbot that without a significant influx of manpower and money, he would not be able to stay in the Holy Land beyond Easter, and begged the abbot to do his utmost to raise more money and troops.

4. Roger of Howden speaks of "sinister reports" that John "had seized the castles of the kingdom, and would have taken possession of the whole thereof if he could have found the opportunity" (2:269). See also William Marshal, 499.

5. Guy did not walk away empty-handed. He received the kingdom of Cyprus as a consolation prize.

6. Walter Map tells the unlikely tale that the Old Man and his followers were about to convert to Christianity, when the Templars killed the priest sent to carry out the baptisms— "lest (it is said) the belief of the infidels should be done away and peace and union reign" (67).

7. See letter from the Old Man of the Mountain to Leopold, duke of Austria, in Roger of Wendover, 2:129–30.

8. "What could the king do," commented Ambrose, "save in his turn to make another song concerning them that through envy thus assailed and mocked him?" (141).

9. William of Newburgh says that Richard's enemies accused him of having "connived with Saladin for betraying the Holy Land and, there, would not proceed to the siege of the Holy City" (601).

10. For Richard's trip home and capture, I have drawn upon the accounts of Roger of Howden, William of Newburgh, and Roger of Wendover. Each makes its own contribution to the story, but Roger of Wendover heard his version directly from Richard's chaplain, Anselm, who accompanied Richard (Roger of Wendover, 2:124).

11. Roger of Howden writes that "many pilgrims who had come away with the king of England from the [Holy Land], returned before the Nativity of our Lord to England, hoping there to find the king; and, on being asked about the king, where he was, they made answer, 'We know not' " (2:278).

12. Whom William of Newburgh names as Mainard (606), while Henry Hohenstaufen, in a letter to Philip of France (see chap. 9, note 4), refers to him as Maynard of Gortze (Roger of Howden, 2:278).

13. Roger of Wendover, 2:124.

14. These details are from Henry Hohenstaufen, in his letter to Philip of France (Roger of Howden, 2:279–80).

9. A WORLD OF ENEMIES

Selected sources for this chapter: Roger of Wendover; Roger of Howden; William of Newburgh; Rigord; Guillaume le Breton, *Continuation de la vie de Philippe II Auguste* [henceforth cited as Guillaume le Breton], trans. from Latin by François Guizot (Clermont-Ferrand, France: Paléo, 2003); Gillingham, *Richard I*; Flori, *Richard the Lionheart*; Bradbury, *Philip Augustus*.

1. Roger of Wendover, 2:125.

2. Roger of Howden says he was captured while asleep (2:270).

3. "Hail, king of England, in vain do you disguise your person, your face betrays you!" (William of Newburgh, 606).

4. The emperor's letter to Philip of France seems to have been the first official word of the capture (Roger of Howden, 2:278–79). Interestingly, a copy of this seems to have made its way to the archbishop of Rouen, who quickly forwarded it to interested parties in England (Letter of the archbishop of Rouen to the bishop of Durham, in Roger of Howden, 2:279–80). Obviously, the archbishop had some well-placed spies in the French royal household.

5. As William of Newburgh put it, "For it was never before heard that any Christian king or emperor made captive another Christian potentate, who was merely returning home through his territories from service in the Holy Land" (608).

6. Roger of Howden, 2:287.

7. William of Newburgh, 607; Roger of Howden, 2:281, 287. On hearing this news, Richard was understandably upset, but then added, "My brother John is not the man to subjugate a country, if there is a person able to make the slightest resistance to his attempts" (Roger of Howden, 2:281).

8. John "always predicted that he [Richard] would never return" (Roger of Howden, 2:289).

9. According to Roger of Wendover, Leopold delivered Richard to the custody of his soldiers, "with orders that they were to keep a most strict guard over him, with drawn swords day and night" (2:126).

10. William of Newburgh comments that the emperor, "alleging that it was not fitting for a king to be detained by a duke, though it was no disgrace to royalty to be under the custody of an emperor, took measures to get the noble captive into his possession" (608).

11. The pope promptly excommunicated Leopold and threatened to place the emperor and all of his empire under interdict unless Richard was speedily released. He also threatened Philip and his kingdom with interdict if he did not cease from persecuting Richard (Roger of Howden, 2:284–85, 290). None of this seemed to carry much weight with any of the offending parties.

12. Roger of Wendover says that it was sixty thousand pounds of silver (2:126), while Roger of Howden says it was a hundred thousand marks (2:282). Both work out to between twenty-five and thirty tons of silver (see chapter 6, note 13).

13. Roger of Howden, 2:282.

14. Roger of Howden, 2:282; Roger of Wendover, 2:127–28. It seems to have been on this occasion that Richard produced a letter from the Old Man of the Mountain, absolving Richard of all part in Conrad of Montferrat's murder (Roger of Wendover, 2:129–30).

15. Roger of Howden adds, "The king made answer with such frankness, such self-possession, and such intrepidity, that the emperor thought him worthy not only of his favour and pardon, but even of his praise. For he raised the king when bending before him, and received him with the kiss of peace" (2:282).

16. Philip seems to have offered to equal or even exceed the sum that Richard had promised (William of Newburgh, 610). See also Roger of Howden, 2:294–95.

17. Roger of Howden, 2:295. Roger of Wendover says the final ransom was 140,000 marks (2:128).

18. In addition, according to the final ransom terms, Richard was to give his niece, the daughter of Geoffrey, in marriage to Leopold of Austria's son, and was to set free Isaac of Cyprus.

19. Roger of Howden, 2:297.

20. See chapter 11, note 11.

21. Berengaria does not even seem to have been present at Richard's second coronation, following his release from imprisonment. Eleanor, however, was seated opposite the king (Roger of Howden, 2:322).

22. Rigord calls her Ingeburge (149). Roger of Howden (who calls her Botilda) says that Philip intended that her father, the king of Denmark, "might be induced to invade England with a naval armament" (2:304).

23. The cause of Philip's sudden aversion to Ingeborg is unknown. William of Newburgh says that "some affirm that it was on account of her unpleasant breath; others, that he repudiated her from some secret infirmity, or because he did not find her a virgin" (599). Guillaume le Breton blames the whole business on evil spells and sorcery (40).

24. Probably a hundred thousand marks. See Roger of Howden, 2:297, 305. Hostages had been given as security for the remainder (Roger of Wendover, 2:133).

25. According to the treaty's terms, if the silver were lost in Richard's territories, it would have been at his risk; only if it were lost in imperial territory would it have been at the emperor's risk (Roger of Howden, 2:296).

26. "Behold, how they loved him!" Roger of Howden caustically remarked (2:307).

27. According to Roger of Howden, the emperor required Richard to include England in the homage: "Richard, king of England, being still detained in captivity by Henry, emperor of the Romans, in order that he might escape from this captivity, by the advice of Eleanor, his mother, abdicated the throne of the kingdom of England, and delivered it to the emperor as the lord of all, and with his cap invested him therewith. However, the emperor, as had been pre-arranged, immediately restored to him . . . the said kingdom of England, to hold the same of him for five thousand

pounds sterling, yearly, payable as tribute. . . . However, the said emperor, at his death, released Richard, king of England, and his heirs from these and all other covenants whatsoever" (2:286).

28. Roger of Wendover, 2:134.

10. LIONHEART'S RETURN

Selected sources for this chapter: William of Newburgh; Roger of Howden; Léopold Delisle, *Catalogue des actes de Philippe-Auguste* [henceforth cited as *Actes de Philippe-Auguste*] (Paris: A. Durand, 1856); Orderic; Lemarignier, *Recherches sur l'hommage en marche et les frontières féodales*; Judith Green, "Lords of the Norman Vexin," in *War and Government in the Middle Ages*, ed. John Gillingham and J. C. Holt (Woodbridge, UK: Boydell, 1984); Musée de Normandie, *Les Châteaux Normands de Guillaume le Conquérant à Richard Coeur de lion* (Caen, France: Musée de Normandie, 1987); Roger of Wendover; Landon, *Itinerary of Richard I*; Ambrose; Gillingham, *Richard I*; Gillingham, *Richard the Lionheart*; Gillingham, "Some Legends of Richard the Lionheart"; Flori, *Richard the Lionheart*; Bradbury, *Philip Augustus*; Kate Norgate, *Richard the Lion Heart* (New York: Russell & Russell, 1969 [first published 1924]); Kate Norgate, *John Lackland* (London: Macmillan, 1902); Stapleton, *Rolls of the Norman Exchequer*; Archer, *Crusade of Richard I*; Powicke, *Loss of Normandy*; Rigord; Guillaume le Breton.

1. Roger of Howden says that upon hearing that Philip was laying siege to Verneuil, Richard "hurried on to that place with all haste," more swiftly than "the discharge of a Balearic sling" (2:325).

2. Roger of Wendover says he took it "by storm" (2:136). Landon, *Itinerary of Richard I*, gives a different order of events (95).

3. Richard had destroyed its walls six years before.

4. See illustration in chapter 4. Henry II is credited with building the circular stone donjon on this site, whose ruins still remain, but Château-sur-Epte had been part of the major line of defenses along the Epte since William Rufus's time (see Orderic, 6:233).

5. Orderic, 6:217, and Roger of Howden, 1:324. A portion of Andely's original fortifications, these two semicircular turrets and some wall still can be seen along the Rue des Remparts, on the town's northern side.

6. Lemarignier, *Recherches sur l'hommage en marche et les frontières féodales*, 43, 44n45. See also Green, "Lords of the Norman Vexin," 49. Orderic states that there was a castle at La Roche-Guyon, on the French side of the Epte's junction with the Seine, almost a century before the fortress, whose ruins still exist, was built—not surprising, considering this fortress's strategic position (Orderic, 5:215).

7. According to the Musée de Normandie, Henry II's donjon at Gisors is the only Norman example of a twelfth-century polygonal donjon—a form that was far more common in England (*Les Chateaux Normands de Guillaume le Conquérant à Richard Coeur de lion*, 70).

8. Roger of Howden gives the terms, 2:329–32.

9. Henry had leaned upon the pillar of an upper window, which gave way (Roger of Howden, 2:404–5).

10. The Church seems to have stepped in only after Richard wrote the pope (Roger of Wendover, 2:138–39). The hostages appear to have been promptly released, but the silver was another matter. On January 25, 1195, Richard wrote the archbishop a thank-you letter, in which he took the opportunity to urge him to use his influence to make sure Lionheart got his money back (see Landon, *Itinerary of Richard I*, 101). Roger of Howden writes, however, that some of the hostages were offered four thousand marks of the ransom money to take back to Richard, but that "on account of the perils of the journey, they had not dared on any account to take charge thereof" (2:347).

11. Ambrose, 26.

12. Gillingham, *Richard the Lionheart*, 7. See also Gillingham, "Some Legends of Richard the Lionheart," 60–65.

13. Roger of Howden describes Richard's sin as "filthiness." Howden states that Richard was "sensible of the filthiness of his life" and confessed "the filthiness of his life" to God in the presence of all the churchmen who were with him in Messina. For, as Howden puts it, "the thorns of lustfulness had departed from his head, and it was not the hand of man who rooted them out, but God, the Father of Mercies" (2:176).

14. See the Letter of Pope Celestinus to the archbishops and bishops of England, in Roger of Howden, 2:283–84.

15. Roger of Howden, 2:356.

16. Flori, who is cautious about reading a modern-day mentality into medieval texts, takes issue with most of the grounds for the recent claim that Lionheart was homosexual. Nevertheless, he concludes that the denizens of the twelfth century would have understood the hermit's warning about Sodom as a specific reference to homosexuality (*Richard the Lionheart*, 378–93). Gillingham strongly disagrees ("Some Legends of Richard the Lionheart," 61–62).

17. As Roger of Howden puts it, Richard "took back his wife, whom for a long time he had not known: and, putting away all illicit intercourse, he remained constant to his wife" (2:357–58). William of Newburgh simply says that, from that time forth, Richard "wished to render his couch more chaste" (633).

18. Delaville Le Roulx, cited in Landon, *Itinerary of Richard I*, 101.

19. Philip lined up his tower with the Château des Tourelles, a twelfth-century fortification (extensively remodeled in the fifteenth century) across the Seine, so that each of these defenses guarded its end of the bridge that linked them. Remnants of both, along with Vernon's old bridge, which suffered severe bombing damage during World War II, can still be seen.

20. Gillingham, *Richard the Lionheart*, 255–56.

21. In mid-1195, the emperor sent Richard a golden crown ("a massive crown of gold, of great value, as a token of their mutual affection"), accompanied by a message urging him to make war on Philip. Richard, quite wisely, feared a trap: "For it was well known to the king of England that the said emperor, above all things desired that the kingdom of France might become subject to the Roman empire; while, on the

other hand, the king of England conjectured that if an alliance were formed between the emperor and the king of France, the whole would redound to his own detriment" (Roger of Howden, 2:369).

22. Richard seems to have preferred Welsh and Flemish mercenaries, although Mercadier was Provençal. Curiously enough, the *Rolls of the Norman Exchequer* indicate that Richard employed Saracens as well; but according to Stapleton, this should not be taken literally, as the term seems to have been generally used as a reference to any band of foreigners who fought for hire (*Rolls of the Norman Exchequer*, 1:clix; 2:xiii).

23. "In process of time," notes Stapleton, "the personal service was allowed to be commuted into a money payment at the option of the tenant of the fief, and thus a certain sum came to be customarily charged upon all fiefs in aid of the army wherever the sovereign raised his banner in war" (*Rolls of the Norman Exchequer*, 2:xi).

24. In 1198, Richard placed a levy on his kingdom to produce three hundred knights for one year, or the monetary value thereof—namely three shillings "English money" per knight for each day (Roger of Howden, 2:415). This would have been the equivalent of about twelve shillings Angevin.

25. Stapleton, *Rolls of the Norman Exchequer*, 2:xl. In addition to the examples already given, the *Rolls of the Norman Exchequer* record a single knight receiving the lordly sum of 72 pounds for 240 days, and a company of twenty men-at-arms receiving 2 pounds 13 shillings and 4 pence for 4 days (2: xliv, xvi). A shilling was reckoned at 12 silver pence, and the English Standard Pound as 20 shillings (see Archer's discussion of medieval coinage in *Crusade of Richard I*, 369–71).

Weapons were also expensive. Mangonels, crossbows (and their sturdy square-headed arrows, known as quarrels or bolts), and spears for the use of Richard's army at Pont-de-l'Arche and Vaudreuil in 1195 cost almost 1,500 pounds. Spurs cost a shilling a pair (Stapleton, *Rolls of the Norman Exchequer*, 1:cxlvii).

26. Commenting on one particular truce between Richard and Philip, William of Newburgh writes: "Through the endeavours of good men, a truce for two months was agreed upon, in order that the vintage might be attended to" (646).

27. William's lands, although not large, were strategically placed between Normandy and Flanders on the lower Somme.

28. Roger of Howden, 2:371–72.

29. Rigord, 171; Landon, *Itinerary of Richard I*, 108.

11. THE ROCK OF ANDELY

Selected sources for this chapter: Robert de Monte; R. Allen Brown, "The Norman Conquest and the Genesis of English Castles," in *Castles, Conquest, and Charters: Collected Papers*, ed. R. Allen Brown (Woodbridge, UK: Boydell Press, 1989); Robert Liddiard, *Castles in Context: Power, Symbolism, and Landscape, 1066 to 1500* (Macclesfield, UK: Windgather Press, 2005); Robert Liddiard, ed., *Anglo-Norman Castles* (Woodbridge, UK: Boydell Press, 2003); Musée de Normandie, *Les Châteaux Normands*; R. Allen Brown, *English Castles*, 3rd ed. (London: B. T. Batsford,

1976); Landon, *Itinerary of Richard I*; Power, *The Norman Frontier in the Twelfth and Early Thirteenth Centuries*; Roger of Howden; Rigord; Guillaume le Breton; Roger of Wendover; William of Newburgh; Powicke, *Loss of Normandy*; Gillingham, *Richard I*; Gillingham, *Richard the Lionheart*; Norgate, *Richard the Lion Heart*; Flori, *Richard the Lionheart*; Bradbury, *Philip Augustus*; Flori, *Eleanor of Aquitaine*; Kelly, *Eleanor of Aquitaine*; Stapleton, *Rolls of the Norman Exchequer*; Orderic; Dominique Pitte, "Un brève histoire du château," in *Château-Gaillard: "Découverte d'un patrimoine"* (L'exposition organisée par le musée municipal A. G. Poulain et le service régional de l'archéologie de Haute-Normandie avec l'aide de la direction régionale des affaires culturelles de Haute-Normandie du conseil général de l'Eure, 15 novembre 1995–6 février 1996); M. Dieulafoy, *Le Château Gaillard et l'architecture militaire au xiiie siècle* (Paris: Imprimerie nationale, 1898); R. A. Brown, "Royal Castle-Building in England, 1154–1216," *English Historical Review* 70 (1955): 353–98; Martin S. Briggs, *The Architect in History* (New York: Da Capo Press, 1974 [first published 1927]); John Harvey, *The Mediaeval Architect* (New York: St. Martin's Press, 1972); Lon R. Shelby, "Mediaeval Masons' Templates," *Journal of the Society of Architectural Historians* 30 (May 1971): 140–54; Douglas Knoop and G. P. Jones, *The Genesis of Freemasonry* (London: Q. C. Correspondence Circle, 1978); Giraldus Cambrensis, *De Principis Instructione Liber*; Barraclough, *Origins of Modern Germany*; *Actes de Philippe-Auguste*.

1. Brown, "The Norman Conquest and the Genesis of English Castles," 87. Although recent castle historiography now prefers to emphasize castles' symbolic and residential rather than military functions, there still seems to be agreement that the Normans introduced the motte and bailey castle to England—consisting of an artificial mound, or motte, rising from an enclosed area, or bailey, and topped by a palisade and usually a tower. Yet there is disagreement over whether the Normans simply copied what they were building at home or were adapting to the needs of the Conquest. Such fortifications could be quickly built and handily defended, even when the defenders were vastly outnumbered, and some scholars believe that motte and bailey castles—although an attractive option for the Normans in England—were rare or nonexistent in pre-Conquest Normandy. The Musée de Normandie, however, points out that although there remain no written references to mottes in Normandy before 1050, recent archaeological finds show that numerous mottes were built there before the middle of the eleventh century (*Les Châteaux Normands*, 19). See also Brown, *English Castles*, 37–39, 55, and Liddiard, *Castles in Context*, 1–3, 5–7, 17.

2. The hulk of Montrichard still dominates its small town on the banks of the Cher, while the ruins of Montbazon (on the Indre, near Tours) similarly draw the eye. Langeais is worth looking up for its very antiquity: once the oldest known surviving castle in Europe (this title is now held by its Loire valley neighbor, Doué-la-Fontaine), it dates from the 990s, or possibly a decade or two later (not to be confused with its fifteenth-century replacement nearby).

3. Landon, *Itinerary of Richard I*, 111.

4. Despite the ancient political settlement of the Treaty of St-Clair-sur-Epte, the whole of the Vexin—French and Norman portions alike—remained under the ecclesiastical authority of the archdiocese of Rouen (see Roger of Howden, 2:386–87; also Power, *The Norman Frontier in the Twelfth and Early Thirteenth Centuries*,

116–17). Those readers recalling the role of the Abbey of Saint-Denis as overlord of the French Vexin (see chapter 4), should be assured that such an arrangement was neither unusual nor incompatible, since the abbey's jurisdiction here was feudal rather than ecclesiastical (those lords—after 1076, the French king—who held lands directly of the Abbey of Saint-Denis served as its advocate). The French Vexin was a fief of the Abbey of Saint-Denis but ecclesiastically part of the archdiocese of Rouen, which in turn held Andely (in the Norman Vexin) as its fief.

5. Walter of Coutances, archbishop of Rouen, to Ralph de Diceto, cited in Landon, *Itinerary of Richard I*, 114. Since the archbishop made no mention of Richard's several appearances at Andely, one may conclude that Lionheart was still proceeding warily and had not yet begun to build there.

6. Roger of Howden says she was the daughter of the German duke of Genest, 2:373. The French chroniclers call her Marie and say she was the daughter of the duke of Moravia and Bavaria (Rigord, 174; Guillaume le Breton, 45).

7. In exchange for demanding more than forty days' service from these English lords, Richard said that none should bring more than seven knights with him (see Landon, *Itinerary of Richard I*, 112, and Roger of Howden, 2:317). In other words, fewer men for longer service.

8. "And so the two kings played at castle-taking," remarks Roger of Wendover, 2:145. Despite, according to William of Newburgh, "the inclemency of the weather, which was more severe and lasting than usual," and "the famine which was raging beyond measure throughout the provinces" (650). Newburgh describes this severe famine and the torrential rains that caused it (662–63).

9. Richard—who did his own reconnoitering—was reconnoitering Gaillon when he was struck.

10. Raymond VI, also known as the count of Saint Giles, or Saint Gilles.

11. Raymond had previously been married to Bourguigne of Lusignan, whom he repudiated and divorced in order to marry Joanna. What Joanna thought of these events is not recorded, but the marriage certainly proved tumultuous. After giving birth to a son, she became pregnant a second time. Yet instead of remaining at home in peace during her pregnancy, she took her absent husband's place in besieging a castle (a task she apparently handled quite competently). Betrayed by his men and forced to flee for her life, she hastened north to her mother, Queen Eleanor, but died moments before her child was born. This second child, a boy, lived only long enough to receive baptism (see Roger of Howden, 2:394, 400, 463; Kelly, *Eleanor of Aquitaine*, 354–55).

12. Orderic, 6:217.

13. Stapleton notes that "Andely was the manor specially set apart for the supply of the table of the Archbishop; hence the occupation of the island and a great part of the demesne land was regarded by him as an outrage not to be borne" (*Rolls of the Norman Exchequer*, 2:xiv).

14. Noting the size of the sum borrowed to cover the costs of this expedition (some 1,200 marks, or more than £3,000 Angevin), Stapleton surmised that the outcome was "in some measure" brought about by well-placed bribes (*Rolls of the Norman Exchequer*, 2:xiv).

15. William of Newburgh reports that the pope told Archbishop Walter: "The unjust captivity of the king of England, on his return from the East, where he has been warring for Christ, . . . and the plundering he has undergone, while suffering a heavy and lengthened captivity in a German dungeon, are known to all the world. It would be more discreet, therefore, for you to dissimulate for awhile, even if he should have attempted greater things than these of which you speak" (665). See also Roger of Howden, 2:396–98.

16. Vestiges of the curtain wall still remain, although they are not accessible; the island is privately owned and no longer connected to either shore.

17. The island of Gardon no longer exists: the narrow strip of water between it and the shore has since been filled, either by man or by Nature, and Gardon is now at the tip of the peninsula.

18. The Rolls of the Norman Exchequer contain fascinating details about Richard's building program in Andely, including exact costs (2:xxxix–xlii). See also Pitte, "Un brève histoire du château," 13–42.

19. This pond no longer exists.

20. As William of Newburgh notes, Richard's fortifications were "wonderfully assisted by the nature of the ground" at this site (671).

21. The crossbow was banned by papal edict in 1139, on grounds that it was "too murderous" a weapon, but no one paid much attention. Significantly, this ban extended only to Christian targets; the Church had no problem with Christian warriors using crossbows against the infidel.

22. The Rolls of the Norman Exchequer give the total cost as £48,878, 13 shillings and 8 pence (2:xxxix). Gillingham points out that Richard spent about £7,000 sterling on all English castles during the course of his entire reign. Dover received the most of any English castle overall (around £8,000 sterling), but this expenditure began years before Richard's reign and was spread over a half-century (*Richard the Lionheart*, 264–65). The total expenditure for English royal castle-building between 1154 and 1216, a period of great activity in royal castle-building, amounted to around £46,000 sterling. Henry II's average annual income amounted to around £10,000 sterling. See Brown, "Royal Castle-Building in England," 158.

23. According to Martin S. Briggs, in his classic study *The Architect in History*: "For every medieval building of any importance there was an architect," who also usually acted as builder (55, 78). Briggs notes, "The architects of most of our medieval buildings were originally drawn or promoted from the mason's craft." This was logical, since "a medieval building of any size consisted chiefly of masons' work" (64, 74).

24. Pay, except for the most highly ranked among the skilled workers, was for work done and by the day. During winter (calculated from Michaelmas until Lent), when the working hours were shorter, the pay correspondingly declined.

25. The name possibly derived from the freestone (finely grained limestone and sandstone) they customarily worked. According to Knoop and Jones, freestone can be freely worked in any direction, making it the finest stone available for carving and cutting (*Genesis of Freemasonry*, 14).

26. This sum represented the cost of shipping timber as well as stone (Stapleton, *Rolls of the Norman Exchequer*, 2:xl).

27. Stapleton, *Rolls of the Norman Exchequer*, 2:xxxix–xl. Carpentry remained especially labor intensive, for saws were not yet commonly used. John Harvey notes the existence of sawmills in northern France by the early thirteenth century (*Mediaeval Architect*, 72), but these may not yet have been available to Lionheart's carpenters. Until the arrival of sawmills, carpenters shaped each piece of construction timber from its own log, rather than longitudinally sawing larger logs into matching timbers.

28. Guillaume le Breton, who was a vivid eyewitness of Gaillard and its site, notes that the name Boutavant (the name of Gaillard's second advance fortress) means "push forward, as if to say: I am stretching forward in order to recover my lands" (57).

29. This phenomenon probably was the result of red sand and dust swirled into the upper atmosphere by North African winds and carried aloft until deposited in northern Europe as red-tinged rainfall—a not uncommon occurrence.

30. William of Newburgh remarks that "the king was not dismayed at this, nor did he relax in promoting the work in which he took so great delight, that (unless I am mistaken) if even an angel from heaven had persuaded him to desist, he would have pronounced anathema against him" (672).

31. Centuries after leprosy in Andely had disappeared, the religious facilities once built for Andely's lepers became a convent.

32. Louis VII, who died in monk's garb, was more consistent than most.

33. Even though "the bodies of the dead were lying unburied in the squares and streets of the cities, which caused a great stench amongst the living" (Roger of Wendover, 2:165).

34. Pope Celestine pointedly reminded the bishop of this fact: "For, throwing aside the peaceful bishop, you have assumed the warlike knight" (Celestine's letter to Philip, bishop of Beauvais, in Roger of Howden, 2:402).

35. Roger of Wendover says that before letting Philip go, Baldwin insisted that he swear to restore to Baldwin and Richard all the castles that he had taken from them; but that as soon as Philip got back to Paris, he decided to break the agreement—on the grounds that he was not bound to keep an oath made on compulsion (2:168).

36. Giraldus Cambrensis, always a good storyteller, told this particular story (*De Principis Instructione Liber*, 8:289–90).

37. Letter from Celestine cited in Norgate, *Richard the Lion Heart*, 317. Like Leopold of Austria, Henry VI died excommunicate (Roger of Howden, 2:408). As with Leopold, the pope forbade his burial until Richard received full compensation for his ransom, but Richard never received anything back from the Hohenstaufen coffers. According to Roger of Howden, the body remained unburied, at least for a time (2:414). In the spring of 1198, Pope Innocent III attempted to prod Leopold's son and Henry's younger brother into making financial restitution to Richard, but nothing came of it (Landon, *Itinerary of Richard I*, 128–29).

12. THE TREASURE OF CHÂLUS

Selected sources for this chapter: Landon, *Itinerary of Richard I*; Guillaume le Breton; Norgate, *England under the Angevin Kings*; Roger of Howden; Roger of

Wendover; Powicke, *Loss of Normandy*; *Actes de Philippe-Auguste*; Rigord; Gillingham, *Richard I*; Gillingham, "Some Legends of Richard the Lionheart"; Flori, *Richard the Lionheart*; Norgate, *Richard the Lion Heart*; Bradbury, *Philip Augustus*.

1. Before that, Richard issued his Andely charters from the Isle of Andely (Landon, *Itinerary of Richard I*, 125).

2. Guillaume le Breton says that *gaillard* "is a word which in French expresses liveliness or exuberance ['la pétulance']" (57).

3. Shakespeare made good use of this legend in *King John*, where Richard's illegitimate son is called Philip Faulconbridge as well as Philip the Bastard.

4. Richard's words, quoted in Roger of Howden, 2:430 (although Richard used the royal "we": "in so doing, *we* have put *our* life in peril, and *our* kingdom"). Roger of Howden gives Richard's own colorful account, from a letter from the king to Philip, bishop of Durham (2:429–30).

5. Roger of Howden, 2:430.

6. Powicke, *Loss of Normandy*, 185. Gillingham has a slightly different translation, but with the same meaning (*Richard I*, 319).

7. According to Roger of Howden, Aimar actually offered a significant part of the treasure to Richard, but Richard refused this, saying that he ought by right to have the entire thing—terms that Aimar "would on no account agree to" (2:452).

8. See Gillingham, "Some Legends of Richard the Lionheart," 66–68, and Flori, *Richard the Lionheart*, 203–15.

9. "As a present to the inhabitants of Rouen on account of the incomparable fidelity which he had always experienced in them" (Roger of Wendover, 2:178).

10. Roger of Wendover says that this remarkable deathbed confession was made to "some of his intimate followers" under "a promise of secrecy" (2:178).

13. PHILIP AND JOHN

Selected sources for this chapter: Landon, *Itinerary of Richard I*; Gillingham, *Angevin Empire*; Giraldus, *Historical Works*; Rigord; Roger of Howden; Roger of Wendover; Guillaume le Breton; W. L. Warren, *King John* (New Haven, CT: Yale University Press, 1997); John Gillingham, "Historians without Hindsight: Coggeshall, Diceto, and Howden on the Early Years of John's Reign," in *King John: New Interpretations*, ed. S. D. Church (Woodbridge, UK: Boydell Press, 1999); Kate Norgate, *John Lackland*; Bradbury, *Philip Augustus*; Flori, *Eleanor of Aquitaine*; Kelly, *Eleanor of Aquitaine*; Anton Ervynck, "Medieval Castles as Top-Predators of the Feudal System: An Archaeozoological Approach," *Château-Gaillard: Etudes de Castellologie médiévale* 15 (1992): 151–59; Madeleine Pelner Cosman, *Fabulous Feasts: Medieval Cookery and Ceremony* (New York: George Braziller, 1976); *Actes de Philippe-Auguste*.

1. Not unreasonably, Arthur mistrusted John, who had a consistent track record of treachery (see Gillingham, *Angevin Empire*, 88).

2. Giraldus, *Historical Works*, 162–63.

3. Roger of Howden briefly tells the tale, 2:464–65.

4. Among wildfowl alone, they regularly downed several types of heron, swan, and wild goose, in addition to eagles, cranes, storks, woodcocks, pheasants, game hens, pigeons, quail, various songbirds, and even peacocks (although the latter were more usually displayed in full plumage than eaten). Anton Ervynck gives a list of the full range of fish, fowl, and animals consumed by the elite based upon the bones found at a number of castle archaeological sites ("Medieval Castles as Top-Predators of the Feudal System," 153). He also notes the common—and wasteful—practice among the privileged of eating their animals young and tender, before they were full-grown and productive (154).

5. To create this particular wonder, cooks would have taken the meat from capons, hens, mallards, woodcocks, and other fowl and thrown it into a huge crust. Then they would have finished off the marvel with mutton and marrow, hard-cooked egg yolks, dates, raisins, prunes, cloves, mace, cinnamon, and saffron (Cosman, *Fabulous Feasts*, 60).

6. Philip had a son and daughter by Agnes.

7. As of October 1203, Philip still had no idea of whether Arthur was alive or dead (*Actes de Philippe-Auguste*, no. 783).

8. Roger of Wendover, 2:206–7.

9. Philip's barons supported him in this decision (see *Actes de Philippe-Auguste*, no. 762).

14. LIONHEART'S PROUD DAUGHTER

Selected sources for this chapter: Roger of Wendover; Guillaume le Breton; Rigord; William of Newburgh; Stapleton, *Rolls of the Norman Exchequer*; Warren, *King John*; Gillingham, "Historians without Hindsight"; Gillingham, *Angevin Empire*; Daniel Power, "King John and the Norman Aristocracy," in *King John: New Interpretations*, ed. S. D. Church (Woodbridge, UK: Boydell Press, 1999); Norgate, *John Lackland*; Bradbury, *Philip Augustus*; Powicke, *Loss of Normandy*; Dieulafoy, *Château Gaillard*; Jean Mesqui, *Châteaux et enceintes de la France médiévale: de la défense à la résidence*, 2 vols. (Paris: Picard, 1991).

1. Guillaume le Breton, who was Philip's chaplain, gives an extraordinary eyewitness account of these events (56–57, 61–72).

2. Rigord says there were ten such towers (216).

3. In preparing to defend itself in 1198, Évreux had equipped its castle with 90 salted carcasses of hogs (called bacones), 63 English cheeses, 15 tuns of wine (more than 250 gallons to the tun), and barrel after barrel of wheat and dried peas—the latter being the basis for a thick porridge that regularly sustained all but the most well-to-do of northern Europe. Évreux also laid in a good supply of weaponry, including 12 dozen cords for its mangonels, seven slings for its perriers (stone-throwers), 6,002 quarrels (crossbow bolts or arrows), 4,000 regular arrows, one grinding stone (essential for sharpening weapons), and an assortment of darts and spikes (Stapleton, *Rolls of the Norman Exchequer*, 2:clxxi).

4. Or as William of Newburgh remarked, "Whenever kings rage the innocent people suffer for it" (662).

5. These would not have appeared so obvious to nineteenth- and early-twentieth-century observers, who had to see their way through piles of rubble. Only in 1993, following archaeological excavations begun in 1991, was Jean Mesqui able to identify the square tower as the latrine tower (*Châteaux et enceintes de la France médiévale*, 2:176).

6. Historians still are not unanimous on this critical point. Note that the alternative location—the window in the storeroom beneath the chapel—is near the latrines, and can also be interpreted as corresponding with Guillaume le Breton's description of the point of entry (71–72).

EPILOGUE

1. Orderic, 6:243.
2. Roger of Wendover, 2:214.

Bibliography

❧

PRIMARY SOURCES

Ambroise [Ambrose]. *The Crusade of Richard Lion-heart.* Translated by Merton Jerome Hubert; notes and documentation by John L. LaMonte. New York: Columbia University Press, 1941.

———. "The History of the Holy War." In *Three Old French Chronicles of the Crusades.* Edited and translated by Edward Noble Stone. Seattle: University of Washington Press, 1939.

Andreas Capellanus. *The Art of Courtly Love.* Translated, with notes and introduction, by John Jay Parry. New York: Columbia University Press, 1990.

Bernard of Clairvaux. *Bernard of Clairvaux: Selected Works.* Translated, with foreword, by G. R. Evans. Introduction by Jean Leclercq. Preface by Ewert H. Cousins. Mahwah, NJ: Paulist Press, 1987.

———. *The Letters of St. Bernard of Clairvaux.* Translated by Bruno Scott James. Chicago: Henry Regnery, 1953.

Bernart de Ventadorn. *Songs.* Edited and translated by Stephen G. Nichols Jr. Chapel Hill: University of North Carolina Press, 1962.

Bertran de Born. *The Poems of the Troubadour Bertran de Born.* Edited by William D. Paden Jr., Tilde Sankovitch, and Patricia H. Stäblein. Berkeley: University of California Press, 1986.

Delisle, Léopold. *Catalogue des actes de Philippe-Auguste.* Paris: A. Durand, 1856.

Douglas, David C., and George W. Greenaway, eds. *English Historical Documents, 1042–1189.* New York: Oxford University Press, 1953.

Dudo of Saint-Quentin. *History of the Normans.* Translated by Eric Christiansen. Woodbridge, UK: Boydell Press, 1998.

Eadmer. *Eadmer's History of Recent Events in England.* Translated by Geoffrey Bosanquet. London: Cresset Press, 1964.

Edbury, Peter W. *The Conquest of Jerusalem and the Third Crusade: Sources in Translation.* Hants, UK: Scolar Press, 1996.

Étienne de Rouen. *Draco normanicus.* In *Chronicles of the Reigns of Stephen, Henry II, and Richard I,* edited by Richard Howlett. Vol. 2. London: Eyre & Spottiswoode, 1889.

Florence of Worcester. *The Chronicle of Florence of Worcester.* Edited and translated by Thomas Forester. London: Henry G. Bohn, 1854.

Geoffrey of Monmouth. "Geoffrey of Monmouth's British History." In *Six Old English Chronicles,* edited by J. A. Giles. London: Henry G. Bohn, 1848.

———. "The Prophecies of Merlin." In *History of the Kings of Britain,* translated by Sebastian Evans. London: J. M. Dent, 1928.

Gesta Stephani, or *Deeds of Stephen.* Edited and translated by K. R. Potter. London: Thomas Nelson, 1955.

Giraldus Cambrensis. *The Autobiography of Giraldus Cambrensis.* Edited and translated by H. E. Butler. London: Jonathan Cape, 1937.

———. *The Historical Works of Giraldus Cambrensis.* Edited and translated by Thomas Forester. London: Henry G. Bohn, 1863.

———. *De Principis Instructione Liber.* Edited by George F. Warner. In *Giraldi Cambrensis Opera.* Vol. 8. London: Eyre & Spottiswoode, 1891.

Guillaume le Breton. *Chronique* and *Philippide.* In *Oeuvres de Rigord et de Guillaume le Breton.* Edited by H. François Delaborde. 2 vols. Paris: Librairie Renouard, 1885.

———. *Continuation de la vie de Philippe II Auguste.* Translated from Latin by François Guizot. Clermont-Ferrand, France: Paléo, 2003.

Henry of Huntingdon. *The Chronicle of Henry of Huntingdon.* Edited and translated by Thomas Forester. London: Henry G. Bohn, 1859.

Imad ad-Din and Baha ad-Din. *The Life of Saladin: From the Works of Imad ad-Din and Baha ad-Din.* Edited by Hamilton Gibb. Oxford, UK: Clarendon Press, 1973.

John of Glastonbury. *The Chronicle of Glastonbury Abbey: An Edition, Translation, and Study of John of Glastonbury's* Cronica sive Antiquitates Glastoniensis Ecclesie. Edited by James P. Carley. Translated by David Townsend. London: Boydell Press, 1985.

Landon, Lionel. *The Itinerary of King Richard I.* London: J. W. Ruddock & Sons, 1935.

Magni Rotuli Scaccarii Normanniae sub Regibus Angliae [*Great Rolls of the Exchequer of Normandy*]. Edited and translated by Thomas Stapleton. 2 vols. London: London Antiquarian Society, 1840–1844.

Map, Walter. *De Nugis Curialium.* Edited and translated by M. R. James. Revised by C. N. L. Brooke and R. A. B. Mynors. Oxford, UK: Clarendon Press, 1983.

Nicholson, Helen J. *Chronicle of the Third Crusade: A Translation of the* Itinerarium Peregrinorum et Gesta Regis Ricardi. Brookfield, VT: Ashgate, 1997.

Orderic Vitalis. *The Ecclesiastical History of Orderic Vitalis.* Edited and translated by Marjorie Chibnall. 6 vols. Oxford, UK: Clarendon Press, 1969.

Ralph of Coggeshall. *Chronicon Anglicanum.* Edited by Joseph Stevenson. London: Longman, 1875.

Ralph de Diceto. *Opera Historica: The Historical Works of Master Ralph de Diceto, Dean of London.* Edited by William Stubbs. 2 vols. London: Longman, 1876.

Richard of Devizes. *The Chronicle of Richard of Devizes of the Time of King Richard the First.* Edited and translated by John T. Appleby. London: Thomas Nelson, 1963.

Rigord. *La vie de Philippe II Auguste.* Translated from Latin by François Guizot. Clermont-Ferrand, France: Paléo, 2003.

Robert de Monte [also known as Robert de Torigni]. *The Chronicles of Robert de Monte.* Translated by Joseph Stevenson. Lampeter, UK: Llanerch Publishers, 1991. First published 1856.

Roger of Howden [also known as Roger of Hoveden]. *The Annals of Roger de Hoveden, Comprising the History of England and of Other Countries of Europe from A.D. 732 to A.D. 1201.* Translated by Henry T. Riley. 2 vols. London: Henry G. Bohn, 1853.

Roger of Wendover [formerly attributed to Matthew Paris]. *Roger of Wendover's Flowers of History: Comprising the History of England from the Descent of the Saxons to A.D. 1235.* Edited and translated by J. A. Giles. 2 vols. London: Henry G. Bohn, 1849.

Suger, Abbot of Saint Denis. *The Deeds of Louis the Fat.* Edited and translated by Richard Cusimano and John Moorhead. Washington, DC: Catholic University of America Press, 1992.

William of Malmesbury. *William of Malmesbury's Chronicle of the Kings of England.* Edited and translated by J. A. Giles. London: Henry G. Bohn, 1968. First published 1847.

William Marshal. *History of William Marshal.* Edited by A. J. Holden. Translated by S. Gregory. Historical notes by D. Crouch. 3 vols. London: Anglo-Norman Text Society, 2002.

William of Newburgh. *The History of William of Newburgh.* Translated by Joseph Stevenson. Lampeter, UK: Llanerch Publishers, 1996. First published 1856.

William of Poitiers [Gulielmus Pictaviensis]. *The Gesta Guillelmi of William of Poitiers.* Edited and translated by R. H. C. Davis and Marjorie Chibnall. Oxford, UK: Clarendon Press, 1998.

SECONDARY SOURCES

Adams, Henry. *Mont-Saint-Michel and Chartres.* Garden City, NY: Doubleday Anchor, 1959. First published 1913.

Alcock, Leslie. *Arthur's Britain: History and Archeology, AD 367–634.* London: Allen Lane/Penguin Press, 1971.

Anderson, Sven Axel. *Viking Enterprise.* New York: Columbia University Press, 1936.

Archer, T. A. *The Crusade of Richard I, 1189–92.* New York: G. P. Putnam's, 1889.

Barber, Richard. *The Knight and Chivalry.* London: Longman, 1970.

Barlow, Frank. *William Rufus.* Berkeley: University of California Press, 1983.

Barraclough, Geoffrey. *The Medieval Empire: Idea and Reality.* London: George Philip & Son, 1950.

———. *The Medieval Papacy.* London: Thames & Hudson, 1968.

————. *The Origins of Modern Germany.* Oxford, UK: Basil Blackwell, 1966.

Bates, David. *Normandy before 1066.* London: Longman, 1982.

————. *William the Conqueror.* London: George Philip, 1989.

Bloch, Marc. *The Royal Touch: Sacred Monarchy and Scrofula in England and France.* London: Routledge & Kegan Paul, 1973.

Blumenthal, Uta-Renate. *The Investiture Controversy: Church and Monarchy from the Ninth to the Twelfth Century.* Philadelphia: University of Pennsylvania Press, 1988.

Bordier, H. L. *Les églises et monastères de Paris.* Paris: Aug. Aubry, 1856.

Bradbury, Jim. *The Battle of Hastings.* Stroud, UK: Sutton, 1998.

————. *The Capetians: Kings of France, 987–1328.* London: Hambledon Continuum, 2007.

————. *The Medieval Siege.* Woodbridge, UK: Boydell Press, 1992.

————. *Philip Augustus: King of France, 1180–1223.* London: Longman, 1998.

————. *Stephen and Matilda: The Civil War of 1139–53.* Stroud, UK: Sutton, 1996.

Brett, M. *The English Church under Henry I.* London: Oxford University Press, 1975.

Briggs, Martin S. *The Architect in History.* New York: Da Capo Press, 1974. First published 1927.

Brittain, F. *Medieval Latin and Romance Lyric to A.D. 1300.* Cambridge, UK: Cambridge University Press, 1951.

Brøggler, A. W., and Haakon Shetelig. *The Viking Ships: Their Ancestry and Evolution.* New York: Twayne, 1971.

Brown, R. Allen. *English Castles.* 3rd ed. London: B. T. Batsford, 1976.

————. "The Norman Conquest and the Genesis of English Castles." In *Castles, Conquest and Charters: Collected Papers,* edited by R. Allen Brown. Woodbridge, UK: Boydell Press, 1989.

————. "Royal Castle-Building in England, 1154–1216." *English Historical Review* 70 (1955): 353–98.

Brundage, James A. *Richard Lion Heart.* New York: Scribner's, 1974.

Callahan, Thomas, Jr. "The Making of a Monster: The Historical Image of William Rufus." *Journal of Medieval History* 7 (1981): 175–85.

Carpenter, David. *The Struggle for Mastery: Britain, 1066–1284.* London: Oxford University Press, 2003.

Cazelle, Raymond. *Nouvelle histoire de Paris: de la fin du règne de Philippe Auguste à la mort de Charles V, 1223–1380.* Paris: Diffusion Hachette, 1972.

Chambers, E. K. *Arthur of Britain.* London: Sidgwick and Jackson, 1966. First published 1927.

Château-Gaillard: "Découverte d'un patrimoine." L'exposition organisée par le musée municipal A. G. Poulain et le service régional de l'archéologie de Haute-Normandie avec l'aide de la direction régionale des affaires culturelles de Haute-Normandie du conseil général de l'Eure (15 novembre 1995–6 février 1996).

Chibnall, Marjorie. *The Empress Matilda: Queen Consort, Queen Mother, and Lady of the English.* Oxford, UK: Blackwell, 1991.

————. *The World of Orderic Vitalis: Norman Monks and Norman Knights.* 2nd ed. Woodbridge, UK: Boydell, 1996.

Christ, Yvan. *Églises de Paris.* Paris: Diffusion Française, 1956.

Clout, Hugh D., ed. *Themes in the Historical Geography of France*. London: Academic Press, 1977.

Comnena, Anna. *The Alexiad*. Translated by E. R. A. Sewter (London: Penguin, 1969).

Cosman, Madeleine Pelner. *Fabulous Feasts: Medieval Cookery and Ceremony*. New York: George Braziller, 1976.

Coulton, G. G. *Medieval Panorama: The English Scene from Conquest to Reformation*. New York: Macmillan, 1938.

Couperie, Pierre. *Paris through the Ages*. New York: George Braziller, 1971.

Coutil, Léon. *La Ville des Andelys et ses environs à travers les âges*. Les Andelys: A. Briard, 1942.

Crosby, Sumner McKnight. *The Royal Abbey of Saint-Denis: From Its Beginnings to the Death of Suger, 475–1151*. New Haven, CT: Yale University Press, 1987.

Crouch, David. *The Beaumont Twins: The Roots and Branches of Power in the Twelfth Century*. Cambridge, UK: Cambridge University Press, 1986.

Cuttino, G. P. *English Medieval Diplomacy*. Bloomington: Indiana University Press, 1985.

David, Charles Wendell. *Robert Curthose, Duke of Normandy*. Cambridge, MA: Harvard University Press, 1920.

Davis, R. H. C. *King Stephen, 1135–1154*. 3rd ed. New York: Longman, 1990.

———. *The Normans and Their Myth*. London: Thames and Hudson, 1976.

Dieulafoy, M. *Le Château Gaillard et l'architecture militaire au xiiie siècle*. Paris: Imprimerie nationale, 1898.

Dodwell, C. R. *Anglo-Saxon Art: A New Perspective*. Ithaca, NY: Cornell University Press, 1982.

Douglas, David C. "Medieval Paris." In *Time and the Hour*. London: Eyre Methuen, 1977.

———. *The Norman Achievement, 1050–1100*. London: Eyre & Spotteswoode, 1969.

———. *The Norman Fate, 1100–1154*. London: Eyre Methuen, 1976.

———. "The Rise of Normandy." In *Proceedings of the British Academy, 1947*. London: Oxford University Press, 1948.

———. "Rollo of Normandy." *English Historical Review* 57 (October 1942): 417–36.

———. *William the Conqueror: The Norman Impact upon England*. Berkeley: University of California Press, 1964.

Drover, C. B. "A Medieval Monastic Water-Clock." *Antiquarian Horology* 12 (Summer 1980): 165–67.

Duby, Georges. *The Chivalrous Society*. Translated by Cynthia Postan. Berkeley: University of California Press, 1977.

———. *France in the Middle Ages: From Hugh Capet to Joan of Arc*. Translated by Juliet Vale. Oxford, UK: Blackwell, 1991.

———. *Medieval Marriage: Two Models from Twelfth-Century France*. Translated by Elborg Forster. Baltimore: Johns Hopkins University Press, 1978.

———. *La société aux XIe et XIIe siècles dans la région mâconnaise*. Paris: Librairie Armand Colin, 1953.

———. *William Marshal: The Flower of Chivalry*. Translated by Richard Howard. New York: Pantheon Books, 1985.

Dunabin, Jean. *France in the Making, 843–1180.* New York: Oxford University Press, 1985.

Duval, Paul-Marie. *Paris antique: des origines au troisième siècle.* Paris: Hermann, 1961.

Ervynck, Anton. "Medieval Castles as Top-Predators of the Feudal System: An Archaeozoological Approach." *Château-Gaillard: Études de Castellologie médiévale* 15 (1992): 151–59.

Fawtier, Robert. *The Capetian Kings of France: Monarchy and Nation (987–1328).* Translated by Lionel Butler and R. J. Adam. London: Macmillan, 1960.

Ferruolo, Stephen C. *The Origins of the University: The Schools of Paris and Their Critics, 1100–1215.* Stanford, CA: Stanford University Press, 1985.

Flori, Jean. *Eleanor of Aquitaine: Queen and Rebel.* Translated by Olive Classe. Edinburgh: Edinburgh University Press, 2007.

———. *Richard the Lionheart: King and Knight.* Translated by Jean Birrell. Edinburgh: Edinburgh University Press, 2006.

Fornier, Gabriel. *Le Château dans la France médiéval: essai de sociologie monumentale.* Paris: Aubier Montaigne, 1978.

France, John. *Western Warfare in the Age of the Crusades, 1000–1300.* Ithaca, NY: Cornell University Press, 1999.

Gardiner, Robert, ed. *The Earliest Ships: The Evolution of Boats into Ships.* London: Brassey, 1996.

Gies, Joseph, and Frances Gies. *Life in a Medieval Castle.* New York: Crowell, 1974.

———. *Marriage and the Family in the Middle Ages.* New York: Harper & Row, 1987.

Gillingham, John. *The Angevin Empire.* 2nd ed. London: Arnold; New York: Oxford University Press, 2001.

———. "Historians without Hindsight: Coggeshall, Diceto, and Howden on the Early Years of John's Reign." In *King John: New Interpretations,* edited by S. D. Church. Woodbridge, UK: Boydell Press, 1999.

———. *Richard I.* New Haven, CT: Yale University Press, 1999.

———. *Richard the Lionheart.* New York: Times Books, 1978.

———. "Some Legends of Richard the Lionheart: Their Development and Their Influence." In *Richard Coeur de Lion in History and Myth,* edited by Janet L. Nelson. London: Centre for Late Antique and Medieval Studies, King's College, 1992.

Gillingham, John, and J. C. Holt, eds. *War and Government in the Middle Ages.* Woodbridge, UK: Boydell, 1984.

Gold, Penny Schine. *The Lady and the Virgin.* Chicago: University of Chicago Press, 1985.

Green, Judith. "Lords of the Norman Vexin." In *War and Government in the Middle Ages,* edited by John Gillingham and J. C. Holt. Woodbridge, UK: Boydell, 1984.

Grinnell-Milne, Duncan. *The Killing of William Rufus: An Investigation in the New Forest.* Newton Abbot, UK: David & Charles, 1968.

Hall, Hubert. *Court Life under the Plantagenets.* Freeport, NY: Books for Libraries Press, 1970. First published 1899.

Hallam, Elizabeth M. *Capetian France, 987–1328.* New York: Longman, 1980.

Hampe, Karl. *Germany under the Salian and Hohenstaufen Emperors*. Translated by Ralph Bennett. Totowa, NJ: Rowman & Littlefield, 1973.

Harper-Bill, Christopher, and Nicholas Vincent. *Henry II: New Interpretations*. Woodbridge, UK: Boydell Press, 2007.

Harvey, John. *The Mediaeval Architect*. New York: St. Martin's Press, 1972.

Haskins, Charles Homer. *The Normans in European History*. Boston: Houghton Mifflin, 1915.

Haverkamp, Alfred. *Medieval Germany, 1056–1273*. London: Oxford University Press, 1988.

Hollister, C. Warren. "The Strange Death of William Rufus." *Speculum* 48 (October 1973): 637–53.

Hutton, William Holden. *Philip Augustus*. Port Washington, NY: Kennikat Press, 1970. First published 1896.

James, Bruno S. *Saint Bernard of Clairvaux: An Essay in Biography*. London: Hodder & Stoughton, 1957.

Jordan, Karl. *Henry the Lion: A Biography*. Translated by P. S. Falla. Oxford, UK: Clarendon Press, 1986.

Keen, Maurice. *Chivalry*. New Haven, CT: Yale University Press, 1984.

Kelly, Amy. *Eleanor of Aquitaine and the Four Kings*. Cambridge, MA: Harvard University Press, 1978. First published 1950.

Knoop, Douglas, and G. P. Jones. *The Genesis of Freemasonry*. London: Q. C. Correspondence Circle, 1978.

LaBarge, Margaret Wade. *Medieval Travellers*. London: Hamish Hamilton, 1982.

Latouche, Robert. *Histoire du comté du Maine pendant le Xe et le XIe siècle*. Paris: Librairie Honoré Champion, 1910.

Leeper, A. W. A. *A History of Medieval Austria*. London: Oxford University Press, 1941.

Lemarignier, Jean-François. *Recherches sur l'hommage en marche et les frontières féodales*. Lille, France: Bibliothèque Universitaire, 1945.

Le Patourel, John. "Guernsey and Jersey in the Middle Ages." In *Feudal Empires: Norman and Plantagenet*. London: Hambledon Press, 1984.

———. *The Norman Empire*. Oxford, UK: Clarendon Press, 1976.

Lewis, Andrew W. *Royal Succession in Capetian France: Studies on Familial Order and the State*. Cambridge, MA: Harvard University Press, 1981.

Lewis, Bernard. *The Assassins: A Radical Sect in Islam*. New York: Oxford University Press, 1967.

Lewis, C. S. *The Allegory of Love: A Study in Medieval Tradition*. New York: Oxford University Press, 1958.

Leyser, Karl J. *Medieval Germany and Its Neighbors, 900–1250*. London: Hambledon Press, 1982.

Liddiard, Robert, ed. *Anglo-Norman Castles*. Woodbridge, UK: Boydell Press, 2003.

———. *Castles in Context: Power, Symbolism, and Landscape, 1066 to 1500*. Macclesfield, UK: Windgather Press, 2005.

Loomis, Roger Sherman. *Wales and the Arthurian Legend*. Cardiff: University of Wales Press, 1956.

Maalouf, Amin. *The Crusades through Arab Eyes.* New York: Schocken Books, 1985.

Markowski, Michael. "Richard Lionheart: Bad King, Bad Crusader?" *Journal of Medieval History* 23 (December 1997): 351–65.

Marks, Claude. *Pilgrims, Heretics, and Lovers: A Medieval Journey.* New York: Macmillan, 1975.

Martindale, Jane. "Eleanor of Aquitaine." In *Richard Coeur de Lion in History and Myth,* edited by Janet L. Nelson. London: Centre for Late Antique and Medieval Studies, King's College, 1992.

———. "Eleanor of Aquitaine: The Last Years." In *King John: New Interpretations,* edited by S. D. Church. Woodbridge, UK: Boydell Press, 1999.

Mayer, Hans Eberhard. *The Crusades.* London: Oxford University Press, 1972.

Mesqui, Jean. *Châteaux et enceintes de la France médiévale: de la défense à la résidence.* 2 vols. Paris: Picard, 1991.

Morris, Colin. *The Discovery of the Individual, 1050–1200.* Toronto: University of Toronto Press, 1972.

Munz, Peter. *Frederick Barbarossa: A Study in Medieval Politics.* London: Eyre & Spottiswoode, 1969.

Murray, H. J. R. *A History of Chess.* Oxford, UK: Clarendon Press, 1913.

Musée de la Marine de Seine. *La Seine: mémoire d'un fleuve.* Paris: Société d'Éditions Régionales, [1989].

Musée de Normandie. *Les Châteaux Normands de Guillaume le Conquérant à Richard Coeur de Lion.* Caen, France: Musée de Normandie, 1987.

Newhall, Richard A. *The Crusades.* 2nd ed. New York: Holt, Rinehart and Winston, 1963.

Norgate, Kate. *England under the Angevin Kings.* 2 vols. New York: Haskell House, 1969. First published 1887.

———. "The 'Itinerarium Peregrinorum' and the 'Song of Ambrose.' " *English Historical Review* 25 (July 1910): 523–47.

———. *John Lackland.* London: Macmillan, 1902.

———. *Richard the Lion Heart.* New York: Russell & Russell, 1969. First published 1924.

Painter, Sidney. "The Third Crusade: Richard the Lionhearted and Philip Augustus." In *A History of the Crusades,* edited by Kenneth M. Setton, vol. 2. Madison: University of Wisconsin Press, 1969.

Parker, F. H. M. "The Forest Laws and the Death of William Rufus." *English Historical Review* 27 (January 1912): 26–38.

Pirenne, Henri. *Economic and Social History of Medieval Europe.* London: Kegan Paul, Trench, Trubner, 1936.

Pitte, Dominique. "Un brève histoire du château." In *Château-Gaillard: "Découverte d'un patrimoine"* (L'exposition organisée par le musée municipal A. G. Poulain et le service régional de l'archéologie de Haute-Normandie avec l'aide de la direction régionale des affaires culturelles de Haute-Normandie du conseil général de l'Eure (15 novembre 1995–6 février 1996).

Planhol, Xavier de, and Paul Claval. *An Historical Geography of France.* Cambridge, UK: Cambridge University Press, 1994.

Poole, A. L. *From Domesday Book to Magna Carta, 1087–1216.* 2nd ed. Oxford, UK: Clarendon Press, 1970.

Power, Daniel. "King John and the Norman Aristocracy." In *King John: New Interpretations*, edited by S. D. Church. Woodbridge, UK: Boydell Press, 1999.

———. *The Norman Frontier in the Twelfth and Early Thirteenth Centuries.* Cambridge, UK: Cambridge University Press, 2004.

Power, Eileen Edna. *Medieval Women.* Edited by M. M. Postan. Cambridge, UK: Cambridge University Press, 1975.

Powicke, F. M. *The Loss of Normandy (1189–1204).* Manchester, UK: University Press, 1913.

Press, Alan R., ed. and trans. *Anthology of Troubadour Lyric Poetry.* Edinburgh: Edinburgh University Press, 1971.

Reymond, Michel, and Michel Gilles. *Les Andelys d'hier; Les Andelys disparus.* Paris: Société GIM, 1980.

Round, J. H. *Geoffrey de Mandeville: A Study of the Anarchy.* New York: Burt Franklin, 1892.

Rowling, Marjorie. *Everyday Life of Medieval Travellers.* New York: Putnam's, 1971.

Runciman, Steven. *A History of the Crusades.* 3 vols. 2nd ed. Cambridge, UK: Cambridge University Press, 1987.

Searle, Eleanor. *Predatory Kinship and the Creation of Norman Power, 840–1066.* Berkeley: University of California Press, 1988.

Setton, Kenneth M., ed. *A History of the Crusades.* Madison: University of Wisconsin Press, 1969.

Shelby, Lon R. "Mediaeval Masons' Templates." *Journal of the Society of Architectural Historians* 30 (May 1971): 140–54.

Shopkow, Leah. *History and Community: Norman Historical Writing in the Eleventh and Twelfth Centuries.* Washington, DC: Catholic University of America Press, 1997.

Smail, R. C. *Crusading Warfare, 1097–1193.* 2nd ed. Cambridge, UK: Cambridge University Press, 1995.

Sochon, Serge. *Château Gaillard.* Condé-sur-Noireau, France: Éditions Charles Corlet, 1985.

Spufford, Peter. "Financial Markets and Money Movements in the Medieval Occident." *Semana de Estudios Medievales: Viajeros, peregrinos, mercaderes en al occidente medieval* 18 (1991): 202–10.

Stenton, Frank, ed. *The Bayeux Tapestry: A Comprehensive Survey.* London: Phaidon, 1957.

Strickland, Matthew. *War and Chivalry: The Conduct and Perception of War in England and Normandy, 1066–1217.* Cambridge, UK: Cambridge University Press, 1996.

Strutt, Joseph. *A Complete View of the Dress and Habits of the People of England.* 2 vols. London: Tabard Press, 1970. First published 1842.

Tellenbach, Gerd. *Church, State and Christian Society at the Time of the Investiture Contest.* Oxford, UK: Basil Blackwell, 1959.

Thorpe, Lewis. *The Bayeux Tapestry and the Norman Invasion.* London: Folio Society, 1973.

Toy, Sidney. *A History of Fortification: From 3000 B.C. to A.D. 1700*. London: William Heinemann, 1955.

Viollet-le-Duc, Eugène. *An Essay on the Military Architecture of the Middle Ages*. Westport, CT: Greenwood, 1977. First published 1860.

Warner, Marina. *Alone of All Her Sex: The Myth and the Cult of the Virgin Mary*. New York: Knopf, 1976.

Warner, Philip. *The Medieval Castle: Life in a Fortress in Peace and War*. London: Barker, 1971.

Warren, W. L. "The Death of William Rufus." *History Today* 9 (January 1959): 22–29.

———. *Henry II*. London: Eyre Methuen, 1973.

———. *King John*. New Haven, CT: Yale University Press, 1997.

Weiser, Francis X. *Handbook of Christian Feasts and Customs: The Year of the Lord in Liturgy and Folklore*. New York: Harcourt, Brace, 1958.

Index

✦

Note: When there are multiple identical note numbers on one page, they are preceded by the chapter number, e.g., 241:12n7 refers to note 7 in chapter 12.

About the Author

❧

Mary McAuliffe received a PhD in history from the University of Maryland and has taught at several universities. For many years a regular contributor to *Paris Notes*, she has traveled extensively in France and recently published *Dawn of the Belle Epoque: The Paris of Monet, Zola, Bernhardt, Eiffel, Debussy, Clemenceau, and Their Friends.* She is also the author of *Paris Discovered: Explorations in the City of Light.* She lives in New York City with her husband.